The Servants' Hall

SOUTHAMPTON
INSTITUTE

Frontispiece
Edward Prince, carpenter at Erddig in 1792

The Servants' Hall
The Domestic History of a Country House

Merlin Waterson

Foreword by
The Marquess of Anglesey

The National Trust

In Memory of Philip Yorke

First published in 1980
by Routledge & Kegan Paul Ltd
11 New Fetter Lane, London EC4P 4EE
Reprinted in 1980 (twice)

New edition 1990
by The National Trust
36 Queen Anne's Gate, London SW1H 9AS
Set in Monotype Baskerville
and printed in Great Britain by
BAS Printers Limited, Over Wallop, Hampshire

British Library Cataloguing in Publication Data

Waterson, Merlin
The servants' hall : the domestic history of a country house.
1. Clwyd. Wrexham. Country house : Erddig. Domestic
*   servants, history*
I. Title   II. National Trust
640.460942939

ISBN 0-7078-0126-5

Preface to the National Trust Edition

On 10 April 1987 there was a party at Erddig to celebrate the tenth anniversary of the opening of the house by the Prince of Wales. It was an opportunity to assess how repairs had mellowed and how the garden had matured. A sense of constant care and maintenance seemed to have returned to an estate which, in the middle years of this century, was steadily disintegrating. Equally reassuring, the staff clearly still felt possessive about Erddig's special qualities and eccentricities. Over a hundred of us assembled in the garden for yet another photograph to add to the Erddig albums.

Not for the first time at Erddig, there were problems with the photographer. When in 1924 the family and staff gathered on the garden steps to commemorate Simon Yorke's coming of age, the party had to be posed in such a way that Philip Yorke was at right angles to the camera, to conceal, at least partially, his left eye, which was badly swollen as a result of a bee sting (see page 194). In 1987 the photographer recording the tenth anniversary party lost the negative. The only surviving print had to be copied, and in the process acquired a texture rather like the Erddig photographs of the 1880s. The group of 1987 is anyway misleading, with volunteers and others swelling the numbers of full-time staff. But the photographs taken in 1924 can also deceive, as they include staff recruited from Wrexham just for special occasions and celebrations.

These echoes and renewals answer the often-repeated criticism that the heart simply goes out of a house when there is no longer a resident family such as the Yorkes. True, no one lucky enough to have been shown round Erddig by Philip Yorke is likely to forget the experience. However, he and his family were always insistent that Erddig was a home not just to them, but to the community of staff on whom they depended. To convey the nature of this relationship, I always intended that the Yorkes and their staff should be largely left to tell their own story in their own words, through their letters and through their quantities of verse. That extraordinarily rich and evocative archive is one of the things which makes Erddig such a precious survival.

The continuing sense of obligation to the house and its traditions was brought home to me recently by a letter from Mrs Beryl Jones, the great-great-granddaughter of the carpenter, Thomas Rogers, who was rescued from the press-gang by Simon

Yorke and who was still working at Erddig in 1871, in his ninetieth year. An Australian descendent of Thomas Rogers had come across *The Servants' Hall* and I had put the two branches of the family in touch with each other. In the exchange of letters which followed, Mrs Jones mentioned that her son, Kevin, had trained as a cabinetmaker and furniture restorer at West Dean College and was now working for the National Trust: 'Kevin has been desperately busy for some months trying to finish the work before opening day.' She then added, 'The restoration of Erddig Hall changed our lives, I daresay quite a few people say that.' Philip Yorke would have valued that remark as much as I do.

The opportunity to write this Preface to the new edition of *The Servants' Hall* brought home to me how ungenerous I had been in the final chapter of the book, which recounts how the National Trust set about the reconstruction of Erddig. I should certainly have mentioned the work of John Tetley and Gordon Hall, the land agents responsible for the revival of the estate; the contribution of Elisabeth Walters, whose understanding of the needs of visitors ensured that the unconventional way the house was shown actually worked; and the skills of the builders, particularly Glyn Roberts, who carried out the repairs to the outbuildings. There are many others no less deserving of acknowledgement.

The book might never have appeared if Norman Franklin, of Routledge & Kegan Paul, had not taken such a personal interest in it. I am grateful to him, and to Margaret Willes, who has, with this new edition, brought it under the publishing wing of the National Trust.

MERLIN WATERSON
April 1990

Contents

Acknowledgments   xv
Foreword   xvii
Introduction   2

1   Setting Up   22
2   Elizabeth Ratcliffe, Lady's Maid   35
3   Chips from the Block   55
4   Housekeepers, Cooks and Nannies   76
5   Spider-brushers to the Master   98
6   Harmonious Blacksmiths   121
7   Woods and Woodmen   134
8   Gardens and Gardeners Run to Seed   150
9   Liveried Staff   168
10   Failures   187
11   Reconstruction   206

Bibliography and Notes   230
Index   233

Plates

Unless otherwise stated, all photographs are reproduced by permission of the National Trust.

	Edward Prince, carpenter at Erddig in 1792	*frontispiece*
1	The Servants' Hall in 1973 (Alex Starkey, by permission of *Country Life*)	1
2	Simon Yorke, 1696–1767	3
3	Philip Yorke, 1743–1804, by Thomas Gainsborough	4
4	Simon Yorke, 1771–1834, and his sister Etheldred, by Katherine Read	5
5	Simon Yorke, 1811–94, by G. Baldry	5
6	Philip Yorke, 1849–1922, as Placidus	5
7	Simon Yorke, 1903–66	5
8	Philip Yorke, 1905–78 (by permission of *Cheshire Life*)	7
9	The basement passage, lined with portraits of staff, in 1973 (Alex Starkey, by permission of *Country Life*)	8
10	A photograph taken by Gresford Window Cleaners in 1906 (staff listed)	11
11	George Roberts, a gardener, in 1911	12
12	The State Bedroom in 1973 (Alex Starkey, by permission of *Country Life*)	15
13	The State Bedroom in 1977 (by permission of the *Illustrated London News*)	15
14	The New Kitchen in 1973 (Alex Starkey, by permission of *Country Life*)	16
15	The New Kitchen in 1978 (by permission of the *Illustrated London News*)	17
16	The Servants' Hall in 1975 (John Bethell)	18
17	The east front, from the canal (Gareth Jones)	21
18	Joshua Edisbury, builder of Erddig	23
19	John Meller, 1665–1733	23

20	Jane Ebbrell, a mid-eighteenth century spider-brusher	25
21	The tapestries sent from London in 1721 (John Bethell)	27
22	The Gallery in 1973 (Alex Starkey, by permission of *Country Life*)	28
23	The Chapel (Alex Starkey, by permission of *Country Life*)	30
24	John Meller's negro coachboy	32
25	Betty Ratcliffe's drawing of Newnham, in Hertfordshire	36
26	'Two Sardinian Princes teaching a Marmute to dance', copied by Betty Ratcliffe from a mezzotint after Drouais, lent to her by Thomas Pennant	37
27	A drawing by Betty Ratcliffe of Sir Kenelm Digby and his family, after Van Dyck	37
28	'The Chinese Pagoda', signed E.R. 1767 (John Bethell)	39
29	Anne Jemima Yorke (1754–70)	40
30	Francis Cotes's portrait of Elizabeth Yorke (1749–79)	43
31	'The Ruins of Palmyra' by Betty Ratcliffe (John Bethell)	45
32	'The Ruins of Palmyra' (Gordon Robertson)	46
33	'Conway Castle', a drawing by Betty Ratcliffe of 1782	47
34	The arms of Yorke and Hutton, cut out of paper by Betty Ratcliffe and mounted on scarlet foil	48
35	A bouquet of flowers by Betty Ratcliffe, made of silk, paper, wire and wool and mounted in a frame probably by Thomas Fentham (John Bethell)	48
36	John Jones in 1911, thirty-three years after he entered service as a carpenter	54
37	Thomas Rogers, carpenter, painted in 1830 when he was 48	57
38	Tools used by Thomas Rogers and stamped with his name (John Bethell)	60
39	Servants at Erddig in 1852	61
40	The joiners' shop in 1973 (John Bethell)	62
41	The joiners' shop in 1978 (Gareth Jones)	62
42	James Rogers, who succeeded his father as carpenter in 1871	63
43	John Jones, photographed in the joiners' shop	65
44	A sixteenth century table found in an outhouse and restored by John Jones (John Bethell)	68
45	William Gittins, foreman carpenter, in 1911	70
46	Nursery toys, including the train made by the foreman carpenter William Gittins for Simon Yorke's fifth birthday (by permission of the *Illustrated London News*)	75
47	Thomas Jones, butcher to Erddig in the 1790s	79
48	The housekeeper's room (H. A. Thompson)	80
49	Mary Webster, housekeeper during the middle years of the nineteenth century	81
50	Harriet Rogers, lady's maid and then housekeeper	83

51 Harriet Rogers accompanying one of the Squire's sisters on an expedition in the Erddig donkey cart 84
52 Harriet Rogers's lantern, sewing box and the Bible given to her by the Yorke family (John Bethell) 86
53 The second Philip Yorke (1849–1922) 87
54 Miss Brown, who came to Erddig as housekeeper in 1907 and left in 1914 91
55 Lucy Hitchman, nurse to Simon and Philip Yorke, photographed in 1911 with them and with her future husband, the groom Ernest Jones 93
56 The scullery (Gareth Jones) 97
57 A servant's four-poster, designed to fit under the eaves (Gareth Jones) 99
58 Jack Nicholas, 'a constant Porter to the pot' 100
59 The bakehouse (Gareth Jones) 102
60 The wet laundry (Gareth Jones) 103
61 The dry laundry (by permission of the *Illustrated London News*) 104
62 Sarah Davies, affectionately known as 'Lalla' by the Yorke children 106
63 Ruth Jones in 1912, half a century after she came to Erddig as a maid 109
64 Servants at Erddig in 1887 111
65 The workroom, where maids retired in the afternoon to sew and read (Gareth Jones) 113
66 The staff in 1912, each holding their badge of office as their predecessors had done in the daguerreotype taken in 1852 114
67 A garden group of 1912 117
68 The survivors in 1962, half a century later 119
69 Joseph Wright 120
70 A detail of Badeslade's print of Erddig in 1740, showing Robert Davies's wrought iron screen on the west front 122
71 William Williams, blacksmith during the 1780s and 1790s 123
72 The railings supplied in 1781 by William Williams for the entrance front (Gareth Jones) 124
73 Joseph Wright, who came to Erddig as blacksmith in 1886 125
74 The garden fountains, with the lead shells made by Joseph Wright from a cast of an eighteenth century marble basin (the author) 126
75 The screen from Stansty, bought by Philip Yorke in 1909 (Gareth Jones) 127
76 A detail of the Stansty Screen (Gareth Jones) 127
77 The screen when at Forest Lodge (Alex Starkey, by permission of *Country Life*) 128
78 The screen from Stansty, repositioned at the end of the garden canal (the author) 129
79 The blacksmith's shop in 1978 (Gareth Jones) 131

80 The sawmill (by permission of the *Illustrated London News*) 133
81 The Cathedral Aisle 136
82 The agent's office, where wages were paid, accounts kept and where maps of the estate were stored (Alex Starkey, by permission of *Country Life*) 137
83 The Cup and Saucer – a cylindrical waterfall constructed under Emes's supervision in the 1770s – as it was earlier this century 139
84 The view up the tunnel to the waterfall, in 1973 (Alex Starkey, by permission of *Country Life*) 140
85 Jack Henshaw, 'best of beaters' 141
86 Edward Barnes, skilled as a forester, fisherman and brewer 143
87 The saw pit and entrance to the joiners' shop (the author) 144
88 The saw pit (Gareth Jones) 144
89 The timber waggon (Gareth Jones) 145
90 William Hughes, woodman between 1883 and 1903 146
91 Thomas Roberts, sawyer and engineer for forty-nine years 147
92 Mike Snowden, who as head gardener was responsible for restoring the early eighteenth century formal layout (Gareth Jones) 149
93 Badeslade's print of 1740 151
94 The garden as restored to the design recorded by Badeslade (Alex Starkey, by permission of *Country Life*) 152
95 Thomas Pritchard, 'old and run to seed' in 1830 155
96 James Phillips, who succeeded Pritchard as head gardener 157
97 Some of the staff who worked under James Phillips during the second half of the nineteenth century 159
98 John Davies, an under-gardener for over forty years 160
99 Thomas Thomas, a garden boy killed during the First World War 163
100 The Butler's Pantry (by permission of the *Illustrated London News*) 167
101 Edward Humphreys, photographed in 1852 171
102 The Family Museum (Alex Starkey, by permission of *Country Life*) 174
103 George Dickinson's hatchment in the Servants' Hall (John Bethell) 175
104 Nineteenth century liveries, usually hung in the Butler's Pantry (Gareth Jones) 176
105 Frank Lovett, formerly a footman, shortly before he left for Italy 180
106 John Jones, coachman in 1911, with Simon Yorke 183
107 John Jones in livery and Lucy Jones (née Hitchman) in the Servants' Hall in 1943 (*Picture Post*) 184
108 The Nursery corridor in 1973 (Alex Starkey, by permission of *Country Life*) 186
109 Mrs Penketh, cook at Erddig from 1903 to 1907 191
110 Simon Yorke's coming of age party in 1924 194
111 Staff at Simon Yorke's coming of age party 194
112 Albert Gillam, the last head gardener employed by the Yorkes 196

113 Philip Yorke in *The School for Scandal* at the Northampton
Repertory Theatre   198
114 The final flowering of the Yorkes' taste for *Chinoiserie*   199
115 The sawmill in 1973 (John Bethell)   201
116 The haybarn in 1973 (John Bethell)   202
117 The haybarn and outer stable yard in 1978 (Alex Starkey, by
permission of *Country Life*)   203
118 Philip Yorke (by permission of the *Daily Mirror*)   205
119 The garden and Mr Yorke's gardeners in 1973 (Gareth Jones)   208
120 The Drawing Room in 1973, when Philip Yorke was using it as a
bedroom (Alex Starkey, by permission of *Country Life*)   209
121 Philip Yorke in the Drawing Room, a few months before he gave
Erddig away (Gareth Jones)   213
122 The stable yard in 1973 (Alex Starkey, by permission of *Country
Life*)   214
123 The stable yard in 1978 (Gareth Jones)   214
124 The family Rover in 1973 (John Bethell)   216
125 The Rover in 1978 (Alex Starkey, by permission of *Country Life*) 217
126 A nineteenth century shower, with pipes and a pump to circulate
the water (John Bethell)   219
127 Philip Yorke's shower (John Bethell)   220
128 Barry Roberts clearing the garden in 1974   221
129 The Garden House in 1973 (John Bethell)   222
130 Mike Snowden in 1978, outside the Garden House (the author)   223
128 Barry Roberts clearing the garden in 1974 (Bill Leimbach)   224
132 The garden, 1974 (Bill Leimbach)   224
133 The garden, 1978 (Alex Starkey, by permission of *Country Life*) 225
134 Graham Carr remounting the eighteenth century Chinese painted
panels in the Chinese Room (H. A. Thompson)   226
135 Jigsaw puzzles in the State Bedroom (H. A. Thompson)   226
136 The Library (Alex Starkey, by permission of *Country Life*)   227
137 The Dining Room (by permission of the *Illustrated London News*) 227

Acknowledgments

As the last of his family to live at Erddig, Philip Yorke realised better than anyone that its preservation should involve more than just the rescue of material objects. It was also vital to record a mass of information about life at Erddig which earlier generations would have taken for granted, or which his elder brother would perhaps have thought best forgotten. Between 1973, when I first felt a responsibility to write about and photograph what was happening to the house, until his death in 1978, Philip fed my notebooks with facts, anecdotes and occasionally with fantasy. He delighted in his forebears' eccentricities and indiscretions, provided they were not caricatured and were related in a sympathetic way. I hope he would have felt that my attempts to strike that elusive balance have been at least partially successful.

Thanks are due to the editors of *Country Life*, *Smithsonian*, and *Apollo* for permission to use material they first published. I doubt whether those few disparate articles would have finally been drawn together into a book without all the help and advice I have had from the Marquess of Anglesey, who read the whole book in typescript, corrected numerous errors and allowed himself to be persuaded to contribute a foreword. Mr Robin Herbert, the Chairman of the National Trust's Committee for Wales, also gave much-valued encouragement. For guidance on the early history of the house, and for the Index, I am indebted to Miss Elizabeth Pettitt. Gervase Jackson-Stops was characteristically generous with his discoveries among the Erddig archives. Consulting the Erddig papers now in the Clwyd Record Office at Hawarden could not have been made easier by the County Archivist, Mr Geoffrey Veysey. Others who have made important contributions include my parents, Miss Diana Carroll, Mr John Hardy, Mr Peter Howell, Mr H. V. Kitching, Wing Commander F. W. Lovett and Mrs Elisabeth Walters.

It was a stroke of remarkable good fortune that John Bethell, Gareth Jones and Alex Starkey fell under Erddig's spell and recorded its changing faces in their very different photographic styles. Their enthusiasm for the house has fed mine; as has that of scores of others who helped in its rescue or who shared their memories of its past.

I am also grateful to Mrs Angela Booton, Mrs Sarah Watson and Miss Patricia Burke for deciphering my handwriting. Most patient and tolerant of all has been my wife.

Foreword

When I first went to Erddig, twenty-seven years ago, the house and garden were on the verge of total dereliction. That was in the reign of Simon Yorke, the penultimate squire. I had invited myself to lunch (together with the late Sir Grismond Philipps, who was then Chairman of the Historic Buildings Council for Wales), under, I am ashamed to say, false pretences. It had come to my ears that Mr Yorke was extraordinarily keen upon the International Eisteddfod at Llangollen, which he attended every year most assiduously. In 1952 I had been asked to act as 'President of the day'. This entailed making a speech in the pavilion, so I pretended to him (and perhaps half hoped) that he would be able to give me some hints as to what to say.

Sir Grismond's and my real motive for practising this abuse of the squire's hospitality was an anxious desire to assess at first hand how true was the current gossip about the neglect of the house's contents, known to be of exceptional quality. A relation of the Yorkes, the late Ralph Edwards, the celebrated expert on English furniture, told me that an application to gain entry by stating a desire to inspect one of the great houses of Wales would not have been attended by success: hence the mild deceit.

Many and diverse were the rumours about our host's peculiarities. It was said, for instance, that he had employed monies received in compensation for war-time damage to raise the height of the park wall. This was palpably untrue. In fact, it can be taken as certain that during his time absolutely nothing was ever built up. On the contrary everything was falling down. Anyway there *is* no park wall to speak of! Yet such tales as this were not inconsistent with the man's strange character.

But to return to our visit. Had he known that we were what he would have categorised as 'Government spies' – a term which his suspicious mind applied to any persons even faintly connected with officialdom – he would certainly have refused us entry. As it was we were treated to a frugal meal served by a sinister-looking 'butler', the temporary nature of whose employment was manifested by his ill-fitting uniform and obviously limited knowledge of the job.

As we were taken round the house we were shown with real but pathetically childlike enthusiasm many a broken piece of furniture. These, we were assured, were about to be repaired. Upon the great State Bed, I remember, sat three basins and one chamber-pot, collecting the rain-water which was dripping through the canopy from the crumbling ceiling above it. When our eyes strayed from this dispiriting spectacle and focused upon the view from the first-floor windows, the branches of saplings growing from the base of the house almost shut out the scene of desolation presented by the grossly neglected garden.

Soon after our visit I wrote to thank Mr Yorke for his kindness, adding a suggestion that he might apply for an Historic Buildings Council grant towards the restoration of the many contents of the house which were of outstanding national importance. His failure to reply came as no surprise. Not long after his death, however, his more rational, amenable, if only slightly less eccentric, younger brother, Philip, agreed to meet members of the Historic Buildings Council and in due course a grant was offered, though typically not accepted. At that time this likeable but whimsically wayward last of his line was reputed to be driving a private taxi-cab between Wrexham and Madrid! On top of his battered automobile was strapped an equally bruised bicycle. His shirt I well recollect was not of the cleanest. He was, indeed, the only man I ever met whose linen was never really clean nor really dirty. How he managed that, I never discovered. It was nearly always just as impossible to discover how his mind worked.

One thing, though, was beyond doubt. He was determined with an unbending persistence to sustain the appallingly daunting effort required to stop the rot at Erddig. As Merlin Waterson shows in this captivating history of one of the five or six really great country houses in the Principality, without Philip's resolute constancy, the National Trust, when eventually it came to take the place over, would have had nothing to take over, nothing to rehabilitate, nothing to restore. Mining subsidence, vandalism and natural decay would have seen to that.

During the weary years of negotiation with the Trust, I was deputed to carry on – or perhaps wage is a better word – some of the correspondence with Philip. Though at times the frustrating parts of this labour seemed to outweigh even the humorous aspects of it, I came to esteem, almost to love, this peculiar man, who during his earlier life had been a professional actor. His unpredictability, bordering sometimes on perversity, made the transaction of business far from easy, but it banished dullness and excluded pomposity absolutely. His very first letter to me began 'My Lord Marquess' and ended 'Your Lordship's obedient servant, Phil'! His death in 1978 was a considerable personal loss. Thousands of people who visited his ancestral home during the first five years of its ownership by the Trust were privileged to enjoy Philip's presence as a sort of self-appointed guide and to listen to his highly amusing anecdotes. Almost miraculous as is Erddig's regeneration, the atmosphere of the place will never of course be quite the same again, now that its last squire has departed.

This immensely readable book, as its title suggests, is slanted towards the virtually unique relationship between the successive families 'upstairs' and their retainers 'downstairs'. This is reflected in the fact that of all the two hundred or so country houses owned by the National Trust, Erddig is the only one where the visitor enters through the back yard, as if he were one of that devoted band of long-serving servants whose merits (and sometimes faults) were celebrated in verse by squire after squire.

Mr Waterson takes full advantage of the circumstances that have preserved at

Erddig documentary evidence of almost every conceivable description, covering more than 250 years, on a scale lavish enough to dismay a less industrious author. The organisation of his mass of material, and the clear, pithy way in which he presents it, would be remarkable achievements for a seasoned writer. They are particularly notable – and positively rare – in a young man's first book. As the Trust's Historic Buildings Representative in the area, he has borne the brunt of the prodigious undertaking of nursing Erddig from imminent demise to radiant resurrection, a task exceeding in complexity and scale any other undertaken by the Trust in its eighty-five years of existence.

The Marquess of Anglesey
DL, FSA, FR Hists, Hon FRIBA, FRSL
Chairman, Historic Buildings Council for Wales
Vice-Chairman, Committee for Wales of the National Trust

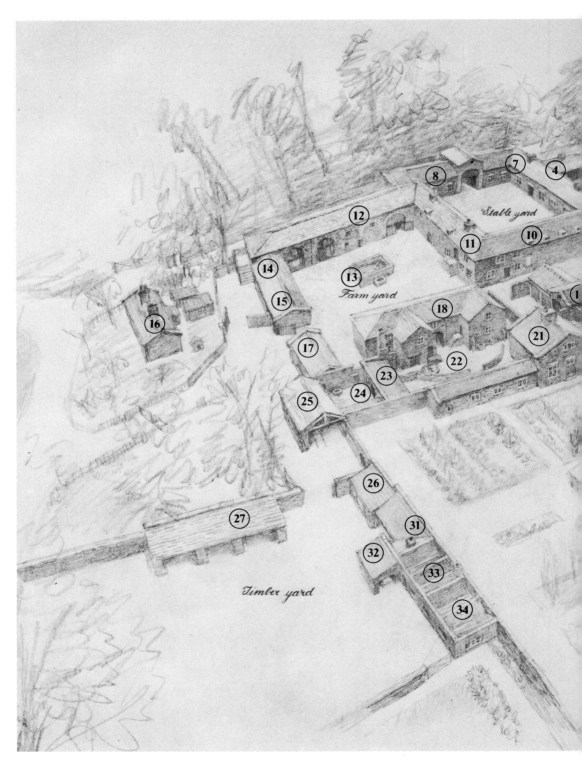

Pleasure garden

Kitchen garden

ERDDIG
The domestic offices and
outbuildings from the south-east
John Bedford 1979

KEY

 1 Cook's room
 2 New Kitchen
 3 Bell Tower
 4 Bakehouse
 5 Wet laundry
 6 Dry laundry
 7 Tack room
 8 Stalls
 9 Coach-house
10 Garages
11 The Bothy Cottage
12 Haybarn
13 Midden
14 Bull pen
15 Waggon shed
16 Coachman's Lodge
17 Slaughterhouse
18 Sawmill
19 Workmen's privy
20 Garden tools store
21 The Garden House
22 Mortar mixer
23 Kennels
24 Dog yard
25 Timber waggon shed
26 Paint store
27 Timber store
28 Vine house
29 Greenhouse
30 Garden machinery store
31 Blacksmiths' shop
32 Saw pit
33 Joiners' store
34 Joiners' shop

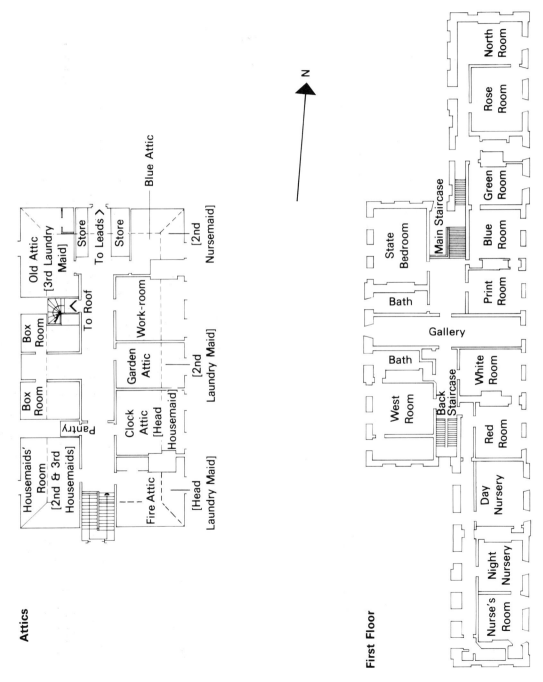

Attics

Housemaids' Room [2nd & 3rd Housemaids]

Box Room

Box Room

Pantry

Old Attic [3rd Laundry Maid]

Store

To Leads >

Store

To Roof

Blue Attic

Clock Attic [Head Housemaid]

Garden Attic

Work-room

Fire Attic

[Head Laundry Maid]

[2nd Laundry Maid]

[2nd Nursemaid]

N

First Floor

Nurse's Room

Night Nursery

Day Nursery

West Room

Bath

State Bedroom

Bath

Back Staircase

Red Room

White Room

Gallery

Main Staircase

Print Room

Blue Room

Green Room

Rose Room

North Room

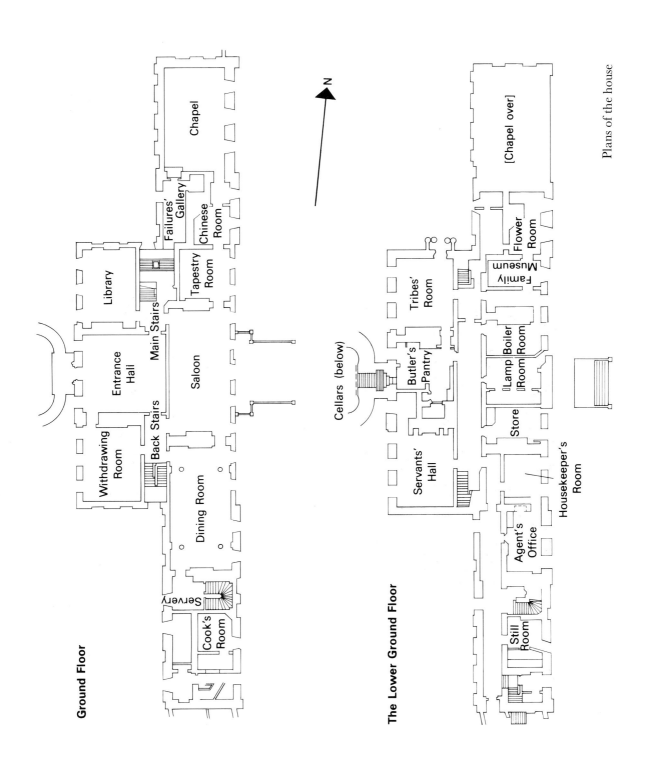

Ground Floor

N

Library
Entrance Hall
Withdrawing Room
Main Stairs
Back Stairs
Failures' Gallery
Chinese Room
Chapel
Tapestry Room
Saloon
Dining Room
Servery
Cook's Room

The Lower Ground Floor

Servants' Hall
Butler's Pantry
Tribes' Room
Cellars (below)
Store
Lamp Room
Boiler Room
Family Museum
Flower Room
[Chapel over]
Agent's Office
Housekeeper's Room
Still Room

Plans of the house

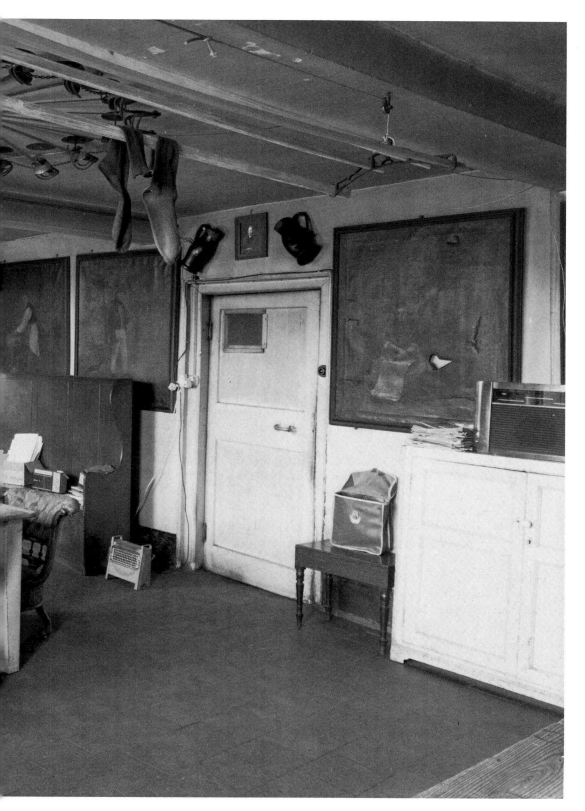

1 The Servants' Hall in 1973

Introduction

While the last Philip Yorke was squire of Erddig, the most important room in the house was the Servants' Hall, the most important meal, tea. Old actor friends, visiting officials and connoisseurs, distant relatives and part-time helpers on the estate would gather there for mounds of bread and butter, jam and cakes. It was the one meal Philip could offer without offending his vegetarianism. At that time, during the late 1960s and early 1970s, the portraits of staff lining the walls were blackened and in places torn. The eyes of Jane Ebbrell, a housemaid painted in 1793, had served as an improvised darts board. Whenever the late afternoon sun rounded the chestnut on the entrance front and streamed into the room, the crude but decorative early eighteenth century portrait of a young negro in livery and the portrait of a gardener Thomas Pritchard, painted 100 years later, would be lost in the gloom of the window wall. More conspicuous were the socks and other clothes dangling from the ceiling on drying frames, and the signs of spasmodic office use: the smartly headed letters spilling out of the half-closed drawers of a battered davenport, the photographs and reports squabbling with motor cycle kit and biscuit tins for every spare inch of table top.

'No wonder the place went to pieces – the family were soft on their servants', I once heard a visitor remark. That crass explanation could scarcely be further from the truth. Indeed, one of the things which persuaded the National Trust to attempt the rescue of the house was its unrivalled collection of servants' portraits. Without this record of the Yorke family's remarkable relationship with their staff over two centuries, the argument that the house was not outstanding architecturally might have prevailed, the scales tipped the other way. Bulldozers and the London sale rooms would happily have speeded its disintegration.

Of all types of employment during the eighteenth and nineteenth centuries, domestic service was the area least scrutinised by philanthropists and by Royal Commissions, least well recorded in diaries, letters and the press. That the Yorkes should have had more portraits painted of their staff than they did of their own family and should have written lengthy inscriptions for them in verse was regarded by their contemporaries as whimsical, to say the least. There was nothing unusual about a country house owner having expensive portraits painted of his horses, his prize-winning bulls or his dogs – they, after all, were the product of careful breeding like their

2 Simon Yorke, 1696–1767

owners – but to extend the treatment to generations of servants was thought to be a symptom of extreme eccentricity.

The continuity in the Yorkes' ownership of Erddig accounts for much of the interest of the record of service there. It would be hard to devise a more straightforward succession than the Yorkes'. The first Simon Yorke inherited from his uncle John Meller in 1733. He was succeeded by his son Philip in 1767. Another Simon followed in 1804, and another in 1834. The second Philip inherited in 1894. On his death in 1922 Erddig passed to the fourth and last Simon and then, the only instance of an eldest son not succeeding, to his brother Philip, in 1966. To simplify things still more, the Simons all tended to be, if decent, rather dim and dull. The three Philips were decent; but rarely dull and certainly not dim. With so uncomplicated a succession I have not felt it necessary to follow a strict chronology. Instead a chapter is devoted to each of the principal categories of staff, rather than to each generation of Yorkes, in the hope that this gives a clearer picture of the organisation of the household.

The verse the Yorkes wrote about their staff inevitably gives a very one-sided account of life at Erddig, perhaps one which is most revealing for what it tells of the attitudes of the squire's family. The staff they recorded were the successes, those whose virtues, loyalty and long service were held up as an example to other staff. Their verse describes the relationship as the Yorkes wanted it to be; not necessarily as it was. Fortunately it has been possible to trace a large number of private letters and diaries to redress the balance. Some of these were among the Erddig papers, others have been made available by the descendants of staff who worked at Erddig. Because letters from those in domestic service elsewhere have rarely survived, not least because staff were often barely, if at all, literate, I have usually quoted in full, rather than paraphrased them. They are of interest for the way they are written, not just for what they say.

3 Philip Yorke, 1743–1804, by Thomas Gainsborough

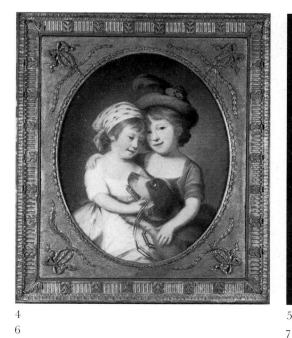

4

5

6

7

4 Simon Yorke, 1771–1834, and his sister Etheldred, by Katherine Read

5 Simon Yorke, 1811–94, by G. Baldry

6 Philip Yorke, 1849–1922, as Placidus

7 Simon Yorke, 1903–66

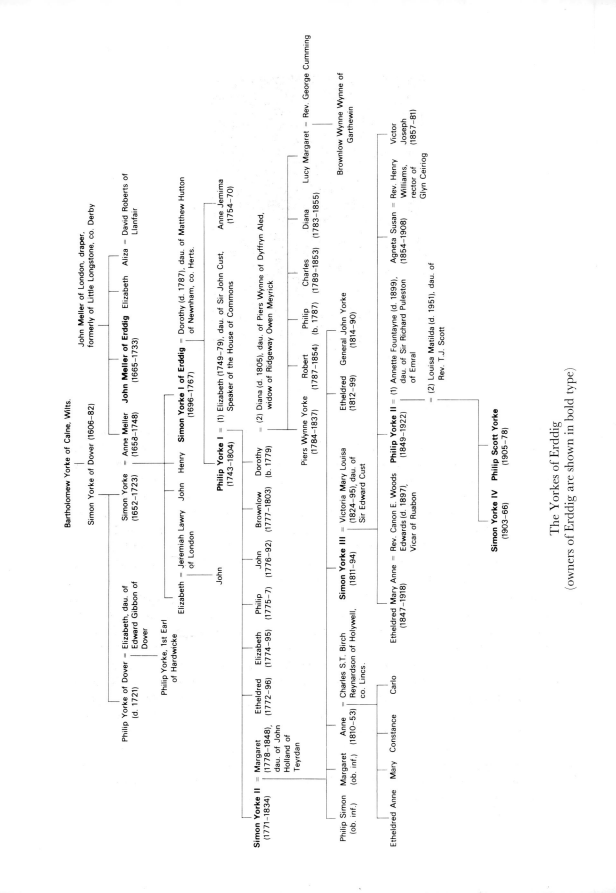

The Yorkes of Erddig
(owners of Erddig are shown in bold type)

8 Philip Yorke, 1905–78

Some of the early letters quoted were included in the two-volume *Chronicles of Erthig on the Dyke* (1914) by Albinia Lucy Cust, a cousin of the Yorkes. Its very length and unselectivity makes the book both invaluable and infuriating. Interested friends and relations were roped in to help transcribe, sometimes with startling inaccuracy, the hundreds of letters and documents she quotes in full. When the authoress wrote to Simon Yorke in 1922 to explain how she had sorted the family archives, she explained that she had thrown away a great deal of recent family correspondence in the belief that 'since the days of newspapers private letters have lost their political and historical value'. She also told Simon that she had destroyed 'by your Mother's special wish all records of a painful character'. Such vandalism is easier to forgive when one remembers that the Yorkes set great store by charity. But no sifting of documents could obscure the fact that there were times when the family's relations with each other and with their staff were very far from happy, very far removed from the image of mutual service and trust presented in the portraits and verse. My penultimate chapter is devoted to what Mrs Yorke would have called 'records of a painful character'.

Most of the letters by Erddig staff which have been preserved were occasioned by events of special importance or stress: by some unexpected kindness from the squire's family, an unfair dismissal, or bereavement. They convey, as the Yorkes' verse does not, the more sombre, serious side of the relationship, and are more telling for being sometimes clumsily and painfully written. The jingling rhyming couplet – that most obvious, most exacting poetic form – is rarely an appropriate way in which to describe human tragedy; and when the second Philip Yorke used it on such occasions, the results were usually disastrous.

9   The basement passage, lined with portraits of staff, in 1973

The verses which line the walls of the basement passage and the Servants' Hall at Erddig were only a small part of the Yorkes' output. Drawer after drawer was crammed with bundles of poems, sometimes printed for them privately in Wrexham, sometimes written out, most frequently typed with a faded blue ribbon by the second Philip Yorke. Confronted with such fertility, perhaps a little pruning may be allowed. Without the occasional prose interlude, the Yorkes' light verse can prove very, very heavy going.

Remarkably, Erddig itself has survived. With the house, the state rooms, its domestic offices, stables, estate yards and workshops still intact and with a wealth of documentary material about their use to draw on, its history can be seen not just through the eyes of its owners, but through those of the whole community who lived and worked there.

The study of country houses has in the past tended to be regarded as the preserve of the connoisseur, the furniture and architectural historian. The social historian has until very recently been the poor relation. The results have been that the preservation of country houses has too often been considered only in terms of grand rooms and imposing façades. The first wing to be pulled down has usually been the one with the domestic offices; the contents of the servants' quarters and the attic bedrooms were frequently the first to be sold or thrown out. Very few houses have preserved more than a random and haphazard selection of relics of their domestic history. Erddig is an exception. Over two and a half centuries, each succeeding generation of Yorkes was largely content to preserve their inheritance, to cherish the curious and personal as well as the obviously valuable, and to throw nothing away. Perhaps this form of complacency was their greatest virtue. Finally, Erddig was supremely well served by the helpless and hopeless way in which the last Simon Yorke failed totally to come to terms with the twentieth century.

How does Erddig compare with other country houses? Can any useful general conclusions be drawn about the organisation of other households and about the relationship between landed gentry and their servants? Admittedly, a family that cultivated their eccentricities as assiduously as the Yorkes may not offer the ideal case study. But what I believe can be deduced is that life in the smaller country houses, especially those more than a day's journey from London, did not slavishly follow the example set by the very grandest establishments. It was not just that they were slow on the uptake. They had their own traditions and values, related to but still significantly different from those of the titled aristocracy. Because the archives of the great pioneering houses have tended to be more accessible, in several cases in published form, they have perhaps received more than their fair share of attention. Generalisations about life in lesser houses cannot safely be made on the basis of such evidence.

The descriptions of the splendid households of the higher nobility in Mark Girouard's *Life in the English Country House* (1978) are now an indispensable yardstick against which to measure other houses. But his accounts of changing attitudes to domestic service cannot be invariably applied to smaller households. Erddig certainly does not conform to his assertion that throughout the eighteenth and nineteenth centuries the gulf between family and staff widened steadily as the last memories of the closely knit medieval household faded, and that at the beginning of the present century 'the two communities still lived independent lives'. Erddig seems to have followed a very different pattern, with John Meller's household of the 1720s far more hierarchical and rigidly divided than Philip Yorke's in the 1780s. The tradition that the first Philip nurtured so carefully of respect and real friendship between family and staff was continued by his son, the second Simon, and was still strong at the end of the nineteenth century.

Further study may in due course suggest that the trend during the late eighteenth century towards greater informality in upper class life may in some lesser country houses have encouraged a less formal relationship with staff. It may also be that differing regional traditions of domestic service, for instance in the West Midlands and the border country, will emerge. The stability of a particular household depended so much on outside factors: on working class mobility in the area, on alternative employment and the wages it offered. The genre of servants' portraits, so well represented at Erddig, Hawarden, Chirk, Dudmaston, Lyme and Chatsworth, all within 100 miles of each other, may well have regional significance.

If this book has a central theme it is that the Erddig household throughout most of its history was genuinely one community. This was an ideal which the second Philip Yorke returned to time and again in his verse about his staff, prefacing his accounts of their service with such lines as

> But yet we introduce a few
> Whom we remark as comers new
> And unto whom we now allude
> To show our sense of gratitude.

That he was also at pains to show that the relationship was more than just a working one comes over particularly strongly in what Philip Yorke wrote of George Roberts, an under-gardener. Roberts's early life had been spent on the Great Western Railway and then at the Cefn quarries, loading trucks with sandstone. When in the 1880s there was a serious recession in the North Wales building industry, he was lucky to find a job at Erddig. He had no special knowledge or experience as a gardener, but his mother-in-law was remembered for her loyal service to the squire's father. Philip Yorke's verse of 1911 describes how parish meetings were deliberately not held at Erddig:

> Roberts, to serve the public ends,
> His home at our disposal lends
> While acting thus the double post
> Of Councillor and genial host.
>
> Then, at our evening meeting's close,
> Foregoing his well-earned repose
> He often, if the night be dark,
> Escorts his chairman through the park,

10   A photograph taken by Gresford Window Cleaners in 1906
Back row, left to right: Williams, third carpenter; Lizzie Copestake, kitchen maid; Jinnie
Fairman, second housemaid; Annie Parry, scullery maid; Arthur Baker, footman; Mrs
Hughes, charwoman; Edith Haycock, third housemaid; Matilda Boulter, head
housemaid; Alice Jones, second laundry maid; Mr Wooton, butler
Front row, left to right: Edward Jones, labourer; George, hall boy; Walter Davis,
bricklayer; Alfred Roberts, second sawyer; Percy Jones, the coachman's son; John
Davis, labourer; Jonathan Davis, bricklayer (son of Walter Davis)

> (The same of whom we here may say
> He is the Author of this Lay.)
> And in much converse we engage
> Of things pertaining to the age.

The charge of hypocrisy could be levelled against Philip Yorke for writing in that
vein when he was paying his staff wages below the average for country house posts. His
butler, Wooton, was receiving £55 a year in 1903, which was not much more than he
would have earned as under-butler at a larger house; while the female staff were
consistently paid below the rates recommended in J. H. Walsh's *A Manual of Domestic
Economy* of 1857 and successive editions of *The Book of Household Management*. Mrs
Beeton gave £18 a year as the wage for a maid-of-all-work in 1900, when the junior
maids at Erddig were receiving between £8 and £15. But such comparisons ought to be
seen in the context of the quality of food and accommodation offered at Erddig, and the

11 George Roberts, a gardener, in 1911. His wife is holding a portrait of her mother, who had been in service at Erddig

opportunities the staff had for saving. During the second half of the nineteenth century two servants at Erddig died leaving substantial sums to their relatives: in the case of the housekeeper, Mrs Webster, £1,300 and of James Phillips, a gardener, £4,000. That those figures are difficult to square with their annual wages is a measure of the importance of additional sources of income, including the commissions, or 'poundage' that a housekeeper could receive from shopkeepers in return for custom from the big house.

The Yorke family also provided such loyal members of their staff as Thomas Rogers with pensions when they retired, as well as a cottage on the estate. The most remarkable instance of this is the annuity of £100 paid to Dorothy Yorke's gifted maid and companion, Betty Ratcliffe, after she left the family's service. It has been suggested that such generosity points to some unrecorded kinship with the Yorkes, perhaps that she was an illegitimate daughter. The records of divorce cases in the eighteenth century show that it was by no means unusual for relations between masters and servants to be paternal in a very literal sense. But I can find not a shred of evidence for any such tie between Betty Ratcliffe and her employers. That it was Dorothy Yorke who paid for her education and who in 1787 left her the legacy makes the suggestion all the more improbable. Surviving letters to and from Betty Ratcliffe point to an entirely straightforward explanation of kindness and affection from several of the Yorkes, and respect for her exceptional talents.

The most tangible expression of the relationship between the family and their staff is found in the physical planning of the house and its outbuildings. The fact that the eighteenth century arrangement of the domestic offices at Erddig was scarcely altered throughout the nineteenth century has social as well as financial implications. The plan of the offices was established in the 1770s, when a new kitchen and laundry yard were built in a block south of, and detached from, the main house. The decision to separate these buildings was dictated more by Philip Yorke's fear of 'the dreadful accident of fire', the subject of two letters to his steward in November 1770, than by social considerations. The Butler's Pantry and the Servants' Hall remained where they had been in the 1720s, when John Meller set up house. The Yorke family do not seem to have worried that only a short flight of stairs separated the servants' quarters from the main apartments, or that the Servants' Hall looked out on the main entrance courtyard. At no time did they consider building a separate servants' wing to isolate themselves from their staff. The only significant change that may reflect a desire for greater segregation was the replanning of the garden to the east of the house in 1861. By laying out a parterre with box hedges on the terrace in front of the saloon windows, the view of the garden from the basement rooms used by the staff was effectively blocked off. But the parterre may equally well have been prompted simply by changing fashions in garden design and be completely innocent of any social scheming.

During the nineteenth century the first Philip Yorke's warnings about fire were forgotten and the space between the new kitchen and the south wing was filled in to make new rooms for the housekeeper. Judging by an inventory of 1726, the housekeeper's bedroom was originally in the attics, along with the maids' rooms. The move into a suite of three rooms at the far end of the building reflects the housekeeper's changing status and may also suggest increasing divisions separating senior and junior staff. However, at Erddig there seems to have been far less distinction and fewer barriers between their different ranks than in larger country houses. Twice in the mid-nineteenth century the Yorkes appointed one of their maids to be nurse, and this led in turn to promotion to housekeeper. Two of their butlers began service at Erddig as footmen. Both the Yorke children and his own junior staff remembered the butler, George Dickinson, with great affection and respect.

The green baize door has become the symbol of a divided household. It is, therefore, tempting to attach significance to the fact that Erddig seems never to have had any green baize on its doors. Moreover, the billiard room, which the first Philip Yorke decorated with coats of arms taken from his book *The Royal Tribes of Wales*, happens to be 'below stairs'. If nothing else, that can be taken to symbolise the contradictions and complexities of the relationship between the squire and his staff.

To generalise about the Erddig household over 200 years is a dangerous exercise; to extend these generalisations to other country houses still more so. The temperament of an individual squire could so colour the lives of all those around him. There is no better example than that of Thomas Apperley of Plas Grono, a contemporary and neighbour of the first Philip Yorke. He had what his son called

> strange fancies respecting domestic servants, some of which were not exactly in unison with a liberal and highly cultivated mind. It would almost appear, indeed, that he associated their situation more than he should have done with that of slaves, inasmuch as, although he fed them nearly to repletion, he too rigorously exacted their services, and seldom acknowledged the performance of them, however valuable they may have been.

Suspecting a junior footman of stealing, he had him 'stripped to the waist, hoisted over the servants' hall door, and very well flogged'.

Sir Watkin Williams Wynn, of Wynnstay, another neighbour, makes a further revealing comparison. The fifth Baronet was a byword for benevolence towards staff and tenants. It was reputedly a saying amongst the poor on his estate that 'If God was to die we should still have Sir Watkin.' Just as the abuses of landlordism in nineteenth century Wales have tended to be mythologised for political ends, so too have the abuses of domestic service. Wynnstay and Erddig may not be typical households; but they cannot simply be dismissed as exceptional and extreme cases of provincial conservatism.

My first visit to Erddig was on a dreary February afternoon in 1971. Half a century had not mellowed the harsh Ruabon brick of the suburbs of Wrexham. Although the lodge at the entrance to the park was derelict and roofless except for a few tiles clinging to its gable ends, a Wrexham Scout troop still had its name in large, unruly letters over the entrance porch. The gate piers ended, not in ball finials, but in the jagged stone of their broken necks. Puddles clustered around the gates, which were loosely secured with rusty chain.

Inside the park, the road disintegrated into a ridge of mud flanked by almost continuous potholes. It led down a steep bank, threaded its way between massive exposed tree roots, across a valley of water meadows, then climbed a hillside of hanging beech woods before emerging abruptly at the house. Fresh white paint on the iron railings leading up to the main door drew attention to the weeds sprouting between the steps and to the variegations of black staining and pale sandstone of the entrance front. Where the shutters of a few of the ground floor rooms were open, reflections quivered in the exquisite imperfections of the old glass. But most of the shutters were closed, many of the windows broken and whole sashes were missing. It was the death mask of a house which faced the two vast slag heaps in the park.

Few park monuments are as telling as those two colliery tips. Erddig was undermined during the 1940s and 1950s and subsidence all but wrecked the house irrevocably. It was scarcely surprising that the National Trust's committees should have baulked at taking on a building that had fallen 5 feet at one end, 3 feet 6 inches at the other, and where a hasty arrangement of pit props in the State Bedroom supported those sections of the ceiling which had not already collapsed; or that the director of a

12　The State Bedroom in 1973

13　The State Bedroom in 1977

14   The New Kitchen in 1973, with girders inserted by the Coal Board to prevent the main walls collapsing inwards

leading national museum should have dismissed Erddig as an 'evil house', which the Trust would be crazy to try to save. But in March 1973 craziness prevailed.

Four years later the house was opened to the public by the Prince of Wales. There were radio and television programmes about Erddig, *The Times* spoke of a 'masterpiece of restoration' and the *Daily Mirror* gave its front page to a picture of the Prince falling off an Erddig penny-farthing. That the change in the house's fortunes should have been so dramatic was not entirely out of character. Since the eighteenth century the Yorke family had delighted in amateur theatricals. The placid, slow-moving middle acts of the drama contrasted strikingly with these melodramatic last scenes of near disaster and triumph.

In my final two chapters I deal at some length with the decline of the house, the dispersal of its staff, and then its revival. As much as any period in its social history, the twentieth century deserves to be recorded. Not least remarkable is the way the community living and working there now is in many respects so similar to that of two centuries ago; and so unlike the skeletal household of the middle years of this century.

Much of the interest Erddig has aroused is attributable to the National Trust's novel approach to its restoration and presentation. As much effort was put into the rescue of its ruinous outbuildings and domestic offices, as was spent on the state rooms.

15 The New Kitchen in 1978

16   The Servants' Hall in 1975

Visitors are obliged to arrive, not at the front door, but through estate, stable and laundry yards, so that the organisation of the whole household at every level can be appreciated. The experience of being treated more like a guest's valet or lady's maid than a titled dignitary has by and large been welcomed.

Philip Yorke, the last squire of Erddig, not only went to enormous trouble to pass on all he knew of the house; he also helped me to trace some of the staff who remembered life in service at Erddig before the First World War. Bessie Gittins, Edith Haycock and Maggie Roberts gave particularly vivid accounts of their work as maids. Theirs is the last generation able to relate at first hand what country house domestic service during the 1900s was like; and this gives their recollections both a poignancy and a bias. They were scarcely out of their teens then and inevitably they remember best the girlish pranks, staying up later than they should to play cards, and keeping in the housekeeper's good books. Staff of another generation might have wanted to talk more about the hardships of those compulsorily retired without pensions, or of loss of employment because of sickness.

In June 1978 I wrote to Philip Yorke to tell him that Erddig had just won the Museum of the Year Award, jointly with the Museum of London. In his reply of 25 June, Philip summed up his attitude to the house: 'I have always thought of Erddig as being the best place in the world, and I do not regard it as extraordinary that the judges still regard it as (almost) outstanding.' He died on 2 July. He was as usual late that Sunday and after a frantic bicycle ride arrived breathless at the quiet and isolated little church of Penylan. He had a stroke during the service. Almost exactly a month before, Bessie Gittins had died.

Fortunately Philip had been able to comment most helpfully on sections of this book, which was nearing completion at the time he died. My principal justification for writing it at all is that some fragments of the history of Erddig and its staff might otherwise go unrecorded.

17   The east front, from the canal

I

Setting Up

Court records and family letters describe in detail Joshua Edisbury's fall from High Sheriff of Denbighshire, with a lavish new house at Erddig, to disgrace and bankruptcy. Only in his very last years is Edisbury lost in the Piranesian gloom of the Fleet Prison. But how did his ruin affect the lives of his household at Erddig, those who had served him for many years and who looked to him for charity when they were no longer fit for work? What happened to his staff while Erddig was mortgaged to Edisbury's creditors? There are only occasional hints at the hardship his servants may have suffered. In 1709, while Edisbury was being hounded in the Court of Chancery, his steward John Williams wrote wearily of the demands of importunate tradesmen and of the calculated insults of a visiting mortgagee, Sir John Trevor. Finally he had to tell Edisbury that he had been forced to find work on a neighbouring estate: 'tho: I have left Erthigg God knows it was with a hevy heart for I had not inclination to leave yor Service and my leaving it was more upon force than Choyse.' The early years of the Erddig household could scarcely have been more inauspicious.

In 1683, when Edisbury was at his most prosperous, he commissioned Thomas Webb of Middlewich to build him a new house 85 feet long and 50 feet deep, at a cost of £677 10s. 9d. The year before Edisbury had been appointed High Sheriff and had decided that rather than try to enlarge his solid, unpretentious family home at Pentre Clawdd, he would do better to build himself a new house worthy of his rank, on a different site. The ideal spot was close at hand. Scarcely a mile to the south of Wrexham a densely wooded hillside rises steeply above the meandering course of the Clywedog. Wat's Dyke skirts its western escarpment. At its northern end the Normans raised a motte, probably that referred to as 'Wristlesham' in the Pipe Rolls of 1161. A house in this commanding if exposed position would leave Edisbury's neighbours in no doubt of his wealth and influence.

To build Erddig and to finance disastrous speculations in lead mining at Trelawnyd in Flintshire, Edisbury borrowed money at crippling rates of interest. Among the most hard-headed of his creditors was Elihu Yale, his near neighbour at Plas Grono. When he was the East India Company's Governor of Fort St George, Yale had corresponded with the Edisburys and exchanged presents with them. On 2 April 1682 he wrote thanking them for 'four Rundletts of Sandpatch Ale', adding

'Tis a precious Comodity that requires present Sattisfaction, wch the trewth
is I cannot now so well discharge as I desire, therefore begg yor and yor Good
Ladyes acceptance of part, in one of ye vessells, fild with our best Mango
Atchar to yor Selfe, & to her a Japan Skreen, wch come upon this Shipp –
Bengall Merchant.'

Yale had later to add a postscript to that letter: 'Since the foregoing tis my misfortune
not to prevail with the Capt to carry the Screens, his shipp being full already, so pray
excuse me till next year.' The outstanding late seventeenth century Chinese lacquer
screen now in the State Bedroom at Erddig may well be that referred to in the letter. In
1699 Yale was forced to leave India after it was discovered he had amassed an immense
personal fortune of over 500,000 pagodas, had been accused of making extortionate
demands on merchants and was under suspicion of the murder of at least one of the
members of the Company Council opposed to him. When he returned to his old family
home at Plas Grono, he was an obvious source of loans for Edisbury. But as the
governors of a struggling college in Connecticut found when they tried to secure a
bequest in return for naming the future university after him, Yale drove a hard
bargain. His demand for £4,000 from Edisbury was in return for a loan of half that
amount.

By the time Yale and Joshua's other creditors had begun to suspect that he had
over-reached himself, his financial difficulties had become bound up with those of his
brother, Dr John Edisbury, a successful lawyer and a Master in Chancery. The final

18   Joshua Edisbury, died *c*.1718.
     Builder of Erddig

19   John Meller, 1665–1733. Thomas
     Gainsborough touched up the hands
     and wig of this early eighteenth
     century portrait

stage in the ruin of both men is summed up in a petition to the Lord Chancellor, dated May 1712, in which John Edisbury

> doth with the Utmost Shame & Sorrow acknowledge his Crimes and abhor himselfe for his breach of Trust in missaplying the money by the Orders of this Court comitted to his Charge, so that he is at present unable to pay ye same.
>
> But forasmuch as your Pet^r was Seduced into that Guilt by affection to his Brother whose Estate yor Pet^r *then verily believed* to bee more then sufficient to reimburse the money lent, and all other Incumbrances whatsoever. . . .

Dr John died in disgrace in 1713; Joshua Edisbury in total obscurity some years later. It was a fellow Master in Chancery, John Meller, who salvaged what was left of Edisbury's estate. In 1716 Meller bought out the principal mortagee of the property, Sir John Trevor, and took possession of Erddig.

Edisbury left the house little more than an empty shell. Meller was free to furnish the state rooms entirely to his taste, to add wings probably to his own design at either end, and to refashion the garden. After its disastrous early years, Erddig was at last put on a stable course. The household established by John Meller was allowed to evolve without any major upsets over the next two centuries. By the time it passed to Meller's nephew, Simon Yorke, Erddig was already a sacred inheritance.

Meller was a wealthy bachelor with the ability, so conspicuously lacking in the Edisburys, to deal firmly with those, including his own family, who did not have his sound business sense. When his nephew, John Yorke, ran into debt, Meller did nothing to dissuade him from leaving the country to seek his fortune abroad. He was equally impatient of his sister's follies. As far as his own considerable extravagance was concerned, it was always within his means, always accounted for meticulously. When he purchased furniture from the very finest London cabinet makers, or indulged his taste for exotic textiles, every bill was most carefully filed away. Meller showed no inclination to share the fruits of this connoisseurship with a wealthy widow whose virtues were brought to his attention by an anonymous well-wisher; although he thought the letter worth keeping. Perhaps the only really attractive things about this hard-headed, self-contained man were his pier glasses, his cut wool velvets and his silvered seat furniture.

More than just fine textiles, furniture and his legal library came with Meller from his house in Bloomsbury Square. He also brought staff with him. Meller's maid, Jane Ebbrell, was still working at Erddig in 1793, when Philip Yorke commissioned her portrait from John Walters, a rough and ready Denbigh painter. She was the subject of one of Philip's *Crude Ditties*:

> To dignifie our Servants' Hall
> Here comes the Mother, of us all;
> For seventy years, or near have passed her,
> Since spider-brusher to the *Master*;
> When busied then, from room to room,

20   Jane Ebbrell, a mid-eighteenth century spider-brusher

She drove the dust, with brush, and broom
And by the virtues of her mop
To all uncleanness, put a stop:
But changing her *housemaiden* state,
She took our coachman, for a mate;
To whom she prov'd an useful gip,
And brought us forth a second whip:
Moreover, this, oft, when she spoke,
Her tongue, was midwife, to a joke,
And making many an happy *hit*,
Stands here recorded for a wit:
O! may she, yet some years, survive,
And breed her Grandchildren to *drive!*

A visitor to Erddig in 1732, John Loveday, recorded in his diary that Meller was 'not very agreeable to ye Countrey'. Self-made and known to have been closely involved in Edisbury's downfall, he wisely did not recruit all his staff locally, so as to ensure that they would not discuss his affairs in Welsh the moment his back was turned. The need for loyalty among his staff was all the greater because Meller was strongly anti-Jacobite, in a county where there was a great deal of sympathy for the Stuart cause, particularly from the most powerful neighbouring landowners, the Williams Wynn family.

Accounts for the annual wages of Meller's staff in 1725 have survived, although it is not clear whether they refer to his house in Bloomsbury, or to Erddig. They are initialled by Simon Yorke, John Meller's nephew, who frequently attended to his uncle's affairs in London. Most highly paid was the cook, who received £21 a year, over twice as much as the housekeeper at £10 a year (a century later their relative status would be reversed). Mrs Wynne, maid to Meller's aunt, was paid £6 a year; Betty Cheshire, presumably a senior maid, was paid £3 a year; Anne Williams, probably a junior maid, and an unnamed laundry maid received £2 10s. Jane Ebbrell is not mentioned by name in the accounts.

The male staff in 1725 included John Jones, probably the butler, paid £10 a year, with a guinea 'allow'd him for Washing whilst in Town'. Birch the coachman was paid £8; James Eustace, William Simms, Richard Jenkins and Samuel Davis, whose jobs are unrecorded, received £7, £6, £6 and £4 respectively. An unnamed postilion was paid £4 and '£1 more if a year', and 'The Helper' £3 a year.

Meller relied heavily on the integrity of his nephew, Simon Yorke, and of his steward Richard Jones, to see that his affairs in London and Wales were in order. Richard Jones kept his master informed of disputes with his neighbours at Erddig, of recent attempts to extract coal from the estate and of progress with improvements to the house and the new buildings around the courtyard. His letter of 1 May 1721 concludes:

> John Evans has undertaken to Paynt the flower Potts and says if your honour would have the faces guilt with Gold the bookes of leve Gold is to be bought 4ᵈ per booke . . . he also wants 100 brass buttons for the window shutters.

Writing again to Meller on 20 June 1724, Richard Jones reported:

> Since your Honour lef Erthig there has been 4 Coaches full of Gentry to see the Hall, the first of this day – 7 nights Mr Mitton of Hailstons and Mr Holland with both their Ladys Mr. Eyton of Leeswood – and som other young Gentlewoman along with em and this day their cam the Lady Billot Madam Edgerton and som 4 or 5 gentlewoman more all desireing their humble services to your Honour My Mistress and the Major they all admired the Hall and furniture Mitily – It has been very uncertain weather for the Hay harvest this weeke last past I hope I have Gott into ye Barne 18 loads of ye Great Meadow hay in very good order, the rest will be in too Morrw night if drye weather –

21   The tapestries sent from
London in 1721. The chairs
with silvered frames were
originally supplied for the
Withdrawing Room

The Ayre pip to ye lesser vault is layd down the bricklayers and Carpenter
have keept prety close to their worke since your Honour has been gon I have
nothing more to add by this but wishing your Honour well at Erthig and yt
soon and beg leave to subscribe my Selfe
    Your Honours Faithfull Humble Servt to comand
        Richd Jones.

The furniture which won his neighbours' admiration was, like Meller's maid, sent
up to Erddig from London. The task of chivvying dilatory upholsterers and cabinet
makers fell to Simon Yorke, who reported frequently to his uncle. On 17 April 1720 he
was able to reassure him that Mr Hurt was making satisfactory progress with the State
Bed; in the following October that the measurements of the tapestries that were to hang
with the bed had indeed been calculated correctly; and on 10 December that

The Tapestry Weaver called here, to acquaint me that ye other Piece of
Tapestry was finish'd; and would have been done sooner, but that he himself
hath been laid-up, with a Fitt of Illness. – I desire to know whether upon

receiving ye Tapestry I may pay him in full – I shall not now send it into ye Country without ord^r because I believe that ye Roads being full of Water the Tapestry may possibly receive damage.

By 1726 Erddig was very fully and very splendidly furnished. Something of its opulence can be imagined by comparing the inventory of its contents made in that year with the impressions of John Loveday, who on a tour of North Wales in 1732 visited 'Mr Millar's Seat of Brick' and noted in his diary:

Y^e Apartments handsome, & furnish'd in ye grandest manner, & after ye newest fashion. Above Stairs a Gallery hung wth ye Sibylls, all lengths. The Stair-case and Rooms are wainscotted wth Oak, & have ye convenience of Dressing Rooms, & Rooms for Servants. They are furnish'd wth Mohair, Caffoy, Damasks, &c. The grand Apartments are below Stairs.

When Loveday arrived at Erddig, he would have swept through a wrought iron screen made by Robert Davies of Croes Foel, into a courtyard flanked by stables (both these and the screen were done away with in the late eighteenth century, when the architect James Wyatt was advising on improvements to the house). The central block

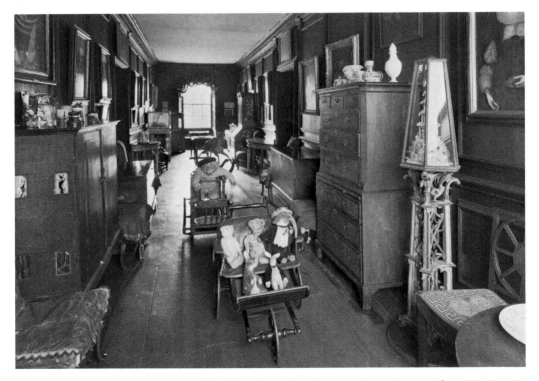

22   The Gallery in 1973. When John Loveday visited in 1732 it was 'hung wth y^e Sibylls, all lengths'

built half a century before by Thomas Webb was by then mellow compared with the fresh pointing and warmer brick of Meller's new wings. The first of the state apartments, the Entrance Hall, was sparsely furnished – a deliberate foil to the lavishly decorated rooms beyond – with ten black leather chairs regimented against the walls, two marble-topped tables on the window piers, a large Dutch table, a pair of backgammon tables, and a three-cornered table for ombre, a card game popular in the eighteenth century. A gilded leather screen offered some protection against draughts.

In the Saloon Loveday admired the set of eight walnut chairs upholstered in caffoy – a cut wool velvet, in this case golden yellow and claret coloured – and the two large sconces, or girandoles, with gilt gesso frames. These had been supplied by John Belchier, a cabinet maker at 'Ye Sun' in St Paul's Church Yard, who charged £14 for each of them on 25 August 1724. From the Saloon Loveday would have proceeded to the Withdrawing Room, furnished with chairs 'ye frames of wch are plated wth Silver', a silvered pier glass and a glass-topped table with 'Mr Millar's Arms work'd in ye middle'.

As was the customary sequence of rooms in Baroque houses, the Withdrawing Room was a necessary prelude to the splendours of the State Bedroom. The room was hung with tapestries, the transport of which had caused Simon Yorke so much concern, and dominated by the bed upholstered by Mr Hurt and decorated with gilded hawk heads probably carved by Belchier. Its ivory coloured embroidered silk may well have been bought from or given to Meller by Elihu Yale, who had taken vast quantities of textiles with him when he hurriedly left India in 1699. Loveday made a curious reference to the 'Hen. 8th's. Dressing-Table . . . of Tortoise Shell thick inlaid wth fine brass'. Above this was another of Belchier's pier glasses decorated with grotesque masks and luxuriant curls of foliage, dispatched to Erddig at a cost of £50 in 1726—'there are here very fine both Glasses & Tables', he noted. The second best bedchamber, with a crimson damask bed and a pier glass scarcely inferior to that in the preceding suite, was like the State Bedroom on the ground floor. Loveday's description concludes:

> The Chappel is not quite finish'd, ye pews &c. of Oak. A large Extent of Ground behind ye House, but not All laid-out as yet; there is much Wall in ye Gardens.

Almost all the pieces of furniture described by Loveday are still at Erddig, although their arrangement changed many times over the next 200 years. The contents of the rooms not grand enough to interest such visitors are all listed in full in an inventory of 1726. It begins with the 'Pantry within the Bakehouse', followed by the 'New Kitchen, Brew House, Cheese Roome, Darry and Sculery, Laundry, Wash House, New Servants Hall, Old Servants hall, Powder Room, Housekeepers Room, Butlers room, Wett Larder, Small Rear Celler, Oven Parlour and Stone Parlour'.

Several of Meller's domestic offices were swept away when Philip Yorke demolished the ranges to the west of the house and in 1774 built his new kitchen, laundry and stable block beyond the south wing. But the present Servants' Hall is almost certainly one of the two described in 1726. At that time the New Servants' Hall

23   The Chapel

contained '1 grate, 3 longe tables, 9 formes, 1 block, 1 iron pestall, 1 iron morter and 1 Horse to brosh Cloiths on'. The senior staff probably had their meals in a separate room and at a different time from the junior staff, because the Old Servants' Hall was similarly furnished with '2 long tables, 1 grate, 2 arm Kane Chares and 8 old Kane Chares'. Both rooms were in the basement, close to the back stairs, as had been normal practice since the architect Sir Roger Pratt had revolutionised country house planning in the mid-seventeenth century.

Meller had fifteen beds for maids in the attic rooms, and eight beds for male staff in the stables and outhouses. The number of beds for men in the 'Bed Chamber next ye Dark yard' are unfortunately not listed, nor are they in the 'Bed Chamber next ye Garden', presumably that used by the junior gardeners; so it can only be guessed that his full complement of staff in the 1720s was in the region of twenty-five to thirty. The lists of contents of all the staff bedrooms are repetitious: 'In the Coachman's Room. 2 Bedsteads, 2 Feather beds, 2 Bolsters, 6 Blankets, 2 Ruggs. Up stairs in ye stable. 3 Bedsteads, 3 Flock beds, 3 Bolsters, 6 Blankets, 2 Rugs'. The maids' rooms were similarly furnished.

One of the coachboys working at Erddig in the 1730s was the negro whose portrait still hangs in the Servants' Hall. His horn, scarlet jacket, braided lapels and silver buttons were the pretext for a decorative if unsophisticated piece of provincial painting. The picture is something of a rarity. Negroes in livery occur frequently enough in eighteenth century portraits, their features serving as convenient foils to the classical profiles and ivory complexions of the main subject. What is unusual about the Erddig negro is that he is painted in isolation. The negro's place at Erddig would be a mystery, were it not for the scroll of verse added at least half a century after the portrait was painted:

> Of the conditions of this Negre,
> Our information is but me'gre,
> However *here*, he was a dweller,
> And blew the horn for Master Meller:
> Here, too he dy'd, but when, or how,
> Can scarcely be remember'd now.
> But that to Marchwiel he was sent,
> And has good Christian interment:
> Pray Heaven! may stand his present friend,
> Where black, or white; distinctions, end;
> For sure on this side of the grave,
> They are too strong, 'tween Lord and slave:
> Here also lived a dingy brother,
> Who play'd together with the other;
> But of him, yet longer rotten,
> Every particular's forgotten;
> Save that like Tweedle-dum, and dee,
> These but in *notes*, could ne'er agree;
> In all things else, as they do tell ye,
> Were just like Handel, and Corelli:
> O! had it been in their life's co'rse
> T' have met with Massa Wilberforce,
> They would in this alone, have join'd
> And been together of a mind;
> Have rais'd their horns, to one high tune,
> And blown his merits to the *Moon*.

A negro is mentioned in a letter to Meller of 16 May 1721, from Humphrey Fowlkes, the Rector of Marchwiel:

I know no reason if the Major send his Black to me to-day, but that he may be Christned this morning, if you go abroad before the Holy days – Whitsuntide was the solemn time among the primitive Christians to Christen the Cate chumens. But we have no number of adult persons to Christen now a days; that day may be public enough.

The Major referred to was the despised husband of John Meller's sister, Aliza. Major David Roberts of Llanfair looked to his brother-in-law to settle his debts and

24   John Meller's negro coachboy. The scroll of verse was added in the 1790s, some sixty years after the portrait was painted

restore his tarnished reputation, usually leaving his wife to write his begging letters. But Meller was quite capable of dealing unsentimentally with his sister's problems. On 7 June 1729 Aliza complained to Simon Yorke of her treatment and called her brother 'hard laced'. A letter with a false note of finality came to Meller from Major Roberts in November that same year:

> I am sure my Company is not very agreable to some people in Wales, so shan't think of seeing it, nor indeed is there any thing or any body in it yt I have ye least desire to see excepting who is at Erthig. I hope Mrs Roberts will send me the three Hundred pound I am instantly obliged to pay & advance me some more money to Carry me abroad where I must endeavour to pass my time as well as I can; I wou'd undergoe any hardship rather y^n she shou'd any and if you and she thinks ye demand I have made too large pray lessen it – doe me ye pleasure of an answer to this. Whatever happens to me I have brought upon myself, so will bear it with spirit, I have renew'd my Cold much. I beg you'l be so good as to see and get my bond from Mrs Drelincourt, else I know not what they may doe, if you my only friend does not stand by me, ye town is very sickly & very empty
>
> My best love & service attends you & Mrs. Roberts & Cos York.
> Yr most affectionate Brother & very Humble servt.
> David Roberts.
> P.S. Let Jones come private & by himself, if I thought things cou'd be done without my meeting him it wou'd be better.

As well as debts to settle, Major Roberts apparently left Meller his negro servant, and in doing so helped to initiate a tradition of recording staff at Erddig which was to be continued for the next 250 years.

2

Elizabeth Ratcliffe, Lady's Maid

The aberrant ambition, the craving for self-advertisement which drove Edisbury to build Erddig and Meller to furnish it so lavishly, were not characteristics of most of the Yorke family. It was their very mediocrity, lack of ambition, and contentment with their status as moderately prosperous Welsh squires which ensured the preservation of Erddig. The epitaph to the first Simon Yorke in Marchwiel church expresses these qualities and limitations with delightful candour:

> A pious temperate sensible country Gentleman, of a very mild, just and
> benevolent character, as the concern for his death did best testify;
> An Advantage which amiable Men have over great Ones:
>   He died July 28th. 1767, aged 71.

Between 1733, when he inherited Erddig from his uncle, until his own death thirty-four years later, Simon Yorke did little to alter or improve the house and grounds. His most significant contribution was to leave Erddig to a son who combined amiability with scholarship, wit, originality and great kindness.

Simon Yorke's wife Dorothy outlived her husband by twenty years. During her lonely widowhood, she depended increasingly on her maid, Elizabeth Ratcliffe, whose niece, another Elizabeth Ratcliffe and so usually called 'Betty the little', also became a constant companion. The Yorke family grew to regard this exceptionally gifted girl with growing respect and affection. Their generosity to her was amply rewarded.

The younger Elizabeth was the daughter of a Chester clockmaker. John Ratcliffe supplied Erddig with at least two long-case clocks, the finest of which was decorated with gilded ball finials and tortoise-shell japanning. It still stands on the landing at the top of the main stairs, its face inscribed 'John Ratcliffe, Chester'. When his daughter was old enough, it was natural that she should seek employment as lady's maid with a family already employing her aunt and who were her father's patrons.

Elizabeth soon showed herself capable of craftsmanship as delicate and exact as her father's. She also developed her own meticulous, observant style of drawing. Given a highly finished mezzotint, she could copy it with such facility that her work was almost indistinguishable from the original print. One of her earliest drawings, a bird's

25   Betty Ratcliffe's drawing of Newnham, in Hertfordshire

eye view of Newnham, a house in Hertfordshire owned by Dorothy Yorke's brother James Hutton, is dated 1754 and records every detail down to the precise design of the Chinese fret railings around its courtyard.

The Yorkes delighted in her talents, supplied her with drawing materials and showed the best of her work to their friends, among them Thomas Pennant. Pennant responded with the interest and spontaneous enthusiasm which made him such a stimulating correspondent for the naturalist Gilbert White. A drawing in the Gallery at Erddig has a label on the back: 'Two Sardinian Princes teaching a Marmute to dance, Coppy'd from a print of – (sic) Pennant Esq. of Downing by Eliza. Ratcliffe, in the year 1765'. Writing to her brother from Chester on 10 May 1768, Anne Jemima Yorke mentions that 'Mr. Pennant has beg'd of Mamma to let Betty Ratcliffe coppy for him, from a print, the youngest of Lord Hardwicke's Daughters. Betty would be much obliged if you would get a sheet of the finest grain'd white Vellum, and send it down by the Fly, as soon as possible.' A month later Anne Jemima reassured her brother: 'Betty is very busy about her drawing & it will be done very soon, the reason it was not done before she waited for the Vellum it is come safe.' Thomas Pennant was not her only admirer to lend prints. Another of her drawings in the Erddig gallery, this time after a Van Dyck group, is labelled: 'Sr. Kenelm Digby and Family coppy'd from a picture in the possession of Miss Longueville By: Eliza Ratcliffe – 1766'.

Although the younger generation of Yorkes and their friends enthused about Betty's work, Dorothy Yorke had misgivings that she might lose her services as a maid. On 17 June 1768 Dorothy wrote to Philip:

> Betty the little, is at work for you; but pray my dear do not imploy her in that way again for one year at least, as all her improvements sink in drawing, & then I shall have no service from her & make too fine a Lady of her, for so much is say'd on that occation that it rather puffs up.

26 'Two Sardinian Princes teaching a Marmute to dance', copied by Betty Ratcliffe from a mezzotint after Drouais, lent to her by Thomas Pennant

27 A drawing by Betty Ratcliffe 'coppy'd from a picture in the possession of Miss Longueville', of Sir Kenelm Digby and his family, after Van Dyck

She begged Philip to remember that his 'good father's admonitions about her to me twas not to set her up to much'. Fortunately, Philip was a great deal more imaginative and perceptive than his father. Dorothy Yorke's letter may well be referring to the family's reaction to Betty Ratcliffe's exquisite model of a Chinese pagoda, which she had completed in 1767. Far from being discouraged, Betty went on to make an even more ambitious model of the ruins of Palmyra.

Betty's Chinese pagoda is so fragile and delicate that footfall in the gallery at Erddig is enough to swing the bells that hang from the mouths of the dragons decorating each storey. It is made of a variety of materials. The base is wooden with parts of the pagoda itself cut out of thick vellum. Mounted on this are crushed mica, fragments of coloured glass and very thin slivers of mother-of-pearl, some of which were probably sold as sequins, ready cut and pierced. The model is loosely derived from an engraving of 'The Great Pagoda as first intended' in William Chambers's *Gardens and Buildings at Kew*, published in 1763. But Chambers's design was considerably elaborated by Betty Ratcliffe, who preferred fretwork rails of a far more complicated pattern and varied them for the different storeys. To allow for all this detail, she changed the scale of the pagoda, reducing it from ten storeys to six and enlarging features such as the bells, which Chambers omitted altogether from the engraving of the pagoda as executed.

There is something of the same simple delight in Betty Ratcliffe's interpretation of Chambers's pagoda that one finds in the drawings of Thomas Robins, who perhaps better than any other topographical artist captured the lightness and frivolity of rococo garden decoration, with its tinkling *Chinoiserie* temples, rustic seats and fences, neat borders of bobbing flowers, and fretwork obelisks trailing honeysuckle. In fact Betty Ratcliffe and Dorothy Yorke were in Bath, taking the waters, when in 1770 Robins died in the city. She may well have encountered his drawings.

Dorothy Yorke's visit to Bath was prompted by ill health frequently referred to in letters to her son:

> Dear Phil
> I fully intend to have wrot to you by last Mondays post but was quite lay'd up on Sunday & all next day with my disorder in a worse manner than ever: was blooded wch has relieved me; & resolved for Bath; got a coach & 4 from Chester for that purpose & set out Monday morng next for Shrewsbery, as to money affairs have enough to set out with, that you need not hurry your payment now & when I am at Bath I will let you know when I want some. I think I could stay very well till yr Tenants pay you at Xmas or longer if I could have that is owing to me from the Gentleman at Bristol. I will take care to leave everything in your house under proper care and order. I take Betty Ratcliffe, B. Bevan & John and Boy with me. I imagine you will like yr servants that are left to be on board wages.
>
> Nov 1: 1768

A few days later she wrote again:

28   'The Chinese Pagoda', signed E. R. 1767

Sunday Nov 13 1768
My dear in the first place I must tell you we got safe to this City on Friday
evening set out on the Sunday before at 7 dreadful bad roads, & tho I had not
been downstairs for a fortnight yet I bore my journey pretty well, tho far from
being so; I have not since I came into my Lodgings on Saturday, put my head
out of doors, very good ones I have got at a Mr. Coes in Millsome Street, I
have a spare bedchamber at yr service and a spare seat in a pew likewise, I
have taken to day: excessive high everything is here & tho I shall not partake

of the grandeur or amusements of this place shall feel the expences of it & believe I shall not relish it at all; The doct I have consulted says I must not drink ye waters till further prepared for them. My spirits are lower than when at Erthig even tho worse & I am every day & night thinking how miserable my poor Brother is. I am sorry for him with all my soul, what says he to my coming to Bath Make our proper compli'ts & good wishes towards him. I rejoiced to see your hand but was greatly disopointed at so few words. Betty Ratcliffe is greatly obliged puts in her own words by my desire one thing puzzled – as we are very short of men acquaintance. as to my part I am quite a stranger to the present world I know not above 3 or 4 persons here.

When Dorothy herself was not well enough to write, her daughter Anne Jemima or Betty Ratcliffe reported to Philip (her letter is partially torn and missing):

Bath Nov 21st 176(8)

Sir,
My Misstress orders me to inform you that she wou'd have wrote herself, but having increas'd the quantity she is to drink of water, finds she cannot hold down her head, the Water seems to Agree very well with her, Miss Yorke is very well, and likes Bath, my Misstress desires S.ʳ that you will write as often as possible that she may know how Mr Hutton does, both M.ʳ Barnston's at my Misstress's request were so good as to set their names to the Letter and have been very Obliging in all respects to my Misstress and Miss Yorke, & who sends her love to you and says she will write very soon. (. . . .) with the very grateful acknowledgment of all fav(ours.)
    Your Most Ob(edient. . . .)
      E. Rat(. . . .)

29   Anne Jemima Yorke (1754–70)

Anne Jemima wrote as promised on 3 December:

Dear Brother,

As Mamma dare not hold down her head for the waters she deputes me to return you a great many thanks for your kind letters which she says are a great comfort to her & begs you write as often as you can I would have wrote sooner but we have been sadly frighted by Betty Ratcliffe having been dangerously Ill but thank God the Doctor thinks her in a very good way at present, Mamma thinks the waters agree with her pretty well but is Oblig'd to have the Doctor sometimes we sent John to Bristol last Saturday to know how Mr J Edwards did he says he is got quite well and proposes to keep his Christmas at Glyn tinne he talks of coming to see Mamma before he goes we have got Mrs Wymondsold's Musling and Gloves and would be very glad if you would put us in a way to send them to her, I am very sorry my Uncle is so indifferent pray give you my Duty and my Mammas best love to him, Miss Lawry came here last Thursday we have seen her once, I am just going to the Play with Mr and Mrs Wiliams who are exceeding civil to us. Mamma Desires her kind love & accept the same from
  Dear Brother your Affectionate Sister,
   Anne Jemima Yorke

It was more than just family affection which led Dorothy Yorke, Anne Jemima and Betty Ratcliffe to inquire so often after James Hutton's health. Although years of dissipation and extravagance had earned him the nickname 'Little Profligacy', Hutton was still the owner of the valuable Newnham estate in Hertfordshire, much fine furniture, silver and pictures, and a London house in Park Lane. He was unmarried, but had an illegitimate son. For months and years the Yorkes watched his decline with the gravest concern: they knew that his fortune and theirs were at stake.

'I am very much grieved at your Uncles odity proceeding; from his dreadful excess in drinking', Dorothy wrote to Philip in July 1768. 'I do not for his whole fortune, wish you to be much with him lest it should taint your sobriety.' But Philip's own future hung on his uncle's whim. He was much in love with Elizabeth Cust, the sister of his university friend Brownlow Cust and the daughter of Sir John Cust of Belton, in Lincolnshire. His marriage, as both parties understood, would depend on his chances of bettering a comparatively modest inheritance from his father. Brownlow, with characteristically eighteenth century frankness, did not hesitate to remind Philip how desirable it was to complement true love with wealth:

tho' your un-le's intention sh—^{d} be ever so good towards you, and his resolution of making you his heir so strong as not to be shaken by the most earnest and most artful endeavours, yet who can tell how much that intention may be frustrated? Even forgery is what nescessitous rogues will not stick at. You have often told me that you have fear'd lest yr un-cle sh—^{d} lose his understanding before his life, what an advantagious situation wd that put a nescessitous hanger-on in? You must to be sure therefore at all events be upon the spot whenever your uncle is thought to be in danger, to watch every body about him as narrowly as a cat watches a mouse. I am very well aware that this business to a mind like your's will be very hateful, but the declining to cope with rogues that mean to use every wicked art to defraud your family, is not only weakness but injustice to yourself, your Mother and all your family: and the way to combat with them is to watch every motion they make, for circumstances that appear little and trifling in general may hereafter be of the greatest consequence, it is impossible therefore that you can trust any eyes or understanding but your own.

Their worst fears proved to be unfounded. James Hutton made provision in his will for his natural son, but the bulk of his fortune went to his sister. In 1770, within the space of a few months, Philip married the girl he adored and secured a generous inheritance from his uncle.

Perhaps it was the occasion of Philip's marriage which prompted a special commission from Betty Ratcliffe. She wrote to Philip Yorke from Chester on 12 July 1770:

> Hon.^d Sir,
> I yesterday received the honour of your Letter and will do the utmost of my power and endeavour to execute, what you are pleas'd to request instead of Comand, as I shall ever think it my Duty, to a Family, I am so particularly oblig'd to. I have been here a few days and shall return on (. . .) day. I am afraid you will be disappointed with the quantity of Apricotts. . . . I rejoic'd to hear you have hopes my dear Mistress will yet get over her heavy Afflication, none Can wish it more than myself, and I greatly long to see her, my most Respectfull Duty, waits on Mrs Yorke to which Lady, S.^r with Yourself, I most sincerely wish the greatest Felicity, and am Hon.^d Sr Your Ever grateful and Oblig'd
> Hum. Ser.^t
> Eliz.^a Ratcliffe.

The following day she added a postscript:

> Sir,
> Since I wrote the above, I Rece'd a Letter from my Misstress, in a very low Spirited Style indeed, which gives me great uneasiness. I know not anything wou'd relieve her so much, as a Visit from yourself and Lady, soon, She desires I will go to her as soon as possible. I will take care to preserve as many sorts of Fruits, as are ready, before I go, and leave directions for the rest.

During the next nine years Elizabeth Yorke bore Philip seven children. She also saw to it that Erddig, until her arrival scarcely altered since John Meller's day, was at

30   Francis Cotes's portrait of Elizabeth
Yorke (1749–79)

least made aware of the changes in fashion there had been over the preceding forty
years. Even before her marriage she wrote to Philip with all the impatient fervour of a
new mistress of the house:

> Saturday night, March 23, 1770.
> Trades-people of every branch are most tiresome to deal with – I sent several
> messages after my Chair since I wrote, but not receiving satisfaction, I went
> myself yesterday, & drag'd Anne with me (for I am nothing without her), all I
> cou'd get for my trouble was to hear it was impossible to be done; however, I
> did set right some mistakes, the man promis'd me to send the drawing of the
> Sopha which I wish'd to send you to night, that you might not fancy I had
> been Idle; it is not forthcoming. *It is all* very *right*. One must have somebody to
> scold (as it is a very constitutional Exercise) and a Cabinet maker as well as
> any. Whilst I am in this humour (i.e. out of humour) don't expect to escape
> tho' so distant; I did expect the account how much paper would be wanted for
> the *new* Dressing Room because I promis'd to send the Man word. I know you
> had many things to think of but my Dressing Room – I hope it was not a wilful
> forgetfulness; People are apt to return to a wrong way of thinking; an
> adequate exchange is all that is desir'd: an Eye for an Eye; and a Tooth for a
> Tooth and a Room for a Room – very fair. – I am glad your Cold is wearing
> off – You know I shou'd rejoice to hear Mrs Yorke's spirits were better; I ought
> to have her ease much at Heart, & I thought we had agreed before we last
> parted, no alteration shou'd be made on that account, till we came down; you

only propos'd the Paint brush for the Parlour; if that cou'd be done without being offensive, it wou'd be fitter to receive the new Chairs, than in it's present state; you who are in the House can best tell. I dare say Mrs Yorke will have pleasure in giving up the place to you, and me; I can easily imagine, & feel that a Place (-) a pretty one too (that is to please you Beauty will always attract the attention at ye first) one has habited, & esteemed for sometime quiting must be irksome, & I join with you in wishing *that* to be as much reliev'd as possible.

Under Elizabeth's influence the State Bedroom was moved from the ground floor to a first floor room at the top of the main stairs, which was redecorated with a hand-painted Chinese wallpaper and where Betty Ratcliffe's flower embroideries were hung. The old Saloon and Withdrawing Room were thrown together to make one large Saloon. In the adjoining room were hung the tapestries from the old State Bedroom, with the silvered pier glass from the Withdrawing Room between the windows. Again, Chinese wallpaper was used in the small, intimate room beyond, in this case composed of painted vignettes, mounted on a pale pink ground and with a European block-printed floral and butterfly border to frame them. On either side of the chimney piece were grey and green brackets loaded with Chinese porcelain. With their passion for *Chinoiserie*, it is not surprising that the Yorkes were delighted by Betty Ratcliffe's pagoda.

When Betty Ratcliffe wrote to Philip Yorke of 'what you are pleased to request instead of Command', she was probably referring to her most ambitious model, that of the ruins of Palmyra. She seems to have made the change of style from *Chinoiserie* to neo-classicism with an ease characteristic of the 1760s and 1770s. The model carries the inscription 'Ruins of the Temple of the Sun at Palmyra E.R. 1773'. Again her inspiration came from one of the most influential architectural publications of the day, Robert Wood's *The Ruins of Palmyra*, of 1753. There is no illustration in the book which she copied directly; she seems to have used plate XXI, a view of the site, for the general composition, and plate VII for the details of the doorways. As with the pagoda, she treated the scale of the various architectural features, recorded with such scrupulous accuracy by Wood, cavalierly. Decorative details and a romantic sense of decay were what really interested her. Acanthus leaves, Corinthian capitals and the swag frieze are reinterpreted in a delightfully carefree way, and the ruins are festooned with trailing vegetation conspicuously absent in Wood's illustrations.

The Yorkes' pride in her models was reflected in the stands they bought for them. The tripod supporting the pagoda is decorated with green and white fretwork, claw feet and silvered dragons as animated as they are grotesque. Such carving must be by one of the best London cabinet makers of the 1760s and similarity to an Italian cabinet at Alscot Park makes an attribution to Linnell at least a possibility. The stand of the model of Palmyra is by another craftsman, almost certainly Thomas Fentham. Until his label was found on the back of an Erddig picture frame, Fentham's work was virtually unknown, apart from references in London street directories of the 1770s, 1780s and 1790s, which describe him as a frame maker and glass grinder at various

31 'The Ruins of Palmyra' by Betty Ratcliffe. The gilt stand for this model of 1773 was
probably bought by Philip Yorke from the London carver Thomas Fentham

32 'The Ruins of Palmyra'

addresses in the Strand. The frame at Erddig with his label was supplied to Philip Yorke in the 1770s for a pastel portrait of Simon and Etheldred Yorke as children, by Katherine Read, one of the few successful female English artists of the late eighteenth century. Its mounts are virtually the same as those on the Palmyra stand and on the frames of two flower embroideries by Betty Ratcliffe, one of which is dated 1774. Fentham must also have made the frame of an arrangement of flowers made of silk, paper, wire and wool labelled 'El. Ratcliffe 1775'. This is one of her prettiest things, with the forms of the flowers and details such as the caterpillar and minute ladybird beautifully observed. The Yorkes valued it so highly that they hung it in their State Bedroom. In her later work Betty Ratcliffe returned happily to earlier styles. The tops of a pair of pier tables almost certainly supplied by Fentham are decorated with *Chinoiserie* scenes in mother-of-pearl and are initialled E.R. 1778. Her view of Conway Castle, in pastel, is naïve enough to be mistaken for one of her early drawings; but the frame is in fact dated 1782.

During the 1770s several important changes were made to the exterior of Erddig. The brick of the west front, exposed to any bad weather blowing over from the Long Mountain, must have been showing signs of deterioration; and the formality of the courtyard, shut in by stables and a wrought iron screen, was now decidedly old-fashioned. James Wyatt, the architect consulted by Philip, clearly persuaded him that the house could be refaced to give it the appearance of a neo-classical villa, framed by the natural undulations of the surrounding beech woods. Wyatt's ambitious design for colonnades flanking the central block and leading to pedimented pavilions was never carried out; and a much duller, but less destructive, solution was executed by an otherwise little known architect named Mr Franks.

What led Philip to favour this conservative approach? Perhaps a letter to him from Elizabeth, written 'Saturday night, May 19, 1770', offers an explanation:

> You give a sad account of Bath but you are such an *unfashionable creature*, I don't mind you: I am glad you *still retain* a good opinion of me – only think I quite forgot (being *overwhelm'd* with *business*) to inform you in my last, of a great Disappointment; it is with *deep* sorrow I tell you now, the Masquerade is defer'd till next Year.

With the passing years Philip became increasingly bored by fashion. At the same time he developed an extremely strong historical sense and this ensured the survival of much early eighteenth century decoration at Erddig. His attitude is revealed particularly clearly in a letter of 4 February 1771 to his agent Caesar:

> I would not have, upon Recollection, any Rummage *yet* made in the Lumber Room; among the many old, and strange things there. Perhaps somewhat on my view, may strike my convenience and therefore I wish, nothing should be parted with from thence, till I have duly considered it.

33   'Conway Castle', a drawing by Betty Ratcliffe of 1782

34 The arms of Yorke and Hutton, cut out of paper by Betty Ratcliffe and mounted on scarlet foil

35 A bouquet of flowers by Betty Ratcliffe, made of silk, paper, wire and wool and mounted in a frame probably by Thomas Fentham

Philip's friendship with Thomas Pennant, who paid him tribute in his *Travels in Wales* (1810), encouraged these antiquarian interests. He was elected a Fellow of the Society of Antiquaries and in 1799 he published an elegantly illustrated history, *The Royal Tribes of Wales*. But the most important consequence of Philip's antiquarianism was his insistence that changes at Erddig should be carried out with care and restraint. He became increasingly preoccupied not only with the history of the house, but with the history of its household.

His inheritance of a share of his uncle's fortune ensured that when Philip purchased new furniture and pictures for Erddig, he could afford to buy the best. Cobb supplied the set of chairs referred to in Elizabeth's letter. Cotes was commissioned to paint his wife's portrait, Gainsborough his own. But it was typical of Philip that he should insist that the greatest portrait painter of his day should spend time while in the house touching up a dull early eighteenth century picture of John Meller. In his pocket book Philip noted on 22 February 1780:

Last pay.t of my own Picture	31.	10.	0.
For new dressing M.r Meller's ditto	5.	5.	0.
Present to servt.	0.	5.	0.

Philip's portrait is as much Elizabeth's memorial as it is his. A few months before Gainsborough painted this sombre and sympathetic picture, the 29-year-old Elizabeth had died, leaving seven children under 9 and a desolate husband. Philip wrote in the family Bible:

Erthig, January 31st. 1779 – (Sunday)
This day at twenty minutes past one, to my irreparable Loss, and very just and great afflication, my most dear and honoured Wife, Elizabeth Yorke, departed this life, having nearly compleated her thirtieth year, being born on the 24th. of February 1748–9 (and married to me, the 2.d July 1770: On the Sunday fortnight preceding her death, She was brought to bed of a Daughter, between one and two months before her expected time, and the Fever which followed her *delivery* (in *itself* very dangerous & critical) left us in a few days, little hopes of her Recovery. Under the strongest Impression of her End, She supported herself (without complaints) with the greatest Composure, and strength of Mind, and with surprising Recollection as to all such things, as became the awfulness of that Time, and occasion; for in the beginning, and towards the conclusion of her fatal illness, she was free from Delirium.
      There was a wonderful sweetness in her manners, in her Countenance, and Disposition, which engaged, & that very soon, all persons of all ranks; and if any comfort can be derived to my deplorable Condition, and that from the very sources of grief itself, she will be extensively, as *really* lamented: With great chearfulness of temper, (the effect of genuine Innocence,) She had a steady, and remitted attention to every humane Duty; was sincere and exact in her Devotions, most diligent in the superintendance, and Instruction of her

children, and active, and accurate, in everything which related to her Family
business: This much I have chosen to note here (not without many tears) of
this most excellent Woman, and in so doing I have weakned, rather than
extended her merits; But my sense of her worth, will be best spoken by what I
suffer in her death; What I chiefly look for in this Testimony of her
Extraordinary Virtue, and my affection, *is*, in the hope that some imitation of
their dear and sweet mother, may from *hence*, be derived from those tender
Pledges she has left me, helpless *indeed*, from the absence of her living
Instruction, and Example; But God Almighty is to me, and them, all in all; To
Whose Wise decrees I desire to submit myself with all humility and
Resignation, and in his good and appointed time to be added to *those* ashes,
wherewith my first Love and wordly affection, is buried.

> Philip Yorke.

Philip had lost his sister Anne Jemima when she was barely sixteen; but
Elizabeth's death was a tragedy which affected the whole household. On the day of her
death Philip Yorke issued the following orders to John Caesar:

Mr. Yorke understood from good Authority, that John Jones the Plumber did
not deal fairly concerning the Leaden Coffin that he made for the late Miss
Yorke (his Sister). This action was passed over by Mr Yorke as it was too
delicate an Affair to stir in; but it is not forgotten; and it becomes of more
necessity for Caesar to look very sharply to all such things, as his Master cannot
in this melancholy cases help himself at the time; or well complain afterwards.
Mr. Yorke depends on Caesars accuracy & Fidelity; of which he has never had
reason to distrust; and hopes it will be exerted in his Master's present very
afflicted and distressed Situation.

Desires that the measurement of things necessary may be proper and by *no
means straitened*.

There should be some well seasoned Boards brought to make the shell
Coffin tomorrow; they may be of a light but durable kind. There must be
likewise some good stout Oaken boards bought to make the Outward Coffin:
this to be covered with Black Cloth – and made strong. Mr. Yorke desires there
may not be any Glaring Ornaments, but all the furniture Black, except a small
Silver Plate (which may be had from Mr. Ratcliffe's at Chester) on which is to
be Engraved.

> Elizabeth Yorke
> wife of Philip Yorke, Esqr. of Erthig.
> Born Feby. 24th. 1749 – died Jany. 31. 1779

Caesar must examine the Vault early tomorrow and see if it will hold
three more Coffins, to those already there – If it will, no occasion to look
further at present – If not – Mr. Yorke will give further Orders. The Vault to
be immediately brick'd up again after examined.

Mr. Yorke means to allow Five Guineas for Mourning to the following

Persons; and wishes they would supply themselves from Mr. Thos Lloyds accordingly.

Nelly Caesar
Mrs Thompson,
Mrs Richardson,
Mary Rice,
Betty Thomas,
Betty Jones (The Housemaid)

NB. Mr. Yorke does not chuse the other Maids or Men should be put into Mourning, but means to give them a small Token.

Mr. Yorke desires Caesar to accept Five Guineas for Mourning
To John Newns Five Guineas
To John Jones (Gardiner) Five Guineas for Mourning . . .

Caesar to give particular Orders to have the dimensions of the Gallery Window taken and have it so contrived that the Atchievement may be fastened & see it fixed up himself, with strict orders that they do not wound the stonework by driving in nails hooks or spikings into any of the Joints or any part of the stone work.

NB. If any difficulty in fixing up the Atchievement on the Window frame: it may be made Easy by nailing accross the upper part of the window some planks of wood to fasten the nails to But not to let the boards appear from under the Atchievement.

Three days later, on 3 February, he added to his instructions:

Mr. Y. did not intend the following Maids into Mourning thinking a Gratuity would be more acceptable: but as it is represented to him to prove otherwise, desires the following wou'd supply themselves with necessarys immediately from Mr. Lloyds – and Caesar to give them Three Guineas each.

Jane   Nurserymaid.
Betty   Housemaid.
Molly   Kitchenmaid.
Nancy   Laundrymaid.

Dorothy Yorke, for all the accounts of her deteriorating health, outlived both Elizabeth and her own daughter, Anne Jemima. Writing from Sunning Hill on 19 November 1784, Betty Ratcliffe described to Philip preparations for yet another expedition to Bath:

Sir,
By my dearest and best friend's desire I address this to you, to return her thanks for both your obliging letters, & to acquaint you that according to the tenor of your last, she means to attempt a Bath journey on monday next, in her own chariot with post horses, as the warmest method of travelling. I am sorry

to add it seems a very necessary undertaking for her weak state of health would deter her from removing so far at this season of the year, her expedition will depend upon her powers for performing the journey, as will her stay at Bath upon the benefit she receives. Mrs Corbett has taken a small house for her, No. 2 Northumberland Buildings, on the same footing as lodgings, by the week. Mrs Yorke desires her affectionate love to yourself, Mrs Yorke and all her dear little Grandchildren, has great pleasure in hearing such promising accounts of them, and has been much disappointed that her illness should prevent her the satisfaction of seeing Master Yorke, but we sincerely hope him & the young Ladies will reach you in perfect health at Christmas. Mrs Yorke commissions me to beg that your bountiful present of a Hog from Newnham may be with-held this winter as she will not be in town to receive or her cook to cure it. Mr Birch who is come to see Mrs Yorke before she goes to Bath desires his best love to you & Mrs Yorke. I shall be obliged to you Sir to make my respectful compliments to her with thanks for her last favor. My aunt desires to join in the same with

> Your much obliged & grateful
> humble servant
> E. Ratcliffe.

Dorothy's decline was slow and painful, as her letters constantly reminded her son. 'Nothing better have I to expect at my time of life, monstrous deal of pain I have endured from my foot, now easy but very weak', she wrote of her 'new Companion the Gout'. Betty Ratcliffe's patience and loyalty during these trying years were to be generously repaid. When Dorothy finally died in 1787, she bequeathed Elizabeth Ratcliffe 'whom she had made her companion and educated' (in the words of the draft Deed) an annuity of £100 for her natural life, to be provided by an investment of £2,000 administered by Trustees. It is some indication of the generosity of that bequest that in 1910 the annual wage of a maid at Erddig was £12.

Following the death of his mother, Philip decided that the finest of the furniture and pictures in the Park Lane house ought to be preserved at Erddig. These included some of the Huttons' seventeenth century portraits, which were to displace Meller's 'Sibylls' in the Gallery; a large Delft vase by Adriansz Koeks, which had been given by Queen Anne to Mrs Wanley, an ancestress of the Huttons; and all the models made by Elizabeth Ratcliffe while her mistress was living in London. Responsibility for their safe dispatch fell to Betty Ratcliffe, who wrote to Philip from Park Lane on 26 April 1787:

> Sir
> enclosed is the account of the goods that are packed to go down, at least that are nearly finished & I thought you would chuse to know what quantity to expect. We have not seen Mr Willock, but have hastened the men as much as possible, they had no Idea so many cases would be wanted, nor upon enquiry did Mr Willock know what you had to be packed. We suppose by the

Thermometer being marked *that* is to go, we have only put up the things that you mentioned to us, namely Plate China books linen & Glass, as you will (see) by (the) Catalogue, they make a great load, & there should be people with the Waggon that can be trusted, with so many valuable articles, if one Waggon will contain them. . . . The stand for the Pagoda and Candle stands will all pack in one case, & the temple itself in another slight one, if you chuse to have them sent, & the thermometer can be put up with them, they wait for an answer about them. We have attended punctually to all the packing, & I hope observed every thing that you wished to have done. My Aunt put up all the books & linen to forward matters as much as might be, & yet we could not take our places with certainty till to'day for monday next, no one has been to look at the house, we hope for the pleasure of finding all things meet your approbation, & that the goods will arrive safe. With my Aunts & my respectful compliments to Mrs. Yorke & Yourself I remain

    Sir

      Your sincerely obliged

        humble servant

          Elizabeth Ratcliffe.

Philip Yorke more than honoured his mother's wishes and by a Deed of his own made the house in Park Lane available to Elizabeth Ratcliffe during her lifetime. However, she finally decided against staying in London and a letter of 1804 reports that 'she has made up her mind to become an inhabitant of Wales.' When last mentioned in the family's correspondence Betty Ratcliffe was living in Liverpool, having chosen not to retire to Erddig.

That the Yorke family continued to cherish her models is shown by Lady Sykes's journal of a tour of Wales in 1796. She wrote enthusiastically of Betty Ratcliffe's Palmyra model, then in the Withdrawing Room, and of her pier tables and candle stands:

This ingenious Lady Was Governess to the late Miss York, and after her death continued with Mrs York as companion. This was told to me by Mr Simon York Grand Son to the above named Lady, he also said they preserved these curiosities with unwearied care, they are a monument of great taste and ingenuity.

36   John Jones in 1911, thirty-three years after he entered service as a carpenter

3

Chips from the Block

The names of carpenters who worked at Erddig during the late seventeenth and early eighteenth centuries appear occasionally among contracts and bills. But they are usually names only, and faceless. There is Philip Rogers, a carpenter from the village of Eyton, some five miles from Erddig, who on 17 March 1685 contracted with Joshua and Francis Edisbury

> to doe all yᵉ Carpenter's work for two banqueting houses to be erected at Erthigg that is say he is to fall square raise & finish as agree'd onely two out dores to be omitted yᵉ sᵈ Josua Edisbury is to find all boards saw'd & timber when made loadable by yᵉ sᵈ Philip and yᵉ work to be sufficiently perform'd at yᵉ sight of Thomas Webb of Middle-wich.

When Thomas Badeslade drew his aerial view of Erddig in 1739, Rogers's banqueting houses were still principal features of the garden, at either end of one of the main paths. But at some stage during the next 150 years they must have fallen into disrepair and been demolished.

John Prince, the first recorded house carpenter at Erddig, is a less shadowy figure. He gave evidence during the bankruptcy proceedings against Joshua Edisbury, in a deposition of 2 October 1715:

> The next was one John Prince, a Carpenter who had been a Workman under Mᵣ Edisbury att his house att Erthigg & elsewhere Above 24 years & saith that Erthigg Hall was built abᵗ 30 Years Agoe & saith that Since the Same was built he had made Some Alteracions and Amendmᵗˢ in the roofe of the said Hall & done other necessaryes in the Said Hall & out buildings thereunto belonging by means whereof he Came frequently there & well knoweth the Said Hall & that the Same Containes Eight Roomes on a ffloor besides Clossetts & that the roomes on the first & Second ffloores are all well Wainscotted & one room fineered & ffloord with Wallnutttree & that All the harths and Chimneys are Curiously fitted up Some with Marble & others with face stone & that the house is the best fitted up of any house in that Country & Saith that

the house as it is with the Outhouses Gardens & alls thereto belonging were never built & finished as they now are for lesse than the sume of 8000£ & saith the hall & Outhouses are now in good repair.

Among estate accounts of 1723 to 1725 there are small payments to five carpenters: William Rogers, William Davies, Charles Prince, Richard Hughes and Robert Jones. Charles Prince, whose dark complexion led John Meller to coin the name Black Prince, was head carpenter at Erddig during the middle years of the eighteenth century; and he may well have been the son of the John Prince who worked for Edisbury. Perhaps William Rogers was related to the Philip Rogers who built the banqueting houses; or to Thomas Rogers whose family were to be such important members of the Erddig household during much of the nineteenth century. In view of the long traditions of service in both families these are all possibilities.

By 1779 Charles Prince had been succeeded by his son, Edward, whose own son was by then already working under him. The head carpenter was at that time the highest paid of the outdoor staff at Erddig: Edward Prince was receiving 1s. 6d. per day for a six day week; Edward Prince junior 1s.; and two other joiners, Robert Jones and John Jones, both 1s. 4d. The gamekeeper, John Henshaw, and the six gardeners were paid 10d. a day, as were the farm workers. John Williams – almost certainly the Erddig blacksmith and another case of father being succeeded by son – was paid 1s. a day. In an account of 1784, when he was still being paid 1s. 6d. a day, Edward Prince is described as being 'self working' and was therefore not under the direct supervision of Philip Yorke's agent, John Caesar. When Elizabeth Yorke wanted to know how much paper to order for the 'Garret over the Room that is to be Her dressing Room' her husband instructed Caesar to take the necessary measurements with Prince's help; and again in 1771 ordered him 'with Prince to measure the Old Wrought Bed'.

There is a far more vivid record of Edward Prince than these occasional references in the family's accounts. His portrait by John Walters of Denbigh still hangs in the Servants' Hall. Casually held in place by a pair of dividers is a scroll of verse:

> One labour more thou muse of mirth;
> That broughtest dogg'rell into birth;
> And before you leave us, enter,
> To record our old Carpenter:
> 'Tis threescore years, then young in grammar,
> When here at first, he held an hammer,
> Under his father, dead long since,
> Who was entitled – the *black Prince*.
> A *raiser this*, indeed of *Houses*,
> That has already had four Spouses;
> And if the present, don't survive,
> Hopes to rebuild them up, to five:
> From these bold strokes, arise a race
> Of *Princes*, to adorn the Place;

37 Thomas Rogers, carpenter, painted in 1830 when he was 48. He was to work at Erddig for the next forty-four years

> Who thrive beneath their parent stock,
> And make good *Chips*, from that old *block*.

Prince was 73 when, in 1792, the picture was painted.

Portraits of staff were occasionally commissioned at other houses in the eighteenth century. There is a particularly beautiful picture at Knole of a footman and maid, eventually to be man and wife, in profile, facing each other. The Legh family of Lyme Park, in Cheshire, recorded their gamekeeper, Joseph Watson – renowned for having driven twelve brace of stag from Lyme to London for a wager – in a dark and unprepossessing picture, appropriate to that severe, ungentle house. In 1719 George Alsop painted 'The Wolryche Fool', of Dudmaston, in south Shropshire, holding a large drinking glass which, remarkably, has still survived. The examples closest to those at Erddig hang in the Servants' Hall at Chirk Castle, only a few miles away; but the three portraits of staff there are so damaged and blackened with smoke that they are scarcely decipherable.

Although Philip Yorke's decision to paint his staff may not have been an original idea, his verse inscriptions were certainly novel. How did he come to write verse about his staff? A possible explanation is that it was an offshoot of Philip's passion for theatricals, from the most amateur to the most professional, which he shared with his neighbour, Sir Watkin Williams Wynn. During the 1770s several Shakespeare plays were staged at Sir Watkin's house, Wynnstay. In the production there of *The Merchant of Venice*, in 1778, Philip Yorke took the part of Antonio, while the Duke was played by Mr Apperley, the father of Charles Apperley, who under the pen-name 'Nimrod' was to be one of the most successful sporting writers of the nineteenth century. Garrick was invited on at least two occasions to witness and to take part in these productions. Writing to her mother during a visit to Erddig in the 1770s (and thoughtlessly failing to date her letter) Frances, Lady Brownlow reported:

> I mention'd in my last that we were going to Wynnstay, we staid all night, & returned yesterday to dinner, S.ʳ Watkin was so obliging to have the Theatre illuminated & shew'd us all the Scenes, of w.ᶜʰ there are great variety & extremely pritty, I should have liked very much to have been present at the plays, w.ᶜʰ have been perform'd there about a month ago, in w.ᶜʰ M.ʳ Yorke was an Actor, and Garrick a spectator. There are to be plays again at Xmas in w.ᶜʰ Mr. Y. is to have a part, S.ʳ Watkin takes great delight in the stage tho I find he is but a moderate performer and Lady Wynne never acts herself.

Philip organised his own productions at Erddig, with parts allotted even to the youngest of his children. In January 1786 they played *Henry V*, and for this occasion Philip himself wrote a prologue, to be spoken by his 9-year-old son Brownlow Yorke. Teasing but affectionate references were made to their cook, Mary Rice, to John their gardener, and to a housemaid, Betty Jones:

> To please you all, from Eton, have I run,
> Through mire and dirt, to kick-up Christmas fun:
> To be the Prologue to my Brother's play,
> And make you, as the season asks, be gay.
> You cook for me, and shall not I again,

Give Mary Rice, some pleasure for her pain;
Her pies indeed, are excellent, and good,
And I will pay her in dramatic food.
To Gard'ner John, I own but little less,
I prog his peaches, and his apple dress;
His fairest apricots, I pull, and plunder;
That boys love fruit, pray where the mighty wonder?
To Betty Jones, I am as much in debt,
I daub her hearths, and give her many a sweat;
Thro' me, her stairs, require successive scrubbing,
And all her floors, reiterated rubbing:
For so much mischief, you must charge my years,
And I in time, will pay you all arrears.

The reaction among the staff in the audience must have been one of delighted surprise; and when five years later their portraits were being painted, Philip decided to explore that same facetious, light-hearted vein again.

Philip's partiality for jaunty, jerky stanzas was inherited by his eldest son, Simon, who succeeded to the Erddig estates in 1804 on his father's death, and lived there uneventfully for the rest of his life. Following the pattern set by Philip, in 1830 he commissioned portraits of his gardener, Thomas Pritchard, his woodman Edward Barnes, and Edward Prince's successor as carpenter, Thomas Rogers. Simon's verse runs:

Another Chip from Nature's Block
Is added to the Parent Stock.
Apprentice first unto a Wheel-wright
This here might have been a Keel-wright.
And, like the London man of yore,
Have pluck'd the Lion's Heart in gore.

But soon he did out-strip his Trade,
And next our Carpenter was made.
To all our jobs he gives his Fiat,
To prove himself a second Wyatt;
He now assumes the Painter's art,
And brushes up the gates and carts.

Of brown and green to make the fixture,
Which Brisco sells him as a mixture,
To clean our walls he finds a washing,
Yellow and white the colours dashing.
Like other builders of a House
He too has got Prolific Spouse,

Who brings us forth a younger race,
To follow him in equal pace.
When Time hath sounded the Last Trump,
And laid their Sire upon his stump.
Tho' Life be lengthened to the longest span,
The House itself must fall as well as Man.

Thomas Rogers began his seventy-three years of service at Erddig in 1798, working at first as a pig boy and then as a thatcher's assistant and as a slater. His long association with Erddig was very nearly cut short disastrously when he was still in his early 30s. In 1815, while working on estate cottages at Plas Grono, he was seized by a press-gang operating from Liverpool. Rogers begged to be allowed to see his master before he was carried off. The request was granted, Simon Yorke intervened on his behalf, and then paid the ransom necessary for Rogers's release.

In his portrait Rogers is shown at his work bench in the joiners' shop. On the wall behind him are racks for his tools: chisels, a saw, clamps, a square and a slate for noting measurements. An adze is propped against the bench. Many of these tools, stamped with Rogers's name, were passed on to his son, James, and have remained in the possession of his descendants ever since. The joiners' shop depicted in the picture is probably that still used today. A late eighteenth century plan of the outbuildings at Erddig shows the saw pit, carpenters' and joiners' shops nearer to the main house, in what was later to become the outer stable yard; but early in the nineteenth century the joiners' shop was moved to a new timber yard, built almost certainly by the 1830s, which has remained in use ever since.

In 1852 the third Simon Yorke to own Erddig had the daguerreotype group portrait taken of his staff on the entrance steps. Thomas Rogers, by now a portly figure dressed in a suit, waistcoat and large bow tie, but holding a saw as his badge of office, stands second from the right in the front row. James Rogers was at this time already working in the joiners' shop alongside his father; and Harriet Rogers, later to be one of

38 Tools used by Thomas Rogers and stamped with his name

39   Servants at Erddig in 1852. Thomas Rogers is second from the right in the front row
and is holding a saw

40   The joiners' shop in 1973

41   The joiners' shop in 1978. Peter Smith, the head carpenter, is at the far end

42   James Rogers, who succeeded his father as carpenter in 1871

the most highly regarded of Erddig's housekeepers, was then nurse to Philip Yorke, the child seen with his parents at an open window in the daguerreotype.

At the age of 90, Thomas Rogers retired and was granted a pension. When he died four years later, on 19 March 1875, Simon Yorke wrote from Leasowe Castle:

> James Rogers,
> It grieved me much to hear this morning of the death of your good Father who had been a faithful servant of mine and a friend so long.
>
> I should wish to provide his coffin and to defray the expences of his Funeral. Tell your Mother how sorry we are for her in her trouble. I shall continue her allowance as before.
>
> I should wish his death advertised in both the Wrexham Papers, stating how long he has been in the service of my Father and Myself.
>
> Yours Faithfully,
> S. Yorke.

The Erddig carriages were, on Simon Yorke's instruction, used for the funeral.

James Rogers's service at Erddig ended unhappily. When the second Philip Yorke wrote about him after his death, he was generous in his praise:

James Rogers claims our high respect,
As all who knew him might expect.
Full half a life-time in the past
His lot on this estate was cast.
His good wife who in earlier years
Amidst an old-time group appears,
As Sarah Evans, here did come
To rear the young sparks of this home. . . .

As Master of the 'Timber-band'
He did conduct with skillful hand,
And much which this estate can show
We to his composition owe . . . .

Rogers fell out not with the Yorkes themselves but with their agent, Hughes. The family moved to Wrexham, where they struggled to run a small grocery store occasionally patronised by the Yorkes. Then Sarah died, the store failed and James left the area. The contents of their house at Bryn Goleu, a charming but ramshackle timber-frame building on the edge of the park at Erddig, were sold at auction. A birdcage and a leather bag, lot 11, made 3s. 6d.; lots 12 to 27 included a cupboard and bookshelves, a hanging lamp, a small square table, a bench and chair, six other chairs, an arm chair, a small oak table, cushions, a swing crib, an oak leaf table, a screen, a case clock, firewood, bottles and jars, which in all fetched 33s. 3d. An American clock was sold for only 1s. 0d.; but a second case clock made 8s. 6d. The few tools needed for their smallholding fetched more than their cottage furniture: £1 for a straw cutter, £1 6s. for a turnip pulper. One cow was sold for £10, another with calf for £10 15s., forty-seven chickens at 4s. 6d. each for £5 5s. 9d. and an old brown mare for only 2s. 0d. After £3 1s. 3d. had been deducted for bills and posting, advertising, portering and commission, the whole sale brought them £37 12s. 9d.

However, the Rogers family did not lose touch with Erddig, not least because Harriet had proved herself such a valuable member of staff. In 1895 the second Philip Yorke provided James's son Thomas with a mortgage of £2,200 at 4 per cent per annum interest. There is no record of his ever having been in service at Erddig, so this assistance must have been given out of respect and gratitude to young Thomas's grandfather and his aunt.

During the last quarter of the nineteenth century Erddig was served by two carpenters, who with their different skills complemented each other ideally. William Gittins, although a competent joiner in his own right, was also estate foreman with as many as a dozen men working under him. He was quite capable of building new houses and cottages, as well as dealing with the more routine jobs of repairing walls and roads, making fences and re-roofing. John Jones on the other hand was almost exclusively a joiner and carpenter. He was one of the staff photographed in 1887, and merited eight verses by the second Philip Yorke:

43　John Jones, photographed in the joiners' shop

John Jones, (tho' not alone), the same!
Our Coachman also bears that name:
'Tis one well known midst hills and dales
Of this our famous land of Wales.
A third yet answers to our call,
At this time dwelling at our Hall.
We in our household once had five,
And others still might be alive.

For him we have a great regard
As veteran of our Timber-yard,
For two & thirty years have sped
Since first he enter'd at our shed.
Yet never failed his course to pace
'Twixt Marchwiel village and this place,
Save when ill-health has been his share,
Which heav'n be thank'd, has been but rare.

The timber from the forest hewn,
Or haply by the tempest strewn,
When to his Bench it has been brought
To Work of excellence is wrought.
And all repairs which we have plan'd,
When once entrusted to his hand,
Are carried out with utmost haste,
And always in the best of taste.

Each field and meadow on the Estate
To his attention owes its gate,
With brand denoting date of same,
Initial'd with the owner's name.
Each Farm and Homestead on our ground
Some benefit from him has found,
By due repairs, both small and great,
To rescue from disastrous fate.

A master of the arts is he
In skillful handling of the Bee,
And well does he supply our home
With honey and the honey-comb.
By him the workers of the Hive
In sweet contentment live and thrive,
And, as the poet used to say,
'Improve each shining hour of day'.

We now in recent time have won
The good assistance of his son,
A youth who will, we trust, aspire
To be as useful as his sire:
Though, sad to tell, while yet a boy,
He met with hurt in our employ,
And worse it might with him have fared,
But this in mercy has been spared.

Though lost one once familiar face,
A daughter fills her Mother's place,
And strives to make the home once more
As happy as it was before;
And when, by Calendar, the page
Of middle life gives place to age,
Then may he every blessing see
Upon his home and family!

His daily work with saw and plane,
Less for his own than others' gain,
Concerns the good of many a home
For generations yet to come,
When we, beholding these no more
Have join'd the ones now gone before,
And rest with them in that same Ground
Which girds our village Church around.

When joinery work was needed in the house, it was usually to John Jones that the Yorkes turned. Such repairs by a humble house carpenter very often do not match up to the work of the finest cabinet makers and can be easily criticised by connoisseurs inclined to attribute anything clumsy or amateurish to his rough and ready efforts. Certainly, mistakes were made. It is hard to justify the decision of the Legh family to let their carpenter, Mr Rowlinson, imitate in plywood seventeenth century plasterwork elsewhere in the house, when he was entrusted with the renewal of the Long Gallery ceiling at Lyme. However, in that particular case the room had been unused and derelict for a number of years and the family could not have afforded, even if they could have found, sufficiently skilled craftsmen to do the job properly. Further decay was arrested only because Mr Rowlinson was willing to do his best. Similarly at Erddig, furniture which might otherwise have been discarded as irreparable, was rescued and made usable again by the house carpenter. The Yorkes' practice over 200 years of conserving the less grand, less obviously precious pieces of their inheritance, of never throwing anything away if they could possibly help it, owed much to the humble skills of staff such as John Jones.

When, early in the present century, the battered remnants of a carved sixteenth century table were found in one of the outhouses, cabinet makers in Wrexham pronounced it beyond repair. John Jones was undaunted. A top was made out of oak panelling removed from one of the servants' attic bedrooms after a fire. Jones carved the elephantine feet to designs by the second Philip, who no doubt also suggested how repairs to the decorated frieze should be tackled. The table now stands, incongruous but unashamed, in the Entrance Hall at Erddig, as much a tribute to the resourcefulness of John Jones and Philip Yorke, as an affront to the delicate neo-classical plasterwork of Joseph Rose, Robert Adam's plasterer.

Another curiosity is the staircase leading to the nursery wing. On one side there are generous, well proportioned balusters that certainly date from Joshua Edisbury's time. On the other are slender balusters which are clearly a much later addition. In fact they were rescued by Philip Yorke from Bishop Heber's house when it was being demolished in 1898. It was in the Old Vicarage, Wrexham, that on Whit Sunday 1819 Reginald Heber wrote his hymn, so loved by the Victorians, 'From Greenland's Icy Mountains', for a meeting of the Society for the Propagation of the Gospel the next day. The Old Vicarage was sold to the Wrexham, Mold and Connah's Quay Railway in 1880 and then pulled down. But Philip Yorke was determined that the memory of Bishop Heber should at least be revered at Erddig.

44   A sixteenth century table found in an outhouse and restored by John Jones

Reginald Heber was also remembered by the Yorke family for his association with the Ancient Society of Royal British Bowmen. The Society had been founded in 1787 by Sir Foster Cunliffe, whose daughter, Emma, kept a charming illustrated diary of their proceedings and was herself adept with the bow, winning prizes on more than one occasion. A print, after a drawing by J. Townsend, records the Bowmen's meeting at Erddig on 13 September 1822.

The Bowmen's meetings were an excuse for elegant fancy dress, with the feathers of their patron, the Prince of Wales, prominently displayed, for much eating and drinking, for the singing of songs composed specially for the occasion, and, perhaps rather less seriously, for archery contests between both gentlemen and ladies. Reginald Heber was the Society's laureate. Even as he was waiting for a ship to take him to his bishopric in Calcutta and an early death, he composed a song to be sung on 20 June 1823, at the first Bowmen's meeting after his departure:

> The Bard is gone! and other bards shall wake the call of pleasure
> That prompts to Beauties' lips the smile and lends the cheek its glow
> And strikes the woodland Harp with louder livelier measure
> And wears the oaken wreath which he must now forego –
> But yet tho' many a sweeter song
> Shall float th' applauding tent along
> Forget not them who doomed to part
> Will wear engraven on their heart
> The sons and daughters of the British Bow.

A print after Bishop Heber's portrait by Thomas Phillips hangs at the bottom of the staircase which John Jones and William Gittins re-erected in his memory.

Gittins's early working life was spent as a general builder and it was only the recession of 1870 that forced him into service at Erddig. For the next forty years he ruled the estate yard and joiners' shop. His bench was on the window wall, John Jones's on the opposite wall, with two apprentices, one of them in due course Gittins's son, Willy, at the far end. Templates, pieces of carving salvaged from furniture beyond repair and iron brackets hung from nails on the walls. Shavings carpeted the cobbled floor and duck boards. The blacksmith's shop was next door, the saw pit immediately outside, and ranged around the rest of the yard were the paint store, lean-tos under which guttering and other materials were stacked and a shed in which creosote was kept.

By the beginning of this century many of the more laborious estate workers' jobs were being performed by heavy machinery. The saw pit gave way to the sawmill in the outer stable yard. It was while de-scaling its large steam boiler, an unenviable job that usually fell to the most junior of the estate staff, that young Willy Gittins found himself wedged upside down in the manhole, where he remained until his muffled cries were eventually heard by his colleagues. Another important acquisition was the large cast iron mortar mill, collected from Wrexham station in the early 1900s by Gittins and his staff. In it were mixed the ashes from the house, lime and sand which went into scores of buildings on the estate and which were used for such decorative additions to the garden as the scalloped gables at either end of the parterre.

Even more ambitious than the garden gabling was the boathouse, designed by Philip Yorke and built by Gittins at the far end of the canal. It is true that its eaves came so low that it was virtually impossible to manoeuvre a boat inside without the oarsmen lying flat; but as an eyecatcher seen from the state rooms, it was much admired. So too was the model train which William Gittins made as a present for Simon Yorke's fifth birthday. The second Philip's verses about Gittins, written in 1911 and some of his most appreciative, stress the range of his talents:

> In portrait here we illustrate
> Our worthy foreman of th' Estate
> Of swarthy build, robust in frame,
> And William Gittins is his name.
> 'Tis five-and-twenty years or more,
> Since first he entered at our door,
> Eighteen were spent with present Squire
> The earlier period with his Sire.
>
> Rhos-llanerchruggog is his home
> Which, (un-pronounceable for some,)
> At each Eisteddfod takes a part
> Renowned for Music, Song, and Art,
> And at that place a goodly throng
> Of cottages to him belong.
> In truth, a worthy Land-lord he
> As all his tenantry agree.

45   William Gittins, foreman carpenter in 1911

Objects of Art within our Hall
Places of interest recall
As formed of fragments deftly wrought
Which were from ruined houses brought.
And are productions of his hand
Assisted by his able band
(Of whom some members here are seen,
Who longest have his helpers been).

If any should the wish impart
To see a sample of his Art
Behold that Boat-house of his make
Reflected in the garden lake
Whose fabric, graceful in design,
Does elegance with use combine
And from the windows of our Hall
An ornament impart to all.

Our boats engaged his earliest Art
And hosts of pleasure still impart
While many have the joy to know
How here they learn'd to punt or row.
His Coracle you yet may see
Worthy of any on the Dee
His sledge is greatly in request
When Winter Sport is at its best.

For all repairs both great and small
On Mr. Gittins straight we call
Nor does his talent e'er despise
The toys that charm our Children's eyes.
Of furniture, for cost and date
We on his guidance do await
And when at sales we him consult
We need not fear but good result.

When each return of Spring demands
House-cleaning and the painters' hands,
His vigilence sees all things right
No rust or crack escapes his sight.
And if decay should cause alarm
At barn or Cottage, Lodge or Farm,
To him we look for due repair
Entrusting all into his care.

> Not e'en the best does Trial spare,
> Of sufferings, he has had his share
> Tho' happy in his wedded life
> With second Spouse, his present wife,
> Who, once attended at our Hall
> Where the respect she well did gain
> Will ever in our minds remain.

In early April 1915 Gittins caught a chill while out fencing on the estate. He had fallen off the timber waggon, seemed to be suffering from paralysis in one arm, but insisted on seeing the fence completed. That night the doctor was summoned and, after first complaining of being called out just for a cold, decided that Gittins was seriously ill. The next day his wife wrote to warn Mr Yorke that he would be off sick for at least a fortnight, at the same time thanking the squire for his 'very kind message' and 'great kindness and consideration for us at all times'. Philip Yorke kept two of the letters subsequently written to him by William Gittins's widow, the first undated:

> Sir
> I feel I cannot express in words my feelings of gratitude for all your great kindness and kind consideration of me and my children in my sad and heavy trial I thank you Sir for the kind offer you gave me for the Education of one of my children but at the present I am unable to give an answer I cannot feel grateful enough to both Mrs. Yorke and yourself and Master Simon and Master Phillip for the most beautiful wreath and cross so kindly sent in laying my dear Husband to rest and your extreme kindness at all times.
> I beg to remain,
> Yours most obediently
> Louisa Gittins.

The second was written on 2 December 1915:

> Sir
> I thank you for your kind letter last evening, and I am most thankful to you for your very kind considerations of allowing me a pension of £4 annually, which will help me a great deal as the loss of my Husband meant so much more to me than I can explain. had either of my children been old enough to have earned a little would have been a help to me, as at the present time everything is so very much advanced in price.
> I also thank you *Sir* for your kind offer to pay for an advertisement should I wish to go into service again but as my health is anything but good, I do not see that I should benefit by doing so as it would take all I could earn, to put my two children out to board & lodge & see to them and again it would mean me to break up my home, then both my children & myself would be without a home, but I will try and do whatever I can, to keep our home untill such times

as my boy can earn a little and then I trust if we have our health life will look
a little brighter. Again thanking you Sir and Mrs. Yorke for your great
kindness & consideration you have of me.

    I beg to remain,
        Yours Most Obediently
        M. L. Gittins.

Mrs Gittins's pension was raised to £6 a year in 1917; and in 1918 young Willy Gittins
was appointed estate carpenter.

46   Nursery toys, including the train made by the foreman carpenter William Gittins for
Simon Yorke's fifth birthday

4

Housekeepers, Cooks and Nannies

'A large house in Wales is ye worst thing in ye world to manage', complained Dorothy Yorke to Philip in a letter of 1765. Yet for all its inconvenience, the Yorkes succeeded in living reasonably comfortably at Erddig for over two centuries and for most of that time the domestic arrangements of the household ran smoothly and well. The Yorkes readily admitted in the verses they wrote about their staff that this was largely due to the virtues of that linchpin of their establishment, the housekeeper.

In a relatively small country house such as Erddig, the housekeeper enjoyed a higher position than she would have done with a wealthier family. At the beginning of the eighteenth century the great houses were still employing a house steward, whose status, although declining, still owed much to the very considerable authority the post had held during the Tudor period. But John Williams and Richard Jones, the stewards employed by Edisbury and Meller, were preoccupied with estate matters and the supervision of outside staff such as the gardeners and woodmen. This left the housekeeper to shoulder responsibility for most day-to-day matters indoors.

Although her wages at £10 a year were not high, Meller's housekeeper was at least being paid the same as his butler, John Jones, and twice as much as the junior maids and the postilion. Her responsibilities included the supervision of the female staff, the custody of much valuable china and linen, the ordering of provisions and the planning of lavish meals. In capable hands these responsibilities could be taken for granted by the family. But when, as happened in the 1900s, a succession of housekeepers proved incapable or untrustworthy, the delicately adjusted machinery of life at Erddig came grinding to a halt. A good housekeeper held the key, not just to some of the Yorkes' most valuable possessions, but to their peace of mind.

'An account of the linens delivered to ye Housekeeper March 4th 1726–7' runs to four pages. It begins with the bed linen: '11 pair of fine Holland sheets; 14 pair of fine Irish Holland sheets' (a total against which the housekeeper noted, 'but 13 pairs'), '16 pair of flaxen sheets, 25 pair of coarse sheets', and so on, making a total of '66 pair of sheets'. Then the coarse linen was listed: one of the fourteen huckaback table cloths was missing, as was one of the napkins, out of a total of thirty fine table cloths and thirty napkins. In a chest in the passage room were a further eight fringed table cloths, three dozen ordinary huckaback napkins, five pairs of ordinary Holland sheets, four pairs of coarse sheets and six round towels. The next three pages go on to list a further 120 diaper napkins, 132 damask napkins, 42 diaper table cloths, '2 Huckabuck Towels of a Pretty figuremen(t), one much burnt; 1 more found', and '2 damask Table-cloths of King Charles II^d in the Royal Oak'. A note was added to the second page that 'all ye preceding linens formerly in ye charge of the housekeeper were deliv^ed to ye Laundring M.^d'. John Meller had linen enough to satisfy a regiment of the most fastidious bachelors and for all of it the housekeeper was ultimately answerable.

The aftermath of hospitality could be almost as demanding as the preparations. When the family was not in residence, the state rooms had to be partially dismantled and the more vulnerable furniture carefully protected. There were 'white cloth covers' to go back on the chairs and settee in the Withdrawing Room, a walnut cover for the glass topped table there, and 'yellow stuff covers' to put over the caffoy upholstery in the Saloon. Care was taken to guard against the damage caused by light and dust, and for much of the time 'Sprigg'd callicoe blinds for windows' had to be drawn. The housekeeper's role was very much that of a curator of a precious collection of textiles and works of art.

Then there were the larders to stock. Many of the entries in the housekeeper's accounts kept by Mary Salusbury from 1798 to 1804, and continued until 1806 by her successor Sarah Lloyd, are for the luxuries that could not be supplied by the Erddig estate:

June ye 25, 1798	Ducks 15 at 12^d cuple	7s	6d
	2 Lobsters	2	0
June 28	3 cuple of chickings	4	0
	Cockles	1	0
	Cakes	4	0
	Muffins	0	8
	Eggs	2	0

and later

July ye 10	4 Geese	5	6
	fish	3	6
	herrins	2	6
	Chickings	6	8
	Salmon & Ells	6	3
	Muffins and cakes	4	10

But Mary Salusbury was dealing with all manner of other household matters: paying Mary Jones 1s. 4d. for two days sewing, and the washerwoman 3s. 'The boys that found the Duck' were rewarded with 1s. On the 24 July 1798 she paid 10s. 6d. for 'a Side of Vensons', 1s. 6d. for 'Musher Rooms' and also gave 1s. to the poor. She was responsible for giving the Yorke children their pocket money (1s. 2d. to Miss L. Yorke on 25 May 1801), for paying Mr Challinder 10s. 6d. for tuning the harpsichord the same month, and for dealing with the sweeping of twelve chimneys at 9s. Between 18 June 1805 and 14 July 1806 Sarah Lloyd had to account for outgoings of £82 11s. 3d.; more than three times her own annual salary.

When writing to his agent while away from Erddig, Philip Yorke often included instructions to be passed on to the cook and housekeeper. Their neighbours' children were to be given 'Raspberry Jam, & Currant Jelly', but the maid 'will take care they do not make themselves sick'. On 14 November 1782 Philip wrote from Dyffryn Aled, the home of his second wife, formerly Diana Meyrick:

> Your mistress would have Molly Salusbury look-out her White Negligee Sack, and the Hoop she wears with it; also a pair of White Silk Shoes, and the Blue Leathern ones, and the old laced Ruffles that she used to wear with it, if they be at Erddig; also a black pair of dropp'd Ear-rings, and a necklace of the same. I would have you, on my part, bring me over a pair of black satten Breeches, which you will easily find without disturbing the other things, among the Packages lately come f.rm London, that Enclose my new Cloathes.

Mr Thomas Jones, one of the tradesmen who supplied Erddig in the 1790s, merited a portrait in the Servants' Hall, and inclusion in Philip's *Crude Ditties*:

> In Nature's chain, a double link,
> For Tom provides both *meat* and *drink*,
> Moreover was a stout freeholder,
> Which makes him rather cock his shoulder:
> In voting matters, had connections,
> And roar'd loudly, at elections,
> 'Sir Watkin ever, none shall touch her!'
> And might have made a *Borough butcher*,
> But that he scorn'd such *rotten* places,
> And only join'd in County cases.
> Tom, in his figure, not emaciate,
> Is rather somewhat calefaciate;
> But honest, active in his calling,
> Nor ever given to forestalling;
> In trade, as proper is, a winner,
> And tho' a Publican, no Sinner.

The original arrangement of the housekeeper's room and domestic offices at Erddig is a matter of conjecture, and certainly considerable changes were made when the New Kitchen was built in the 1770s; but since then the various basement rooms have been little altered. Far from being the wildly unpractical arrangement that a casual look at country house basements can suggest – all endless subterranean passages, kitchens hundreds of yards away from the dining room and scores of apparently anonymous, troglodytic basement rooms – the plan was carefully thought out and worked well.

The position of the housekeeper's room was strategic. It is situated in the basement corridor, with a door linking it to the adjoining agent's office, where

In Nature's chain, a double link .
For Tom provides both *meat and drink*,
Moreover was a stout freeholder,
Which makes him rather cock his shoulder;
In voting matter had connections,
And roared loudly at elections,
"Sir Wa——in ever, none shall touch her!"
And might have made a *Borough butcher*,
But that he scorn'd such rotten places,
And only join'd in County cases.
Tom in his figure, not emaciate,
Is rather somewhat calefaciate,
But honest, active in his calling,
Nor ever given to forestalling,
In trade, as proper, is a winner,
And tho' a Publican, no Sinner.
A Borough Broker one who deals
In the sale of rotten Boroughs   1793.

47   Thomas Jones, butcher to Erddig in the 1790s

accounts were kept, wages paid and the work of the outdoor staff organised. These two rooms were the administrative hub of the household. Beyond the agent's office a staircase leads from the basement to the servery and thence to the dining room. Then comes the still room and further down the passage, the kitchen; on a different floor certainly from the dining room, but with a short staircase and later a lift going up to the servery. Nearest to the housekeeper's room in the other direction is the Servants' Hall.

When in the 1770s James Wyatt was advising the first Philip Yorke on his improvements to Erddig, he was expressly consulted about alterations to the domestic offices. There is a letter in Wyatt's handwriting which, as well as suggesting how the

48   The housekeeper's room

chimneys on the main roof ought to be rebuilt, gives detailed instructions for opening up a door from the housekeeper's room into the old larder in order to give the housekeeper more space and to provide a new china store. Neither Wyatt nor Philip Yorke thought it below their dignity to be involved in the reorganisation of these basement rooms.

The daguerreotype of staff taken in 1852 shows the housekeeper, Mary Webster, holding a brace of fowl. The accompanying verse was written by the second Philip Yorke:

> Upon the portly frame we look
> Of one who was our former Cook.
> No better keeper of our Store,
> Did ever enter at our door.
> She knew and pandered to our taste,
> Allowed no want and yet no waste;
> And for some thirty years and more
> The cares of Office here she bore.

Thrift was a very necessary virtue in a housekeeper to the Yorkes, who during the second half of the nineteenth century were in no position to indulge in extravagance. But Mary Webster was also parsimonious in her own affairs. As a widow with a daughter to care for she had to be: she would almost certainly have been dependent on her own savings had she ever become unfit for work. Without something to fall back on she could in old age have been forced, like so many other domestic servants, to throw herself on the charity of relatives or to accept the ignominy of the workhouse. What was revealed at her death in 1875 came as a shock not only to the other staff, but to the Yorkes themselves:

49   Mary Webster, housekeeper during the middle years of the nineteenth century

A peaceful time she here did spend
And here it peacefully did end.
Few days she on her couch was lain
And passed away without much pain.
At Knockin she was lain to rest
'Midst those with whom she once was blest
And some who longest here had been
Went, and were present at the scene.

And at the reading of the Will
In Bank, (we do not mean a Hill,)
Were more than thirteen hundred pounds
'Gainst rainy day! tho' strange it sounds
This was by weeping kins-folk claimed,
As 'parties therein after named',
But whether spent on 'rainy day'
Or 'a fine time' we cannot say.

The Yorkes did not have to advertise for a replacement for Mrs Webster. Instead they promoted the daughter of their trusted and long-serving carpenter, Thomas Rogers. Harriet Rogers had succeeded her sister as nurse to the children of the third Simon Yorke and had then been for twelve years Mrs Yorke's personal maid. Her letters, books and some of her more precious personal possessions, now all carefully preserved by her great-great-niece, reflect a life of determined struggle for education and the independence it could bring. Harriet Rogers's service with the Yorkes, their encouragement of her reading and the opportunities she eventually had for travel abroad, offered an escape from the confined world of her parents, who were barely literate, and of her sister-in-law, who signed her marriage register with a cross. But it was an escape bought at a high price. Like so many girls who went into service for the chances it gave for self-improvement, Harriet in fact exchanged her family's narrow horizons for a post which, although it brought her into contact with all the privilege and cultivation of country house life, was in its own way just as inhibiting. Her choice was between being trapped by lack of education, or being trapped in the service of the kindly, considerate Yorkes.

Harriet's early letters are earnest and correct, their style more what one would expect from the Yorke children; but they are also full of real affection. On 31 October 1844, when she was barely ten years old, she wrote to her sister Eliza, then in service in Liverpool:

My dear sister
It is with pleasure I take up my pen and to write these few lines to you hoping this will find you enjoying good health as it leaves us at present. We have killed a fat cow and you must come home for this winter to help us to eat it. I think Maria is going from home this winter and mother would be very glad if you

50　Harriet Rogers, lady's maid and then housekeeper

51   Harriet Rogers accompanying one of the Squire's sisters on an expedition in the Erddig donkey cart

would come home instead of her. George's leg is getting a deal stronger. Selina Smith has left Mr. Foulkes for telling stories on the servants. He sent her on a minutes notice.

Jane has left Mrs. Brown, her mother is very ill altogether they are very busy makeing wheelbarrows for the Railway. There has been a man bit by a mad dog. There is many dogs going mad in this month. Samuel has been over and told us all the news about Birkenhead. I have knitted a pair of stockings and I am going to knit a pair of mittens next week. No more news at present. I hope the next letter I write you will be more worthy your perusal then the present. Please write as soon as you can.

I remain your affectionate
Sister Harriet Rogers.

The books she was given at that age had titles to cure all but the most determined of any wish for self-improvement: *The Young Traveller; or a visit to her Grandmother, Containing with a variety of incidental topics, a sketch of elements of Zoology, Botany, Mineralogy and other branches of Natural History*, by a Lady, 1816; and *Alfred, or the Youthful Enquirer, In which many of the operations of Nature and Art are familiarly explained and adapted to the comprehension of children*, the title page of which is inscribed 'Miss Harriet Rogers her book January 28th 1842'.

Once in service at Erddig, the obstacles in the way not just of marriage but of friendship outside the household were daunting. Harriet chose to keep a letter expressing frustrations which she herself must have felt just as deeply:

> Tatton Villa,
> Heaton Moor,
> Nr. Stockport.
> July 28th 1871.

Dear Miss Rogers,

If I say I was pleased to receive your letter I should say what I did not feel.

So often have we looked forward to the pleasure of your visit but as often as we have looked we have been disappointed and for what reason? First because Miss Rogers had not the courage to ask Mrs. Yorke for a week's leave.

All things seem impossible, until an effort is made, and as we said when we were speaking about this subject, the longer you remain satisfied with so little liberty the longer you shall be. We do think it hard that neither you nor Mrs. Webster, or any of the friends from Erddig will come and see us. So often as we have called to see them. We have made up our minds that if you do not come and see us, we will never call again. No excuse will free you from the promise you have made to come here.

It will most likely be 6 weeks before we come to Marchwiel again, so you have an opportunity of coming here before that time, you can please yourself when you come, either next week, the week after or the week after that, but you must come or we must carry out the sentence.

Whenever you are prepared to come please write a day or two before and we will meet you at the station.

Please remember us kindly to all friends and believe us,

Yours very sincerely

J. C. Maddocks.

As far as their employers were concerned, such meetings were likely to end in trouble: at best the loss of a good servant to get married, at worst an unwanted pregnancy and all the unpleasantness of instant dismissal. Attitudes changed little until well into the next century. In 1901 the future wife of the second Philip Yorke noted in her diary how outraged her father was to find their cook speaking to her young man at the back door. Harriet Rogers carefully put away her numerous Valentine cards. She seems never to have been formally engaged.

Harriet combined the posts of cook and housekeeper for nearly twenty years. When she finally left Erddig, to become ladies' maid to Simon Yorke's sisters, she took with her a collection of recipe books, including the inevitable 'Mrs Beeton', her beautifully embroidered work box and a small storm lantern which she must have carried countless times up and down the draughty basement passages. But even when she was living in retirement in Wrexham she kept in touch with the family. She was invited to Simon Yorke's christening on 5 August 1903; she helped Philip Yorke

52   Harriet Rogers's lantern, sewing
box and the Bible given to her by
the Yorke family

identify the staff in the group portraits taken in the 1880s when, some thirty years later, he wished to add verse biographies to them; and in 1907 she wrote to Philip acknowledging the gift of a cheque, 'for which I return very many thanks, I think it extremely kind of you to remember me, as well as for sending me such a very handsome present so often.' When she died in 1914, Philip Yorke kept the letter from her niece telling of her death and the funeral arrangements.

During the last quarter of the nineteenth century the third Simon Yorke lived quietly at Erddig, scarcely ever leaving the house, filling notebook after notebook with elevating sermons and depressing verse. Holidays were spent at Barmouth where he was remembered as 'a very good man, who gave us pennies to throw at the Sunday train' – that blasphemous symbol of frivolity and materialism. His wife Victoria, a first cousin, had been lady-in-waiting to Queen Victoria; but when her royal mistress later visited Wales and instead of staying at Erddig accepted hospitality near Llangollen, Victoria was hurt and upset. She lost interest in affairs at Court and subsequently always referred to the Queen as 'Old Mother Bunch'.

Simon's relationship with his son Philip was an uneasy one. Their principal bond was their verse, which Victoria Yorke deplored and tried to suppress. Writing to Philip in 1894, Simon reported that a junior member of the family had come to 'spy upon my poetical conduct'. He added:

> I am quite convinced that your mother loves me dearly – but hath a rather
> curious way of showing it, in regard to my rhyming propensities.
>
> > She whom I most love does not *like*
> > The rhyming of her faithful tyke.

The second Philip's early life was profoundly unhappy. His first marriage, to Annette Puleston, was very much to satisfy his father's wishes and it ended disastrously. The family blamed the rift on Philip's tactless insistence that their honeymoon should be spent painting watercolours, never a particularly sociable activity. Whatever the reason, Annette deserted him shortly after their marriage. Some account of what happened was given in a letter of 15 November 1877:

My dear Mr Campbell,

Finding on my table this morning a third letter from Miss Campbell to my wife, I write in bitter grief to you to tell you that I know nothing of her. She left me a fortnight ago, while we were staying with some friends of mine, the Humberstones of Glan-y-Wern.

She went off with her maid without ever wishing me Adieu or any one else in the house. Since then I have heard nothing of her, beyond that her maid came over to Erddig to ask for her things. I, not unnaturally refused to see the hateful creature (who, I believe, is the cause of my wife's estrangement from me), and as no note came with her, I know nothing more of her, and I must look forward to a lifelong misery and loneliness, as I am doing now.

I am leaving here on Thursday next, to go for a tour on the continent, which I think may do me a little good, if anything will, but I am terribly upset just at present. My sister Lily is going with me.

53   The second Philip Yorke (1849–1922)

You have always been so kind, that I venture to write and tell you and your's, this sad news, As I feel sure I shall have all of your sympathy; & I remain ever, my dear Mr. Campbell

Yours ever truly

Philip Yorke.

With most aff$^{ect.}$ remembrances to Mrs. Campbell and all your family circle.

Annette apparently left in the early hours of the morning begging a lift on the milk float. She and Philip subsequently met only once. They ran into each other accidentally outside the Army and Navy Stores. 'Is it peace, Philip?' Annette asked. 'Madam, let me show you to your carriage', was the reply. They never spoke again.

Philip spent his middle years travelling in Europe and the Near East, writing, photographing and painting. When he did return home, it was not to face unsympathetic neighbours but to undertake charitable work among the poor in London. Although many he had thought of as his friends now ostracised him, he found other loyalties. Out of his own unhappiness grew his concern and regard for his staff at Erddig. With the arrogance and complacency of so many of their generation, his social equals tended to regard such behaviour as just another eccentric quirk. It may not be entirely fortuitous that of all his forebears, the second Philip had most in common with his great-grandfather, another Philip, whose loss of his first wife shook the complacency of an earlier generation.

In 1899 Annette died. Philip was free to marry again. Eligible ladies were invited to a succession of house parties at Erddig, and when they came to leave were presented with a little paper parcel, neatly tied with a ribbon, in which was a proposal of marriage in verse. While the idea of becoming mistress of Erddig may have been attractive, the prospect of marrying a squire who was already in his 50s, and looked every bit his age, was rather more daunting.

Among the visitors to Erddig in the summer of 1899 was Louisa Scott, the daughter of the Rev. T. J. Scott of Chilton Foliat, in Wiltshire. An energetic cyclist and a competent musician, Louisa was a welcome guest. She admired the dignified way in which Philip conducted services in the chapel, and his kindness to the children of the parish and to the inmates of the workhouse, whom he invited to numerous tea parties. 'Mr. Yorke is a paragon of goodness. Each child had a present as well as a good tea, games, boats etc.', she wrote in her diary. She was canoed by Philip on the canal in the garden, they went for twilight walks in the beechwoods, and they visited neighbours, Philip on his tricycle and Louisa on a two-wheeler. At the end of a strenuous day they would gather in the Entrance Hall for their favourite songs, struggling to read in the light of oil lamps the hand-written copies of J. F. Edisbury's 'To the Cyclist':

If you want to know how to cure *real* rheumatic
Please listen to what I am now going to sing –
Just buy a bicycle – with tyres pneumatic
And – with very slight practice – you'll find it *the* thing.

First – go to bed early – get a good nights repose
Then – put on 'Alarum' – to wake you at six:
Then hurry down stairs (not forgetting your hose)
And on seat of machine – yourself steadily fix. . . .

For seeing the country whether England or Wales
The cycle for travelling is really the best
Because you can traverse its hills or its dales
And, when *winded* – you can always 'pull up' to rest.
Then again – there's no mash or feeding required
Or grooming, or stable, or Old Ostler's fees
The Cycle's the friend that never feels tired
And no broken wind – or yet broken knees. . . .

The next year, in July, Louisa returned to Erddig with her parents. She found Mr. Yorke 'wonderfully changed since last year'. Then, for their summer holiday of 1901, the Scotts went to Denmark. It was not until the following January that they again visited Erddig, this time to stay for several weeks. Louisa noted in her diary:

22nd January. I think it was today we all trouped down stairs and looked at the silver and the Hogaph's (sic) prints in the House-keeper's room. We were all much interested. At 4.30 we drove to Wrexham (5 inside & Mr. Yorke on the box) Mr. Yorke dropped a stamp going up the hill so he and I got out and hunted for it. The girls were much amused. The stamp is to be re-called from Ceylon & Kept as a memento.

24th January. Mr. Yorke took me to Chester and we went to a lecture on the Renaissance. It was a little deep. . . . In the evening Mr. Yorke gave us a Magic Lanthern Entertainment. He showed us Norway, Sweden, Denmark & Egypt.

30th. In the evening we had Mr. Yorke's Magic lanthern out. I worked the slides & very much enjoyed it. We travelled through England & Egypt.

2nd February. I wrote out poetry for Mr. Yorke.

9th February. Mr. Pope, Mr. Yorke & I went for a walk in the woods. Mr. Yorke taught us how to measure the height of trees. You make a ring with your fingers at the end of your nose & place yourself where you can see the top and bottom of the tree.

11th February. Mr. Yorke and I went for a most charming walk, through a wood. Bruno & Bruce were very naughty & their master encouraged them in their wickedness.

13th February. We had a delightful drive & Mr. Yorke was most polite. . . .

14th February. (St. Valentine's Day). One of the happiest days of my life. Mr. Yorke & I walked to Wrexham & coming home he said such pretty things to me & called me his 'sister'. . . . In the evening we learned Palmistry & at

12.15, under the picture of the former Philip Yorke (by Gainsborough) he asked me to become his wife. It seems a dream. I can hardly believe it is true. 15th February. The sense of my coming duties & responsibilities almost frighten me, but I have Philip to help me in my difficulties.

They were married on 23 April and spent the first few days of their honeymoon at Windsor, visiting Frogmore and then cycling out to Stoke Poges to see Gray's monument. High winds did not deter them. Philip secured Louisa's bicycle to his tricycle with a rope and pulled her along. Some days they covered only a few miles; on others Louisa proudly recorded a total of twenty-five miles, and on a trip from Salisbury to Sherbourne they cycled a full twenty-nine miles. On 30 May they returned to Erddig, to 'Church bells canoning, crowds of people cheering, two triumphal arches (made by workmen on the estate)'. The Erddig servants unharnessed the carriage horses and themselves dragged the vehicle up the hill leading to the house.

During his father's later years and Philip's own self-imposed exile abroad and in London, the supervision of staff at Erddig had largely been left to the agent, Mr Hughes. There was no housekeeper and when laundry and housemaid had left they had not been replaced. 'I am much troubled about servants', Louisa wrote in July 1902. 'I do not know of a housekeeper yet . . . I shall want a laundry maid, & kitchen maid & housemaid'; and again later in the month, 'I am having great trouble with the numerous servants. Some are too noisy, some too grand, some find the work too much. I wonder if I shall ever be quite settled.' Louisa thought she had found the answer to her problems in Miss Mackreth, who was given the title of 'Lady Housekeeper'. But she only lasted two months. Her replacement, Mrs Jonathan, a Welsh cook-housekeeper, proved equally unsatisfactory. In November Louisa wrote despairingly in her diary: 'Oh! the trouble of the servants at Erddig. It is sad to contemplate. The new housekeeper Mrs Osmond is to leave at once. She will do no work except arrange flowers!' But such faults were venial compared with the criminal dishonesty of her successor, Mrs Penketh, who brought public humiliation and disgrace to Erddig. Then, to their immense relief, Louisa and Philip found in Miss Brown a housekeeper worth the name.

Miss Brown was the last housekeeper to preside over anything like a full complement of staff. In the photograph taken on the entrance steps in 1912, and deliberately echoing the one taken sixty years earlier, she is in the middle of the front row, holding a basket of keys. Philip eulogised her in the verse he wrote that same year:

> Miss Brown does now the same post hold
> Which mistress Rogers held of old,
> And which for thirty years before
> Good Mrs. Webster held for yore,
> Of both which latter here around
> The record of their worth is found,
> Which pictures in that selfsame place
> Is seen each once familiar face.

54   Miss Brown, who came to Erddig as housekeeper in 1907 and left in 1914

When Rogers had her task resign'd
And left, an easier post to find,
Twelve years or more did intervene
Before Miss Brown came on the scene.
And varied changes then we find
Were in that period brought to mind.
Of Housekeepers we estimate
We had in turn no less than eight. . . .

But since Miss Brown her rule begun
Our lot has well and smoothly run,
And the result may now be class'd
As worth the 'fire' thro' which we pass'd,
For she has won respect from all
And is the mainstay of our Hall,
Where, as the present time may prove,
All does in peace and order move.

Miss Brown was usually responsible for three housemaids, three kitchen and three laundry maids, as well as part-time staff taken on when the Yorkes had a house party. The housekeeper's bedroom and sitting room were at the end of the south wing, with a window conveniently over the back door, so that a key could be lowered to any of the maids who had been allowed out late.

The housekeeper was not expected to get up as early as the junior staff, whose work in the early morning was supervised by the senior housemaid. But Miss Brown had to satisfy herself that all the downstairs rooms had been dusted and the fires laid before the staff gathered for chapel at 9.10. Immediately after chapel, at about 9.30, Mrs Yorke would come to the housekeeper's room to agree menus, talk over any staff problems and reassure herself that all was well. For the rest of the day the smooth running of the kitchen, scullery, laundry and bakehouse, as well as the maids' work in the main rooms of the house, were Miss Brown's responsibility.

Although she had to see that the junior staff carried out their work conscientiously, Miss Brown was not disliked. As at most large houses, her post entitled her to be referred to as 'Mrs' rather than 'Miss', but she was a respected rather than an awesome figure. The maids were, however, less well disposed towards her dog Grip, who had a particularly sharp nose for the smell of toffee, cooked illicitly over their attic bedroom fires.

Miss Brown left Erddig at Christmas 1914. Appearances already mattered less by then. For years the Yorkes had had to struggle to find and pay reliable servants; but now, as at many other country houses, they could attribute their running down of staff to patriotism. Their housekeeper proved least dispensable. Two world wars saw the post transformed, until it involved the stocking, cooking, cleaning and catering that forty years before had occupied a dozen or more male and female staff.

The daughter of a butler to the Bishop of Ely, Lucy Hitchman came to Erddig in July 1903, as nurse for the newly born Simon Yorke. Within six months of marrying Philip, Louisa Yorke had had an ovarian cyst diagnosed and had been operated on most painfully. She was in fact pregnant at the time, but the baby survived. The south wing of the house once again became a nursery. A Kate Greenaway paper illustrating the months of the year was chosen for the large day nursery, and the night nursery was papered with pussy cats and given a terracotta-coloured carpet. 'We like Lucy, the nurse, so much. She is young, only 26, but so careful with the little boy', Louisa wrote in her diary.

On 23 March 1905 Louisa had another son, christened Philip Scott Yorke (his

55 Lucy Hitchman, nurse to Simon and Philip Yorke, photographed in 1911 with them
and with her future husband, the groom Ernest Jones

father's name and that of his mother's family). Lucy was much loved both by the boys
and their parents, and she remained at Erddig to look after them until they went away
to school. By then she had developed other ties. As Lucy took Simon and Philip almost
daily for rides on Bobby and the other ponies, she probably saw more of Ernest Jones,
the groom, than she did of most of the other staff. To the surprise of the maids, and even
though Ernest had little of Lucy's education, the two became engaged. When in 1911
Philip Yorke had their photograph taken, both Ernest and Lucy posed with the two
boys. The verse which Philip, their father, wrote to accompany the portrait, speaks
with real affection:

Foremost amid this group we see
'Our Lady of the Nursery.'
Who, by her worshippers enshrined,
Seems now to Pilgrimage inclined.
The highest praise we can award
To Lucy Hitchman we accord,
Our deepest gratitude we owe
To her whose portrait now we show.

Her City, which is Worcester named,
Is for its old Cathedral famed.
And there a monument is seen
To Grantham Yorke, who once was Dean.
Well noted for the Choir, whose name
Resounds Sir Edward Elgar's fame;
While History tells how, in past age
A fiery battle here did range.

Of 'Lea & Perrins' 'tis the town,
Whose 'Sauce' is held in high renown,
And over Christendom we deem
Its Porcelain held in high esteem.
Yet chiefest 'mid its memories stor'd
Is she of whom we here record,
As most in estimation raised,
And prized still more than she is praised.

We here endeavour to find room
For Ernest Jones, our valued Groom,
Who, an abstainer from his youth,
A splendid sample is, in truth,
There, in the furthest distant view
Our Simon, (yea, and Peter too,)
While here, with 'Bobby' at his will,
Rides forth our little Master Phil.

Ernest, with Lucy at his side,
Yet he who does between them ride
Cannot be said to stand between
The 'happy pair' who here are seen,
For circumstances seem to tell
He was the cause of what befell,
Since this arose from mutual love
Which each, towards him, sought to prove.

And when, in time, the Nursery Rule
Yields to the sterner one of School,
And our 'young sparks' no longer heed
The fostering care they once did need,
We trust th' attachment here begun
May last while life its course shall run
And love, to ours so freely shown,
Be spent on children of their own.

When schooling took Philip and Simon away from Erddig, she wrote regularly, telling them that 'the teddys & Bruin and all the pets are cheering me up & I am cheering them.' She continued to write when they went on to university and to send small presents of money (which she could scarcely afford) on their birthdays; even though she and Ernest had by then left Erddig to run a butcher's shop in Acrefair, between Wrexham and Llangollen. The enterprise did not prosper. Simon Yorke was embarrassed by their obvious hardship and avoided them. Philip, however, kept in touch and they always exchanged Christmas cards. Then, during the Second World War, Mrs Yorke found herself responsible for Erddig while her sons were in the Services, and she persuaded Lucy to come back as housekeeper. Lucy accepted the full burden of running the house virtually single handed, just as John Jones, the coachman when she first knew Erddig, had had to take over the roles of carpenter, gardener and estate foreman. In 1943 they were photographed together in the Servants' Hall.

Lucy Jones died in 1957, at the age of 82; Ernest two years later. They had no children. Perhaps the maids who thought Lucy had been unwise to marry below her station were right: after the First World War a groom was an anachronism in most households, and the couple had to rely on Lucy's wages. During her last illness, Ernest nursed Lucy devotedly. She was buried in Esclusham churchyard, on the far side of the Black Brook from Erddig. The last Philip Yorke was recovering from his first stroke at the time and it was with difficulty that he wrote the inscription for her tombstone:

Lucy is in sight of Erddig, where
For forty years she tendered loving care,
Then let us pray, as here her members rest,
Her soul receives a mansion with the blest.

This was to be the last verse commemorating one of the Yorkes' staff. Only a name and the style of inscription distinguish Lucy's tombstone from the scores of other polished granite slabs that crowd round it. Her portrait at Erddig, along with those of her friends and her employers, is a far happier memorial.

56   The scullery

5

Spider-brushers to the Master

The servants' attic bedrooms that John Meller equipped early in the eighteenth century remained in use for the next 200 years. But in Meller's time they were not the only maids' bedrooms. One of the points John Loveday thought worth noting in his diary of 1732 was that the principal bedrooms had their own rooms for servants. This followed the arrangement recommended by Sir Roger Pratt, whose revolutionary planning of Coleshill House was still influential half a century after its completion and who advocated suites comprising a bedchamber, closet and a servant's room, flanking a corridor running along the central axis of the first floor. At Erddig in the 1720s 'Ye Worked Room' (later called the West Room) was furnished with a bed lined with green satin and with a quilted green satin counterpane, walnut chairs and a black japanned cabinet and chest. There was more fine walnut furniture in its dressing room, a walnut writing desk in its closet, and it had what was called 'ye Maids Room within ye Worked Room'. Similarly there was a 'Servants Room within ye Blew dressing Room'.

The need to have a personal maid or a manservant close at hand was also met by providing beds in the passages on the first floor. In the passage between the Breakfast Room and the Green China Room there was in 1726 a 'couch bedstead', with a feather mattress and bolster, four blankets and a calico quilt. There was a 'settee bedstead' outside the Scarlet Room. Such arrangements reflect the transition from the typical organisation of a sixteenth or early seventeenth century household, when servants would bed down on a straw pallet in any odd corner of a landing, and the nineteenth century tendency to banish staff to attics, basements or, at many houses, a service wing, the more remote the better.

Although some of the maids employed by Meller slept on the first floor, the majority occupied the garrets, their plain wooden bedsteads squeezed under the eaves, or between chests for storing linen and odd pieces of surplus furniture. In the garret immediately on the left at the top of the back stairs there were in the 1720s:

2 bedsteads with curtains, valances and bases, 2 Feather beds, 2 bolsters, 2 pillowes, 6 Blankets and 2 quilts, 1 Long box that Holds ye Sheets, 1 chest that Holds ye Table Linnen, 1 Larun clock, 1 Table, 1 Large Case, 3 chares, 1 Looking Glass, a grate in Chimney, 1 Fire pan, 1 pare of Tongues.

57   A servant's four-poster, designed to fit under the eaves

The attic immediately opposite contained a large chest, as well as two bedsteads; and in the adjoining room was '1 large Chest that keep ye corse Linnen'.

The Green Garritt and the Wanscot Garritt, both further down the attic corridor, seem to have been bedrooms for senior maids or even the housekeeper. There was only one bed in the Green Garritt, with a silk quilt and curtains with valances – far more luxurious than the other servants' rooms – as well as a table, looking glass and five chairs. Some of the fifteen bedsteads in the attics were of a pattern similar to a surviving servants' four-poster which has a sloping canopy to fit under the angle of the roof. The design is very close to a stained beech bedstead with turned pillars still being made in the 1790s for attic rooms by the firm of Gillows of Lancaster. Both the Erddig bed and Gillows' counterpart have sacking strung from the frame with cords, and a deal headboard to keep the feather mattress in place. At the upper end of the garret passage at Erddig was a 'table bed', of beech and elm and perhaps similar to Gillows' 'turn-up bedstead', which was a cheaper version of their 'buroe bedstead', an ingenious design of folding bed which when not in use had all the appearance of a bureau, with '5 sham drawers in front'. Like the other servants' bedsteads at Erddig, the table bed was supplied with a feather mattress, a bolster, blankets and a rug.

Although the sleeping quarters of the male and female staff were, in the eighteenth century, kept well apart from each other, many of their domestic duties were shared. A contemporary of Jane Ebbrell, the spider-brusher painted in 1793, was Philip Yorke's kitchen man, John Nicholas:

58   Jack Nicholas, 'a constant Porter to the pot'

Reflected here, as in a glass,
We recognise Jack Nicholas:
Our other Jack; not he, so stout,
Who beats the bushes all about;
But him, that waited on the Cook;
And many a walk to Wrexham took;
Whether the season, cold or hot,
A constant Porter, to the pot:
Then in the Kitchen corner stuck,
He pluck'd the fowl, and drew the duck,
Or with the basket on his knees,
Was sheller-general to the peas:
Now in the garden, all a-squat,
Upon his bum-beridden mat,
(For thus at first, upon his breech,
Was he brought up an arrant stitch,)
The weeds he spudded out of life,
That fell before his stubby knife.
Our Jack by some, tho' thought a tony,
Escap'd the joys of Matrimony.
And tho' a *Soldier* for *one* day
Dar'd not engage in marriage fray
But in these scarcer times of pelf,
Wisely decreed to keep *himself*;
Nor that was all; had cash at anchor,
And Mistress Salsb'ry was his banker:
Few are his cares; delights, enough,
That lie within a little *snuff*;
An *idle* hour, a cup of beer,
And a sure home, and harbour, here.

Philip Yorke's notes on the poem explain that Jack was as a young man bound to a tailor, hence the reference to 'arrant stitch'; and that he was once enlisted in the Regulars but discharged the same day. He was kept at Erddig out of charity, rather than for his usefulness. In 1779 he was receiving 8*d.* a day, the same as John Jones junior, probably still a lad then, and was otherwise the lowest paid of all the male staff. He was 71 when his portrait was painted in 1791.

Although John Walters was not commissioned to paint any of the younger maids who worked for the first Philip, there are frequent references in the family's letters to the loyal service of Betty Jones, Mary Rice, Betty Bevan and Ann Davies. Writing to her son in July 1770, about a recent visit of an old friend of his, Dorothy Yorke did not doubt that 'worthy Mrs. Betty exerted herself in cooking.' Similarly, Philip remarked in a letter of 1778 to his agent, John Caesar, how he believed he could rely in his absence on Betty Jones looking after the house while the Militia were exercising at

Erddig. Three years later, when relations were proposing to stay, Philip told Caesar that 'Betty Jones will take care, of course, of their beds.'

In larger country houses the maids usually kept strictly to their own departments. Only occasionally would the laundry or kitchen maids come in contact with the housemaids, whose position was generally regarded as a superior one. But smaller households had to be much more flexible. Faced with illness or the unexpected departure of a servant, the Yorkes would usually fill the post by promoting one of their staff, or they would move a maid from one department to another. Lizzie Jones, for instance, was taken on temporarily as a laundry maid at a time of crisis, and having proved her worth was appointed a housemaid. Whether they worked in the laundry, the kitchen or the house, the maids all slept in the attic bedrooms and had their meals together in the Servants' Hall.

The new domestic quarters built by Philip Yorke during the 1770s were far more spacious than the earlier offices. His New Kitchen is in fact one of the grandest rooms at Erddig, its only rival architecturally being the Dining Room added by Thomas Hopper for the second Simon in 1826. The kitchen range is set in the middle of three great rusticated arches, with the words *Waste Not* over one arch, and *Want Not* over another. The main dresser is solidly made, the fielded panels to all the doors being painted in a light and a darker tone of brown. The room is lit with two high windows above the dresser, and, at the other end, a finely detailed and proportioned Venetian window, more usual in a saloon or on a main staircase.

After the death of the second Simon Yorke in 1834, an inventory was made of the contents of all the domestic quarters. Some of the kitchen equipment must have survived from John Meller's time, with additional purchases made over the years by the housekeeper. The items listed would surely have been standard kitchen ware between 1770 and the end of the nineteenth century. Included were:

59   The bakehouse

60 The wet laundry

Three copper fish kettles, three copper preserving pans, two copper pots, two brass skillets, twelve copper moulds, four tin moulds, three copper frying pans, one dish, twenty four copper cups, seventine ditto, tin pots, twenty five copper stew pans, grater & two slicers, brass bound bucket, copper fountain, tea kettle, nine bread tins, pair ice moulds, two sieves &c. twelve tin dish covers, six pewter water plates, tin pot, still, spice bag, dresser and cupboards, beaufet, table & five chairs, dripper & hastener table and tea kettle, cooking table, small do, marble morter, cloth twine bag, three mills, fender and fire irons, earthenware, safe.

To have listed the scores of lesser items, the odd knives and forks, skewers, glass bottles and cockroach traps, would have meant covering several pages.

Beyond the kitchen and adjoining the small scullery was the meat pantry, with frames from which to hang game (on 25 January 1835 eight flitches of bacon and eight hams were hanging there). Then there was the bakehouse, the graining of its table deeply furrowed from years of scrubbing, and with piles of faggots stacked in front of the scuffle ovens (so named because after baking the ashes were raked, or scuffled out). On the other side of the little, enclosed yard, were the wet and dry laundries.

Throughout the eighteenth and nineteenth centuries there was a mangle in the laundry. The box mangle there now has an ingenious gearing device so that the handle can be continuously turned in one direction while the great box of stones automatically trundles backwards and forwards on rollers, pressing linen laid beneath them. More refined pressing was done with what were referred to in 1726 as '4 Box Irons (and) 8 Heaters', or, by 1834, 'Seven pair of flat irons'. Cast iron drying racks, which run in and out on wheels and are warmed from below by a small stove, were added during the second half of the nineteenth century. Goffering irons for crimping starched collars,

61   The dry laundry

iron cloths and candlesticks littered the tables under the windows. In spite of the vent in
its roof, steam from the wet laundry next door drifted through whenever clothes were
boiled in the two great coppers there.

As if to compensate for the dearth of verse and portraits recording the female staff
who served the earlier Yorkes – Jane Ebbrell is the only maid commemorated in the
Servants' Hall – two of those included in the daguerreotype of 1852 were given more
than generous literary treatment. Sarah Davies, affectionately known as 'Lalla' by the
Yorkes, lived to a great age and was the heroine of a poem forty-eight verses long, by
the second Philip:

The worthy dame we here portray
At Erthig serv'd in far-back day,
Engag'd with brush and broom and pan,
Just when Victorian reign began;
When thus employ'd she murmur'd not
But was contented with her lot,
Tho', as we gather from her look,
Her life's vocation she mistook.

When she into existence came
Of Sarah she receiv'd the name,
Tho' seldom, as herein is shown,
Was by this appellation known.
Her life was in Ruabon spent
Until she thence to Erthig went,
And in her twenty-second year
As under-housemaid enter'd there. . . .

Our heroine into life was brought
The year ere Waterloo was fought;
The scene of her nativity
Was a Ruabon hostelry;
Of which John Davies then was host
(A name in Wales well known to most);
'Bricklayers' Arms' that Inn is styl'd
Fam'd for Welsh Ale both strong and mild. . . .

One of his daughters found as mate
A keeper on Wynnstay estate;
Their home, from Erthig plainly seen,
Flank'd by the fir-wood dark and green,
Stands close beside a rippling rill
On Vron-deg's steeply rising hill.
And many a sportsman there might find
A luncheon suited to his mind.

Another sister did agree
A Baptist Pastor's wife to be,
Which sect was in Ruabon known
Having a Chapel of its own;
But later he receiv'd a 'call'
Which may have come from Montreal,
The two then sail'd the western main
Nor evermore return'd again.

62   Sarah Davies, affectionately known as 'Lalla' by the Yorke children

Sarah, by this time fully grown,
Had no attachments of her own,
For both her parents now were dead,
Her sisters from the inn had sped.
A brother still pursued the trade
Tho' now requiring not her aid;
Thus she preferr'd no other home
Than Erthig where she then was come.

Erthig, tho' little known to fame,
A passing notice now may claim;
Its beauty did a Bard inspire
To call it 'Jewell of the Shire.'
With whom the writer doth agree,
For 'tis as fair as fair can be;
With valued treasures richly stor'd
All by its owners much ador'd.

Two miles from Wrexham it is found
By those whose course is southward bound,
Its stone-built front all will remark
Rising within its wooded park.
The writer doth the honour claim
Of fifth possessor of his name
Throughout two centuries or near
Since first the Yorkes were settled here.

And Sarah greatly did admire
Two nieces of the writer's sire;
The place where best she lov'd to be
Was with them in the nursery,
And shortly, as we might expect,
She was proclaim'd the nurse elect,
That when these for their home should start
She also might with them depart. . . .

One Sarah, Abram's ancient dame,
Had for some reason chang'd her name,
And this, the Sarah of our rhyme,
Did copy her of olden time,
And now became as 'Lalla' known
As if that name had been her own.
Tho' we our readers would remind
That it was nothing of the kind. . . .

The love for Lalla stronger grew
From children, and the parents too,
Thus she had now become supreme,
Within the family's esteem.
She well might thus disdain the thought
That higher wages might be sought
By leaving these, her luck to try
In a Ruabon factory.

We now record a bright event
Which gave to Lalla much content;
For whilst they all were living here
A third small daughter did appear;
And Lalla was the first to hold
That treasure, worth its weight in gold,
And hers the hands that first did sway
The crib wherein that infant lay. . . .

This faithful friend of years gone by
We hold in estimation high;
Her joy lay in her loving care,
In sorrow too she had her share;
She learnt and labour'd, not in vain,
Her honest livelihood to gain,
And did her duty in the state
Where Heav'n assign'd her humble fate.

Another maid in the group of 1852 was Ruth Jones; and she too was written about by Philip half a century later:

Ruth Jones of whom we now make mention
Is worthy of our best attention
Like one of whom 'tis here recorded
In terms jacose and quaintly worded
That 'seventy years or nigh had past her
Since spider-brusher to the Master';
Tho' not like her with coachman mated
But to our Keeper thus related.

Ruth did the former record break,
For she did here her entry make
As early books of wages show,
Full one and seventy years ago;

63 Ruth Jones in 1912, half a century after she came to Erddig as a maid

As housemaid then for lengthy space
She was a credit to her race,
And 'midst a group her face appears
When younger by some threescore years.

At that far time her hours were spent
In keeping carpets free from rent,
She from our treasures swept the dust
And kept them from the moth and rust. . . .

Her photograph was taken again in 1912. Ruth Jones was by then a widow and was living with her daughter, the post mistress at Gresford.

In 1887 another group photograph of staff was taken. Eliza Sumpter (fourth from the left in the back row) was then head housemaid, and Ann Roberts (the girl third from the right, unable to keep still during the long exposure) was under-housemaid. Elizabeth Evans and Ellena Rogers, at either end of the front row, were lady's maid and young ladies' maid respectively. The other girls were laundry, dairy or kitchen maids. Seated in the centre is Ellena's aunt Harriet Rogers, the highly respected housekeeper and doyen of the staff.

After nineteen years' service as housemaid Eliza Sumpter married the burly bearded Scotsman, Alexander Stirton, seated in front of her in the photograph. Unlike many landed families in the nineteenth century, the Yorkes did not disapprove of marriage among their staff, and in some cases their pride in the traditions of service at Erddig and in long family associations with the house may even have encouraged it. But it would have been thought entirely proper that Stirton should not have married until he had been head gardener for many years and had sufficient savings to offer Eliza reasonable security. When they did eventually settle together in Gresford as man and wife, the Stirtons' health was failing. In her photograph Eliza seems already to show signs of consumption in her frail figure and drawn features.

The damp and sunless basement rooms and small shared attic bedrooms of most country houses were ideal breeding grounds for tuberculosis, or 'galloping consumption' as it was often known. Florence Nightingale was one of those who spoke out against the unhealthy living conditions of many servants, and by 1905 the *Daily Mail* and the *Lancet* had taken up the cause. Records of illness among those in domestic service are extremely scanty, partly because it was one of the few areas of working class employment not investigated during the nineteenth century by Royal Commissions – the subject was too near home for that – and partly on account of the practice of sending staff straight back to their families for nursing if they fell seriously ill; or alternatively, giving them their notice in the knowledge that they could, if necessary, resort to the workhouse. But what was common practice at most country houses was not necessarily the rule at Erddig. In 1912 Bessie Gittins, the second housemaid, went down with scarlet fever, then frequently a fatal illness. Mrs Yorke decided to nurse her with help from another junior maid, Edith Haycock, under the supervision of two doctors from Wrexham paid for by the squire. All the other maids

64   Servants at Erddig in 1887. The bearded gardener Alexander Stirton was to marry
      Eliza Sumpter, who is standing behind him, next to Meacock, the coachman. On
      Stirton's left are Harriet Rogers, the housekeeper, and George Dickinson, the butler

were given beds elsewhere in the house. Bessie remembered Mrs Yorke at her bedside in
the attics, bathing her forehead with eau-de-cologne.

    Bessie Gittins came to work at Erddig in 1909 as a nursery maid. She had worked
previously for Sir Robert and Lady Egerton, who had the lease of Coed-y-Glyn, on the
Wrexham side of the Erddig estate, where she had to spend much of her time scrubbing
stone floors. As she developed an extremely painful weakness in her knees, she was
encouraged by her mother to try for a place at a large house, where more of the rooms
were carpeted. To land a job at Erddig was a stroke of great good fortune. When she
started work there the family were away on holiday. She found a room of her own in the
attics of a largely empty and unfamiliar country house frightening, and so she was
allowed to move in with Edith Haycock, the second housemaid.

    When Bessie was engaged on 2 June 1909 she was paid £8 0s. 0d. a year (Mrs
Beeton's *Book of Household Management*, in 1900, recommended an annual wage of
£18 0s. 0d. for a maid-of-all-work). This was raised on 1 August 1910 to £12 0s. 0d. a
year. By then Bessie had formed such a close friendship with Edith that she plucked up
the courage to ask Mr Yorke whether she could not leave the nursery and join the other
housemaids. This was allowed and in 1911 she was made third housemaid at
£13 0s. 0d. a year. She was then promoted to second housemaid, and by the time she

came to leave in 1914 she was receiving £22 10s. 0d. She returned to work briefly at Erddig in 1915 as second parlour maid, and was being paid £24 0s. 0d. a year in October 1916.

The attic bedroom shared by Edith and Bessie was simply furnished with two iron bedsteads, a dressing table, wash stand, chest of drawers, small table and a carpet. The hip bath, with its own chintz cover, was kept in the corner. Much of the early furniture once in the attics was disposed of during the nineteenth century, and it was with delight that Louisa Yorke once discovered a maid using a folding oak table which was identified as being seventeenth century and was brought down in triumph to the Gallery. The process was reversed when the family tired of pictures or furniture. At the top of the back stairs they hung some of the second Philip Yorke's less successful watercolours and a print after one of Lady Butler's most morbid, most admired works, 'The Remnants of an Army', in which the unfortunate Dr Bryden, the sole survivor of a British force of 16,000, is shown arriving exhausted at the gates of Jellalabad with scarcely the strength to clutch the saddle-bow of his dying horse.

Sleeping in the room opposite was Alice Jones, the head laundry maid. Matilda, or 'Tillie', Boulter, the first housemaid, had the Clock Attic. When the Yorkes were having difficulty finding a reliable housekeeper, Tillie had to shoulder extra responsibilities. At spring cleaning, in June 1907, she reported at length to Mrs Yorke:

> Dear Madam,
> Just a line to thank you for your kind letter. . . .
> I shall be very glad to see you all back at Erddig again which will not be long now and I shall be quite ready and feel sure that Mr. Yorke will be delighted to return. Yes, all picture nails have been seen to and I think we have done all that was on my list. The painters are only today leaving so you see we have had no time to waste and I am glad to think we have almost finish spring cleaning for another year. I have done all I can in case you cannot go next year. . . .

Tillie devoted most of her free time to practising the violin, and would occasionally join Mrs Yorke's father, a cellist, in duets.

During the summer months the peacocks nesting in the Deodar in the garden were usually shrieking petulantly well before it was time for Bessie Gittins, as junior housemaid, to bring Tillie and the others tea, brewed shortly after 6 o'clock in the attic pantry. At 6.30 they would all report to the Servants' Hall, where the mail, delivered by bicycle at about 5.30, would be sorted so that Mrs Yorke could have her letters with her early morning tea. Before breakfast at 8 o'clock all the shutters in the main rooms had to be opened, as many as forty oil lamps collected up for adjustment and refilling, and a start made on cleaning grates and laying fires. These jobs were resumed between breakfast and chapel. At 9 o'clock the housekeeper would join all the house staff in the Servants' Hall, and then lead them up from the basement passage, through the Failures' Gallery – where the Yorkes displayed all the gifts which for one reason or another were not thought worthy of showing in other rooms – and into the box pews on the west side of the Chapel. The family entered their pew through the Chinese Room. Mr Yorke played the harmonium, an instrument he had contrived to make appear grander than it really was by installing above it organ pipes which he had acquired when alterations were being made to Worthenbury church. The estate staff only attended chapel on Christmas day, when the men would try to make the maids giggle by signalling to each other who was singing out of tune, and by putting fingers into their left ears, so that the gesture could not be seen from the family pew.

The rest of the morning was devoted to renewed cleaning both of the ground floor and, after a break for tea at 11 o'clock, the bedrooms. Staff lunch was at 12. The maids then changed into their black and white afternoon dresses and retired to the workroom, next to the Clock Attic, where they were expected to busy themselves mending sheets or making their own dresses, until tea at 4.00. They then prepared first the main rooms for the evening, and, during dinner, the bedrooms, putting hot water bottles in the beds, turning down counterpanes and lighting fires and oil lamps. Staff supper was at 9.00. Before going to bed between 10.00 and 11.00 there was usually time for a game of whist in the workroom.

Although Mrs Brown the housekeeper was known to have proposed to Mrs Yorke that the maids should only be allowed out one evening a week, in practice permission was freely given for them to be in late as many as three times a week. There were also staff parties at Erddig. The Playroom built in the garden by William Gittins came into

65   The workroom, where maids retired in the afternoon to sew and read

its own for the Christmas Servants' Ball, when Mr and Mrs Yorke danced with the senior staff, and young Mr Simon and Mr Phil' waltzed with the junior maids.

Edith Haycock and Bessie Gittins were included in both the group photographs of staff taken in 1912. Of the one on the entrance steps, Philip Yorke wrote:

66 The staff in 1912, each holding their badge of office as their predecessors had done in the daguerreotype taken in 1852

Here History does itself repeat
And Old Times with the Present meet
Behold a group your eyes before,
Like that of sixty years of yore.
All 'tis pictur'd on the self-same ground
Whereon the former scene is found,
Each hold an emblem of the trade
Which marks the corresponding grade. . . .

Behind our Cook stands one whose name
Would sound as though from Wales she came
For she as Alice Jones is call'd,
And as Head Laundress here install'd
She hails from Ludlow, which is known
As Salop's southern Border-town.
Whose Castle does the heights command,
Where stateliest Church is seen to stand.

More than eight years her care has been
To keep our linen white and clean.
Bearing in patience, we might say,
The Burden and the heat of day.
And though, by duty at her post,
She is less often seen than most,
Her tuneful song in accents clear
Is heard within our Chapel here.

Betwixt our Gardener and Cook
We now upon Ann Gittins look.
And like her Uncle William, she
At Erthig plies her industry,
Here for one year she found employ
Attending to our Infant Boy,
Then further tasks on her did come
The care and cleaning of the home.

Clasping a broomstick in her hand
We notice Edith Haycock stand,
Eight years as Housemaid here employed.
We have her valued help enjoyed.
Throughout which time our home has showed
The utmost care on it bestowed.
We trust our hope may not be vain
That she may here a-while remain.

The Erddig household was a conservative one and, as the Yorkes never introduced gas or electricity, the duties of the housemaids probably changed very little throughout most of the nineteenth and early twentieth centuries. Maggie Williams's account of life there in 1920 shows little change from the régime of twenty years before, and her recollections of what went on in the Erddig attics could surely have been written half a century earlier:

> We were allowed fires up there on the condition that each one cleaned their own grate. During my time, the under housemaid cleaned and made these beds. The Under Parlourmaid and under housemaid shared the big room & Head Parlourmaid and Housemaid each had the bedroom opposite. When we went to bed we would all go to one room and have a good natter, sometimes until the early hours of the morning. And often on a warm summer night we would go and sit on the roof, where a lovely view of the Park could be seen, and it was amusing to see the rabbits playing about on the front. We had lots of fun up there. Though we had to do it very quietly so as not to disturb the family. . . . In the winter it was nothing to get up and find all the water in your room solid ice, even the bed chambers would be frozen. Also you would find that some bats had flown in through the open window lieing on the bed or on the floor. During one spring cleaning time the housemaids were doing the attics or glory holes we called them, when they came across a trunk with old fashioned clothes in it, and there was one beautiful tafate silk mauve dress with leg of mutton sleeves. We tried it on, but it would only fit me. So I put on the hat and took the parasole, and downstairs to show it the cook, but as got to the bottom of stone steps, who came round corner, but Mr. Phil. he paused and looked, and gave a very polite bow to which I curtsyed and dashed back upstair. Mr. Phil had come back unexpectanly. So Cook never saw the dress. Mr. Phil he took it to Ireland and lost it.

In the late evening the maids would go out of the door at the far end of the attic passage on to the leads. There they would listen for the grunting of badgers crossing the drive on their way to the river, undeterred by the perpetual, rhythmic beating of the hydraulic ram pumping water up to the house. The only human sounds were the whistles of poachers in the woods. No doubt it all seemed timeless and immutable to Edith Haycock, Bessie Gittins, Emily Pugh, Lizzie Jones and Maggie Williams. But the verse which Philip Yorke wrote to describe the maids photographed in the garden in 1912 ends prophetically:

> The Group now pictured here is meant
> A former one to represent,
> In corresponding order found
> And pictured near the self same ground,
> But several members of the troop
> Are found yet in another group,

67   A garden group of 1912. Edith Haycock and Bessie Gittins are in the middle row, third and fourth from the left respectively. The footman John Jones is on the extreme right

Which at the Entrance steps we show,
With mention of their names below. . . .

Close to our Gardener, just in rear,
Ruth Davies does in face appear
Who tho' not long has been her stay
Gladdened each and every day,
Her task it must be understood,
Is the preparing of our food
And, should necessity arise
The place of our Head Cook supplies.

From County Glo'ster she did hail
Near Lydney in the Severn Vale,
Well famed for pasture rich and green
And corn with Ruth perhaps did gleen.
Here, for her 'land of Moab', come,
To make our Canaan now her home,
We hope she may not wedlock spurn,
Nor widowed to her kith return.

Behind Miss Brown is here portraid
Our House-maid of the topmost grade.
Eight years within this house employed
We have her valued help enjoyed,
Throughout which time our home has showed
The utmost care on it bestowed
And here we hope she may remain
Until some better post she gain.

Her Father for some years had found
Employment on this selfsame ground
But since has crossed the Ocean wide
To try his luck on other side;
And on far off Canadian soil
Gain higher wages for his toil;
For of that Colony 'tis told
That on its plains we gather gold.

Two Maidens on the right we see
May now together mentioned be
For though but short has been their stay
We still find something here to say,
The first is Under-chambermaid
The other does in Laundry aid.
To both of whom, in sep'rate line
We every confidence assign.

She, slightly furthest of the two,
Is Emily, by surname, Pugh,
And, like some others in our home,
She also did from Ludlow come,
A town which, be it understood,
Has furnished many a helper good,
And this one, it may be confessed,
Can rank with any of the best.

Her comrade, Lizzie Jones who came
When we some extra help did claim
Was called, though only for to stay
Till all our Guests had gone away.
But, having then her value proved,
Soon was to higher post removed,
Again now to be raised, instead
Of one just leaving to be wed. . . .

That Dial marks the hour of day
When we this subject did portray
'Twas in October of this year
And the sixteenth as doth appear;
Not so exactly can we date
The Group which this does personate,
But 'twas some thirty years or near,
Earlier than the picture here.

No Motor then approached our door,
Although sometimes a 'Drag and four'
(Though this was mainly meant to show
The 'Style' of hundred years ago)
The Cyclist then was thought to fly
At speed quite dangerously high,
And record for the road was gained
If he twelve miles an hour attained.

Who knows, in thirty years may tread,
An Automatic Staff instead
A button, by a finger pressed,
May bring response to each request.
In those days may our Motor's speed
Even our fastest trains exceed,
And folks may talk in sparing praise
Of these, the slow old Railway days.

68　The survivors in 1962, half a century later. From left to right: Edith Haycock, Bessie
　　Gittens, a former maid so far unidentified, and John Jones

69   Joseph Wright

6

Harmonious Blacksmiths

The early eighteenth century wrought iron of Robert Davies of Bersham, the greatest smith Wales ever produced, may seem poles apart from the routine jobs of an estate blacksmith. Yet the survival at Erddig of gates and a screen that can with reasonable confidence be attributed to Robert Davies is due to the comparatively humble talents of Joseph Wright, a smith whose work was usually utilitarian and allowed for little more decoration than the occasional scroll on a lamp stand or an extra twist to a window latch. It was Wright's willingness to turn his hand to repairs that might have daunted a specialist restorer, that ensured the survival of the finest ironwork now at Erddig.

Robert Davies's own early work was often as humble as that of any estate smith. In the Chirk Castle accounts of 1702 there are payments to Davies, then aged 26, for 'makeing skrew pins, & a new handle, hamering & holeing 2 big plates to secure the beame on the gallary . . . for hookes & hinges for the stable weighing 29 lb. . . . & a new thomb lach to the stable doore'. Such things are far removed from the massively impressive gates at Chirk which he completed seventeen years later. With the Chirk gates to his credit and with his forge at Croes Foel scarcely a mile away, it is no surprise to find that in the 1720s John Meller turned to Robert Davies for a wrought iron screen to run the length of the Erddig entrance front.

The first mention of Robert Davies in the Erddig archives is in a letter of 26 October 1709, a reference of particular interest because very little is known of his activities at that time. The letter relays news from Mr Alport (a tenant of Erddig during the years that Joshua Edisbury was away in London) that 'Robt. Davies desires he may have wt. old iron ye have to spare towards ye money you owe him.' Exactly what had been supplied by Davies before 1709 is not known, and indeed may have been the type of mundane work he had done at Chirk in 1702. But there was nothing mundane about the wrought iron he was to make for Meller.

Badeslade's print of Erddig in 1740 shows the forecourt closed with a pair of gates flanked by screens. This must be the ironwork referred to in the letter of 17 May 1721 to Meller from his agent Richard Jones: 'Robt. Davis the Smith has been ill of an Ague or the Iron Gate had been up before this time.' There are payments the same year to his younger brothers Thomas and John Davies, although their contributions are not

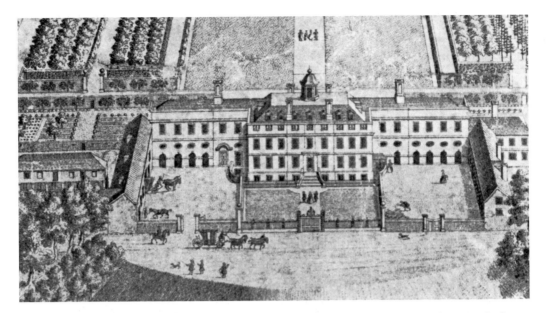

70   A detail of Badeslade's print of Erddig in 1740, showing Robert Davies's wrought iron
screen on the west front

specified. The really large sum, however, was paid directly to Robert and came to the
total of £150 11s. 6d. for pillars, pilasters, one single gate and a frieze, a long frieze,
palisades and a frontispiece.

None of the iron work supplied by Davies for Erddig survived Philip Yorke's
remodelling in the 1770s, when the gates, screens, walls and stables on the west side of
the house were all swept away. Davies's gates at Chirk were also removed in the 1770s
from in front of the Castle, and resited between a pair of park lodges. As the landscape
designer William Emes was working at both Erddig and Chirk at that time, these
changes may well have been proposed by him. What became of the Erddig wrought
iron is unrecorded. Perhaps it was reworked by the Yorkes' smith, William Williams.
For the next 150 years there was nothing to show that Davies had ever been involved
there.

William Williams was among the Erddig staff painted by John Walters in 1793,
and the subject of one of Philip Yorke's *Crude Ditties*:

> This child of fire, Vulcanian imp,
> His old Sire, knew him by his limp,
> Our ERTHIG Smith, who fifty year,
> Was surgeon-general, to the gear,
> And, with ferruginean arts
> Play'd first Physician to the carts;
> High calling, which his father bore,
> And eke his grand-father before. . . .

71   William Williams, blacksmith during the 1780s and 1790s

Of dogs, and horses, much, he knew
To break the one, and t'other shoe,
And, with a setter at his heels,
Preferr'd it far to binding wheels:
Long may he suffer no decay,
And hammer on, from day, to day,
Keep up an everlasting fire,
And be immortal, as his Sire!

Although this seems to imply that Williams was in full-time employment at Erddig, payments of large sums to him in the accounts suggest that he worked by commission, rather than having a weekly wage like the rest of the staff. He may even have had his forge off the Erddig estate entirely, as no blacksmith's shop is shown on the plan of the estate yard made in about 1800. His status was probably somewhere between the complete independence of the Davies brothers, and that of a late nineteenth century estate smith such as Joseph Wright. Williams was certainly in a position in 1781 to charge as much as £43 17s. 6d. for gates and locks, and £38 11s. 8d. the same year for his decent if unadventurous railings for the new steps on the west front.

Joseph Wright's photograph was taken a full century after Williams's portrait was painted. Wright had worked at Erddig since the 1880s, with a versatility recorded in the second Philip Yorke's lines of 1911 about him:

> Our valued blacksmith, Joseph Wright
> Is in this portrait brought to light
> Of swarthy hue and figure spare
> While yet of strength a goodly share.
> A quarter-century has passed
> Since here at first his lot was cast
> Thus early did his anvil sound
> Its note of music o'er the ground.

72   The railings supplied in 1781 by William Williams for the entrance front

73 Joseph Wright, who came to Erddig as blacksmith in 1886

> He fits for use by various arts
> Our waggons, implements, and carts;
> Cyclests who here a visit pay
> Go forth rejoicing on there way.
> Our engine, and hydraulic rams,
> Our tanks, and taps, and water-dams,
> And locks and keys, and hinges too,
> By Wright become as good as new.

The Yorkes also encouraged Wright to develop more refined skills. The lead shells he made for the fountains in the gardens, by taking a cast from an eighteenth century marble basin in the Flower Room, were accorded special praise:

> 'Harmoneus Blacksmith,' him we name
> His work is worthy of the same
> All his additions to the place
> Are full of harmony and grace.
> Within, without, look where you will
> Are traces of his art and skill
> What falleth to the hand of Wright
> He doeth it with all his might. . . .

74   The garden fountains, with the lead shells made by Joseph Wright from a cast of an
eighteenth century marble basin

Hard would it be in words to tell
All he hath done so long and well,
Nor yet within these rhymes to show
The thanks which to his art we owe;
For all the labours of his hand,
Assisted by his able band,
Of whom some foremost here are seen,
Who longest have his helpers been.

Unlike what is in Scripture told
Of Jacob, in the days of old,
Denied the object of his love,
Till he for fourteen years had strove,
Our Joseph won his chosen wife,
After but nine of mutual strife,
And thus a shining link had wrought,
For which a golden ring he bought.

The new gates to the small walled garden at the northern end of the house were
another of Wright's more ambitious projects. But his greatest achievement was the
repair of the gates from Stansty.

Early in the present century coal mining encroached upon the Stansty estate, and, like Erddig in the 1940s and 1950s, subsidence threatened the house, which had eventually to be demolished. Had Philip Yorke not admired the then sadly decayed gates and successfully negotiated their purchase at a cost of £250, they would probably have gone the same way as the house. The surprising thing is that when he bought the gates, Philip Yorke apparently had no idea that they might be by Robert Davies, who had supplied Erddig with fine gates nearly 200 years earlier. At the very last moment Philip was nearly thwarted by a rival claimant, whom he succeeded in appeasing in a letter of 23 March 1910:

My dear Madam,
I am truly sorry to hear from you that the beautiful Iron Gates at the Sontly entrance to this Park, are an un-lawful possession. I did not know anything about you & your claim to them at the time I purchased them from Lady French's trustees. The negotiations however, took so long a time that a claim

75 The screen from Stansty, bought by Philip Yorke in 1909

76 A detail of the Stansty screen

77   The screen when at Forest Lodge

had better have been made, (as it easily might,) before the Gates had actually been removed from Stansty; & even when they had been brought here, a long time was spent in the very necessary & extensive repairs to them, which had to be done by my Blacksmith, in the Timber Yard, here.

Altogether, a whole year had elapsed between the time of my first negotiation, & the setting of them up in their present place. Under these circumstances I do not think it would be a very easy matter to dispute my right to them; but by payment of the price of the purchase, £250, & the extra £30, which is the least at which I can put the cost of the repairs; & another £5, to compensate for the cost I was put to, in the removing of them & erection of them in their present place, you may have them without the trouble of going to Law, assuming of course, that you will also undertake the entire cost of their removal.

With all best respects to you, I venture to think, my dear Madam, that this will be the best course, & one indeed which I shall be very glad that you should adopt; for I have a superstitious dislike to having any unlawfully acquired possessions, (however innocently they may be acquired, so far as regards myself).

With humblest apologies to you, dear Madam, for any trouble & annoyance to which my purchase of the gate may be putting you, believe me to remain, very faithfully yours,
        Ph. Yorke.

Philip Yorke's description of the gates in the letter he wrote to a local paper in August 1908, shortly after their re-erection at Erddig, says much for his perception:

Sir,

The little ceremony which has been so nicely described in your last week's issue was in itself of so homely and private a nature that we had not thought it worthy of a place in your columns. As however you have done us the honour of recording it, may I be allowed to add a few remarks, and through that medium express the gratitude we feel towards the many kind friends who accorded us their good wishes and congratulations on that occasion, (a birthday); and for the valuable assistance of those through whose instrumentality I was enabled to purchase these beautiful Gates, & transfer them from their former place at Stansty where they had for generations been familiar to the public gaze to the place where they now stand, at the Marchwiel end of our Forest Drive. . . .

The removal of the ponderous iron-work and the massive stone-work in which it was set was effected by my Erddig staff of workmen under the super intendance & most able direction of Mr W. N. Capper, the Agent to this Estate, and carried out in so masterly a manner that not a particle of damage was sustained by any portion of it, for which he is deserving of the very highest praise, especially when it is considered into how rusted and brittle a condition it had fallen owing to Stansty having for so many years been without a resident owner.

Great portions of their elaborate ornamentation in that long period of neglect had become damaged, many pieces having even been lost; these have however been cleverly imitated & copied from the original design by the skill and patience of Mr Joseph Wright who for more than 20 years has been Blacksmith to this Estate; and all who had ever observed the fabric closely when in their former place will appreciate and admire the splendid manner in which they have now been restored to their ancient beauty and elegance, being now made by his art as good as new.

The setting up of the Gates in their new position reflects also the greatest

78 The screen from Stansty, repositioned at the end of the garden canal

possible credit on Mr William Gittins, who for nearly quarter of a century has been Foreman to this Estate, and who is so well known and highly respected throughout this district. The Forest Drive is now adorned with an Entrance second only to those of Chirk Castle, Eaton Hall, and Leeswood which are too well-known to need any further mention here. These Gates are of about the same period as those of Chirk namely early Georgian, & possibly dating from between 1710 to 1720, at which time the art of Iron-working reached perhaps its highest degree of perfection, and nowhere more so than in and around this district; The name of the maker is, we believe, unknown, but the excellence of his work will merit the very highest admiration of all beholders throughout generations to come as it has already done in the past; and we rejoice to think that these Gates & their accompaniments should now present an appearance worthy of their handsome neighbours at the Coed-y-Glyn Entrance, familiar to all, and which with all gratitude we remember as having been the kind gift of our Tenants, Friends and Well-wishers in and around Wrexham, on the happy occasion of our Marriage more than 6 years ago.

Wright's repairs were by no means faultless by today's standards. He introduced other metals into the wrought iron work and had casts made for some of the more intricate decoration (although it is only fair to add that Davies himself used cast iron mouldings, obtained from Coalbrookdale). But the vital thing was that the gates were made secure and looked splendid.

The Stansty gates had not one near escape but three, and came perilously close to sharing the fate of the original Davies ironwork at Erddig. During the last war an American army camp occupied the park. Because the overthrow was an obstacle to lorries using the Forest Lodge entrance, Simon Yorke had the gates dismantled and put in store. Although they were re-erected after the war, the estate was already suffering the effects of subsidence caused by coal mining and there was no longer the staff to carry out routine maintenance.

When Erddig was given to the National Trust in 1973, the lead had been stolen from the roof of the blacksmith's shop, tiles had slipped and the bellows breathed only when a tenant needed to repair his own farm machinery. One of the two cylinders no longer functioned. At Forest Lodge, saplings were growing through the side screen, and the overthrow of the gates was tilting alarmingly. As by this time the attribution of the Stansty gates to the Davies brothers had been generally accepted (although there is still doubt about whether the gates themselves were not reworked long before Joseph Wright repaired them), they clearly merited major restoration. Once the blacksmith's shop had been reroofed, Alan Knight was able to work on the gates there, as Joseph Wright had fifty years before. It was at the suggestion of the last Philip Yorke that, largely for reasons of safety, they were sited as a *clairvoyée* at the end of the canal, the central feature of the formal garden laid out by John Meller at precisely the time that Robert Davies was making his original gates for Erddig.

79   The blacksmith's shop in 1978

80　The sawmill

7
Woods and Woodmen

When Charles Apperley, writing *My Life and Times* under his pen-name 'Nimrod', came to describe his neighbour's estate, he had no hesitation in saying that 'the gem of Erthig is its wood'. He went on to relate how when Simon Yorke was presented at Court, George III remarked on how rarely his father Philip came to London. A countryman himself at heart, the King added: 'I am not surprised at it; I have heard of his beautiful wood at Erthig.' That the fame of those hanging beechwoods should have spread so far is not as improbable as it sounds. Travellers in search of the picturesque in North Wales frequently stayed at Wrexham where it was generally known that Philip Yorke welcomed visitors to his park, just on the edge of the town. Erddig's dramatic escarpments, lush meadows and pre-Conquest archaeology usually met with their enthusiastic approval.

Among the visitors to the park in 1784 was Lord Torrington, who had been staying at The Eagles in Wrexham and who wrote in his diary:

> The entrance into these grounds is very pleasant, and the woods and meadows are happily dispos'd. At the house, which seems to be nothing very particular, we found the gardener, and having peeped into the kitchen garden and pluck'd some currants, we took the round of the wood-walks, and pleasure ground, which are well laid out, and only want gravel, (the want of Wales). The views are good, especially from one point, which commands Wrexham steeple; but the dairy house is out of all character, having never held one bowl of milk; and the stream, whose course has been chang'd to flow under the wood, is paltry, and contemptible. The trees are of a fine growth, and many of a Druidical size, and beneath them are to be traced the vestiges of an ancient encampment.

The motte referred to by Lord Torrington is as strategically placed aesthetically as it is militarily, and was bound to appeal to an eighteenth century squire with an eye for a good landscape feature. Badeslade in his engraving of 1740 shows it crowned by a circular tower, with formal terraces along the edges of the motte. There are few signs of very extensive masonry construction on the site now, and the engraving may well record an unexecuted scheme; but the wish to emulate the terraces at Powis Castle, some thirty miles away to the south, is understandable. The yews and straggling box that still survive beneath the dense canopy of beech are the relics of formal walks planted at the beginning of the eighteenth century and then deliberately submerged beneath a later style of landscape gardening.

The landscape designer responsible for these changes was William Emes. He is first mentioned in the accounts in 1767 and he continued advising on planting and on alterations to the mills and watercourses on the estate until the late 1780s. The execution of his proposals was often left in the hands of Philip Yorke's agent, John Caesar, who received regular and very detailed instructions on planting whenever the squire's political and social life took him away from Erddig. A letter of 3 January 1772 to Caesar indicates just how closely Philip Yorke was himself involved:

> Near to where the Old Willow Plantation grew in the French Mill Meadows stand now five Handsome Trees (viz. A Crab; a cherry, an Oak, 2 Ash) I would by all means wish these to remain, and altho' they may grow in the Awkward Line of the Old Hedge Mr. Emes (if he should get so far before I see him) might yet, I should think preserve them by raising the ground a little around em; and throwing in more additional Trees, might make together with them a very Hansome Circular clump.

Surprisingly though, the most impressive feature of the planting carried out in the 1770s was something of an anachronism. On the narrow ridge leading to the motte and bailey, perhaps on the site of a formal walk, an avenue of beech was planted, flanked on both sides by dense woodland. The avenue topped the ridge and when fully mature it appeared from the west like a huge vertical slice out of the skyline. With the fierce competition for light, the beeches grew to a great height and the avenue was aptly named the Cathedral Aisle. Nearby was a Coade stone statue of an old man clutching his beard, other examples of which have survived at The Vyne and Shugborough, where the figure was thought of as classical and called The Philosopher. At Erddig he was always The Druid.

Had Philip Yorke been concerned only with planting, he could probably have managed without Emes. But special expertise was needed for the ambitious diversions of the Black Brook and the Clywedog, which Philip intended should greatly increase the profitability of his King's Mill, downstream. He explained his other motives for these improvements to his friend, Brownlow Cust, whose sister he was courting, in a letter of 24 September 1768:

> I have already finished the last improvement of this Estate; an advance quite adequate to my Expectations, I will not load the Post with particulars; hoping very shortly a nearer conference with you: I was not out of my saddle or the dirt of overflowed fields, for 3 days, but I look over all difficulties; I see nothing insupportable, if it but brings me in the end nearer to one I love dearer than myself. I said I would not particularize and yet I must tell you I am about this Week (under the direction of Vernon) to let my whole Demean, for one Year:

81   The Cathedral Aisle

I shall merely reserve a little Pasture, or the Feild close to my Barn or Stable;
and all this I do, that I may throw my whole Weight, my total Complement of
Teams and Workmen immediately on the Meadows; I mean the improvement
of these Meadows on either side of the French Mill, (under the Eastern view
from the Walk in the woods) Vernon promises me next Spring 50 Shillings an
acre, for all that land, so regulated, as we have planned: The whole piece is
Fifty four acres and what may you think I receive for it now; why 36£
exclusive of the Mill, which brings in £10 pr. an: and a piece (at the hither
end, now in my own Hands) of 8 Acres – so you will easily guess the extent of
this improvement, besides the abolition of an expensive unreturning, Mill, and
a nasty road leading to it, which ruins and deforms that beautiful Spot of
Ground. I *must* verily come and see you at Belton, so don't (unnecessarily) stop
me: the look I ought to be indulged with, to physick a whole Winter's pain,
and absense: When you return to London, I shall move back again hither, and
diligently superintend the Accomplishment of so beneficial an undertaking: I
have also this Winter as I ruin one Mill, to restore and perfect another – My
King's Mill (exclusive of the Land held with it) brings in 110£ pr An:

Much of the day-to-day supervision, when Emes was away working for the Myddeltons of Chirk, in the park at Powis Castle or at Dudmaston, was left in the hands of Caesar, who received frequent letters from Philip, now chiding, now encouraging:

Northaw, Nov.r 16.th 1770:

John Caesar!

Your letter which I received yesterday, brought an agreable account of my Mill, but not so of the House Establishment; which we must think a plan much too ample and extensive in our absence: Mary Rice will deliver to you your Mistres's orders, which is to commence on Board Wages, from Thursday next – You will therefore pay the other Servants (Sam Jones excepted, with whom I have an account, and shall settle myself) their stated and usual Board wages commencing as I said from Thursday next the 22nd Inst and my Household expenses are then suspended. I am very glad you find your Mill Clerk so useful, and I do not doubt you will keep him so, in the full Extent – When any labourer behaves idly or impertinently dismiss him; t'will save the Rest. I am concerned to hear of such sharp Floods; You must strenuously exert yourselves, that no destruction falls on the Woodhouse, which work and

82 The agent's office, where wages were paid, accounts kept and where maps of the estate were stored

precaution may prevent – I have no objection to your employing two more Hands to support the Banks, and works on the River: only, so stipulate, that my other Workmen don't give themselves airs or be induced to it – I do think 10d a day sufficient and nothing shall induce me to exceed it – If workmen (two) will come at that price, at this juncture you may receive them – You say nothing of my Mare; whether she be sold or not; you know I fixed 16 Guineas on her but if 15 Guineas be offered you may let her go, and I must stand to the loss of a Guinea.

Your Mistress desires to know what quantity of Cheese is in the house. The Board Wages as I said must be usual and stated; the *same* as my Servants were first put on when I first articled with them on that head in the beginning of the year 1768 – Let me hear from you, directed as usual, once in every Week – and speak particularly of the new Establishment, when Settled.

I am always
Yr very wellwisher
Philip Yorke –

Philip's regard for his own long-serving and loyal staff should not be mistaken for a high opinion of working men generally. His suspicions that Caesar was gullible and sometimes turned a blind eye to his men's failings were expressed directly and bluntly in several of his letters of the 1770s:

I am ever Jealous of my Workmen; I must insist on your asserting that authority, which is necessary, to restrain any Licentiousness in them, and to make them do their duty towards me – If I am imposed on by them, tis your offence – I am sure you must avoid incurring any such accusation. . . .

. . . I have no doubt you will always make up and Compensate the Absense of the principal by the diligence, and proper *Authority* of the Agent; for mankind are ever to be corrected rather by a distant, and resolute behaviour, than by Intimacy and too much mildness, and easy nature. . . .

and again:

The King is improving S.ᵗ James Park, and I was to-day a Spectator of the shameful profligacy & idleness of the Workmen; I felt it the more for I thought without your general Superintendance, without Worrall & Carmody's particular attendance, & diligence, I might be myself an equal Sufferer; for Workmen are the same in all countries, and will pick your pocket equally, without Remorse. . . .

Philip was determined that his improvements should be as far as possible ornamental. He and Emes devised a series of waterfalls along the Black Brook valley, culminating in the Cup and Saucer, an ingenious and probably novel feature, where the water gathers in a shallow circular stone basin with a cylindrical waterfall at its

83　The Cup and Saucer – a cylindrical waterfall constructed under Emes's supervision in the 1770s – as it was earlier this century

centre, and then emerges from a tunnel several yards downstream. The view from the tunnel entrance, with its finely rusticated keystones, is of a curving transparent curtain of cascading water. 'The Stone Cylinder in the Meadow', as it was called in Philip's accounts, was constructed in 1774. Lavish planting framed Philip's newly excavated streams: in 1778, for instance, Emes was paid £211 1s. 9d. for among other things 'planting scattered trees of tolerable size . . . at the foot of the Hill, west front'. A letter of 31 January 1775 to Caesar from Philip implies that Emes was well looked after when he came to Erddig:

> We propose setting out with Simon, next Sunday morning, and hope to reach home to a late dinner on Tuesday: Betty Jones will accordingly get our own Room Ready, and laid in, as well as the Nursery, & the Child's Bed carefully aired. . . . Your Mistress says, she would not have the Nursery aired, but would have the little Wrought Room aired, and one of the smallest beds in the Nursery removed to that Room, for Simon. Mr Emes is to lie in the Great Wrought Room.

Writing again to Caesar in 1778, Philip remarked, 'I hope that Emes' men are by this time, off your back.' With considerable satisfaction, Philip was able in 1779 to put a notice at the entrance lodges:

> Mr. Yorke having at great Expence, and the labour of many Years, finished the Ground and Wood Walks about *Erthig*, desires to acquaint his Neighbours,

84   The view up the tunnel to the waterfall, in 1973

that they are extremely welcome to walk in the same for their Health and Amusement; All he requires is, that they will enter and return by the Path across the Meadow, over the Wooden bridge; That they will keep the Graveled paths, and not disturb the Grass or Turf; That they will not pull any of the flowers, or meddle with the Trees or Shrubs; Mr. Yorke is satisfied that all the better sort of People will most readily comply with his wishes in this respect; In regard to any loose and disorderly Persons misusing his Indulgence, and wearing irregular Paths and Thoroughfares, or doing other mischief, He has given orders to the Servants who are constantly in the Grounds, immediately to turn such Persons out, to obtain their names, and so send them written notice to keep out of the Walks for the future, and Mr. Yorke has left general directions with his Attorney to prosecute all Persons so offending as Trespassers, whenever they attempt at any time again to come within the Grounds.

One of Philip's staff who witnessed and probably assisted with these improvements was his gamekeeper Jack Henshaw. In 1782 he had offended Philip, who told Caesar: 'If Henshaw wishes to be restored, he must get your Mother or some other Person of

85   Jack Henshaw, 'best of beaters'

character to say a word for him in the shape of a petition to me.' Perhaps the trouble arose from a liking for October brewed ale, referred to in Philip's *Crude Ditties*. Whatever his failing, he was back in favour in 1791, when his portrait was painted by John Walters:

Our Artist here attempts to draw,
That best of beaters – Jack Henshaw;
A lover true to fur, and feather,
Who tired not, nor lost his leather:
Near forty years, through bush and bry'r
He beated for the elder 'Squire
Who now together with his gun,
Hath made him over to his son:
Long may he reign with pole, and bag,
And never in the cover, flag,
Sink his fatigues in strong October,
Nor at night, go home *too sober*.

The house depicted in the picture is not Erddig, but Philip's second wife's home, Dyffryn Aled.

When in 1830 Philip's son Simon commissioned a portrait of his woodman, Edward Barnes, he made his own crude sketch to show the artist precisely how the picture should be composed. Reference had to be made to Barnes's services in the Denbighshire Militia (their swords, supplied by the Yorkes, still hang in radiating circles in the Servants' Hall) and to his prowess as a fisherman. Simon's solution to the problem of how to depict these two roles was to enliven the middle distance of the picture with a second portrait of Barnes, rod in hand this time, rather than wielding his sword. This ingenious iconography Simon explained in his accompanying verse:

Tho' last not least at Master's call,
Here stands the Cerberus of our Hall;
United to his loving mate,
He guarded well the Erthig Gate.
Then to the Meadow House descend,
Where use with Beauty now they blend.

The Brewer's Trade not sought for Gold,
Hath made his Spirit still more Bold;
He knows full well to draw a Cork,
And toast in Port 'The House of Yorke':
A Soldier in his younger Days,
He learn't that art by various Ways;

Would wheel himself to Right about,
And cunningly could catch a Trout,
With Sword in Hand he march'd most ready,
And ever was accounted steady,
Except when 'Cwrw da' He found
(Best Belly-Timber above ground.)

86   Edward Barnes, skilled as a forester, fisherman and brewer

Long may He keep the Woods in Order,
To weed a Walk, or trim a Border,
With Axe and Saw across his Shoulder,
And in Face may ne'er look older,
Until he bows to General Fate,
And falls at last, Himself and Mate!

87   The saw pit and
entrance to the
joiners' shop

88   The saw pit

89   The timber waggon

Barnes must certainly have supervised the ripping of timber over the saw pit, outside the joiners' shop, and the hours, sometimes days, of laborious work with a top-and-bottom saw, before boards could be stacked for further seasoning around the timber yard. Although superseded in the later nineteenth century by the steam-powered sawmill, the pit must have continued to come in useful occasionally, because it was never filled in, and the recesses in the side walls, where the grease pot could be at hand for the bottom-sawyer to lubricate his blade, are still there.

The Erddig timber waggon would also have been familiar to Barnes. It is a hybrid vehicle in two parts, that could be extended to carry a full length tree trunk. When timber was being extracted over rough ground or from dense woodland, only one bob with a single pair of wheels would have been used. The wheel-wrighting of the front bob is far superior to that of the rear one and is probably mid-nineteenth century, as much as half a century earlier than its present companion. On countless occasions the waggon must have been driven by William Hughes, woodman between 1883 and 1903, and described by the second Philip in 1912:

> His Venerable form and face
> Were quite a feature of the place,
> And never was our wood so trim
> As when its paths were kept by him.

90 William Hughes, woodman between 1883 and 1903

Hughes's contemporary, the sawyer Thomas Roberts, was responsible for all the machinery in the sawmill building, after it had been converted from a former hog sty and stable. The steam engine powered not only the saws, but also a corn grinder and the mortar mill used by Gittins and his estate staff. In his verse of 1912, Philip praised Roberts's engineering skills:

> Our veteran Thomas Roberts see
> Whose face will long remember'd be
> For, with the exception of one year,
> He labour'd half a century here.
> At all such jobs as we might deem
> Are best perform'd by power of Steam
> He was the Driver of the Gear,
> And proved an able Engineer.
>
> In his capacity of Sawyer
> He was precise as any Lawyer,
> Well knowing how to 'draw the line'
> And many a 'knotty point' define;
> His Judgement too was ever sound
> Of timber which was grown around,
> And what before his Bench was brought
> Was oft condemn'd as good for nought.

91   Thomas Roberts, sawyer and engineer for forty-nine years

> One of his sons employment found
> For eighteen years within our ground,
> He too was as a Sawyer skill'd
> Which post his father long had fill'd
> Another son in our employ
> First started while as yet a boy,
> But since that time, for many a year
> Served as our Foreman Gardener here.

The Erddig sawmill was given a new lease of life when, in the 1940s and 1950s, Simon Yorke's altercations with the Coal Board about mining beneath the estate led him to forbid the burning of anything but wood in the house. At that time quantities of timber from the estate were cut up in the sawmill. Its voracious boiler was coal-fired.

92   Mike Snowden, who as head gardener was responsible for restoring the early eighteenth
century formal layout of the pleasure ground

8

Gardens and Gardeners
Run to Seed

For its first thirty years the garden at Erddig was never allowed to reach real maturity. The building of the house was disruptive. There were long periods when the garden staff had little if any supervision. Then with Meller's arrival building began again; perimeter walls were demolished, realigned and rebuilt, and whole areas excavated to form ornamental water. Any dedicated gardener might reasonably have given up in despair.

Joshua Edisbury's small walled garden can have brought him even less pleasure than his new house. During his absence in London in 1694 he heard that his melon beds were established, that 'Gillyflour' seeds had been planted and that his workmen were digging the orchard borders. He was even able that year to let a fellow-gardener have some vines from Erddig. But most of the planting that survived the years of neglect after Edisbury's downfall was swept away by Erddig's new owner.

John Meller lost no time in replanning all the pleasure grounds. Like Edisbury he thought automatically in terms of a rigidly formal design, with a central axis leading from the state rooms, paths cutting that axis at right angles, and the whole garden boxed in with perimeter walls. But Meller wanted a garden over twice the size of Edisbury's. The end walls were therefore demolished and their foundation used to form terracing, while at the east end a long narrow canal and a rectangular pool were constructed. Outside what was called 'The Best Garden', there were a walled 'Harty Choak Garden' and a 'Kitchen Garden', as well as orchards. The whole design was similar to that of numerous other early eighteenth century houses recorded by Kip and Knyff, although quite such strict formality was already going out of fashion by the time that Badeslade made his survey of Erddig. The print Badeslade published in 1740 depicts Meller's garden at the moment when his planting was fully mature, by which time Meller himself was dead.

Some of the trees planted by Meller were common enough. On 1 April 1716 his agent Richard Jones paid 'John Hughs Gardener for his Journey to Chirk to see some Yew Trees'. But his fruit trees were to be varied and exotic. The wall fruit listed in the Erddig garden in 1718 included under 'Kitchen Garden':

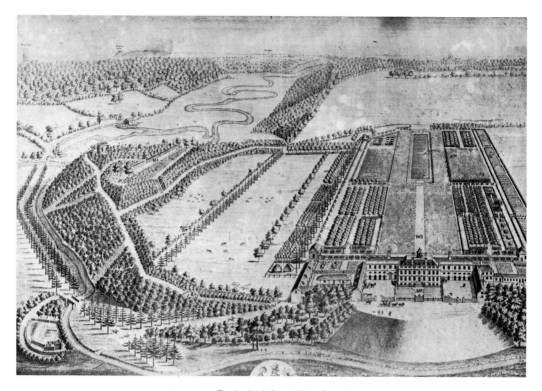

93   Badeslade's print of 1740

South Wall
Kanatian Peach
Old Newington
White Magdalen
3 Burden Peaches
Old Newington
Blew Peralrigou Plumb
Scarlett Newington Nectorn
The Virginall Plumb

East Wall
Queen Mother
Robin Pare
Lemon Pare
Bury Pare
Virh Long Pare
Jargonell Do.
Virtlong
Jargonell
Jesus Coll Warden
Rhine Cland Plumb
Orange Apricock

West Wall
Gross Blanquett pare
White Mogull Plumb
The Petit Russell pare
Blew Mussell plumb
Green Impardigall Do.

Queen Mother plumb
Spanish Musk pare
2 Burgamy pares
Bury pare.

94 The garden as restored to the design recorded by Badeslade

In the Hall Court were 'Roman Nectorns' and 'Cather Peaches'; on the 'East Wall from the Harty Choak Garden Door' were '2 black pares of Worcester' and 'Wrexham and Windsor pares'; on the 'West Wall from ye summer house' numerous different varieties of plums and cherries; in the 'Harty Choak Garden' itself still more plums, pears, apricots and cherries; while in the orchard were vines, nectarines and peaches. The cost of all these fruit trees can only be guessed at, although Meller did note that he spent £2 9s. 9d. between 20 October 1716 and 4 June 1717 on 'Flour and Trees' and during the same period £1 17s. 8d. on 'Flour pots'.

After his uncle's death Simon Yorke continued to improve both the garden and the walks through the woods around Erddig. Writing from Lincoln's Inn on 4 November 1740, Simon's friend Richard Woolfe inquired whether the 'very great storm on Saturday evening' had hit Erddig, and added that he 'shall be glad to hear your Trees about the Roman Fort have escaped'. Two years later he wrote:

> I have heard a great deal of your Grand Assembly at Wrexham, But yet am more pleased with the Account of the Beauty of the Alterations in the Gardens, as I think they will give Mrs. Yorke and yourself a much more lasting pleasure.
>
> Billy Traverse tells me your Billiard Table is arrived, I hope by this time it is put up, And that Mrs. Yorke is become a proficient in the Skill of pocketing.

and writing again from Lincoln's Inn on 1 December 1743:

> [I] hope the milde Season we have had, will greatly have Contributed to the Success of your new plantation; And have often wish't to partake with you in the pleasure of your alterations with Respect to the River.

Another correspondent to report frequently on Simon Yorke's planting was his agent, John Caesar:

> January 22nd, 1750.
>
> Honoured Sir,
>
> Since your absence the weather has been very precarious; consequently

we have not been able to make great proficiency in the Garden; besides nailing the wall Trees and diging that piece of Ground in the Nursery in order to set Gooseberries, Currants, Strawberris &c. Edd Griffiths has been employed ever since your departure in hedging by the furthest Bridge and in the French mill Meadow. Yesterday R: Henshaw and G. Taylor was employ'd throwing the snow off the top of the House, lest it should dissolve and the wett issue into the room. When the Weather Serves we shall carry Gravel for the Firr walk and regulate the New Garden. . . .

    Your dutiful Servant
      John Caesar

          Erddig
       March 1, 1750.

Honoured Sir,

    Since my last information, the Men have gravel'd the Walk in the new Garden from the door to the white Gate; and too day are Graveling from the said Door to the drying yard. too morrow I hope we shall Set the Apple Trees along the Same. Robert Henshaw I believe will make an End of Nailing the wall Trees next wednesday. Edd. Giller and Edd. Griffiths have been along hedging around your Demeons, and have done the out Ring and between the Fields; all to the Hedge between the Wood and the Engine meadows, which they shall do as Soon as the gravel is wheel'd into the Garden.

While it was entirely in character that Simon Yorke should have been content to nurture and enhance the garden he had inherited, it is surprising that his son Philip should have done so little to change a design which his friends would have regarded as absurdly outmoded. During the 1770s Philip was spending large sums of money improving the planting in the park on the advice of William Emes, whose approach was very much that of a follower of Capability Brown. Emes must have been aware of the opportunities for natural landscape gardening on the east side of the house, and how his own pocket might benefit. But Philip insisted on retaining the formal design, limiting change to the demolition of internal walls, which he replaced with the double avenues of limes still flanking the canal. The conservatism of his approach to gardening is another instance of how, with his strong historical sense, Philip could see beyond the vagaries of fashion.

When Philip had to be in London, his sister kept him informed of progress in the garden:

          Erthigg Dec 13th 1763.
My Mamma thanks you for her Letter, and orders me to write in her stead. Papa, and Mamma, are well, and send their love to you, John Jones has made a new Flower Garden, and when you go to London, desires you will send an

ounce of Polyanthus seeds, and a few Anemony, and Ranunculus roots, Your
Colts, and setting Dogs are well, and Speck as cross as ever, one Hare has been
sent to my uncle James, since you went.

    I am, Dear Bro:r
        Your affect:te Sister
        Anne Jemima Yorke.

Once back at Erddig, Philip's preoccupations were easily guessed by his cousin, Simon
Lawry:

>   Great Russel Street,
>   April 20, 1765.
>
> I hope it will not interrupt my dear Cousin Yorke too much in the planting of
> his trees & planning his Green-House just to enquire after his, My Uncle,
> Aunts and Miss Yorke's healths, as I think it is a great while since you went
> into Denbighshire, & we have not heard anything of you; to be sure you have
> had very fine weather for the works without doors, tho' not so Agreable for you
> to stand to see your Workmen perform them, if you have had as much rain in
> your part of the world as we have here. . . .
>
>   As you love planting I make bold to send you from Ovid a collection of
> Forest trees & other plants, Tho' my Papa assures me that all of the Larger
> growth are already found in the woods & gardens of Erthig: but if there are
> any in my catalogue of the smaller kind which you have not already, they are
> much at your service.

Writing on 27 September 1784 at Dyffryn Aled, his second wife's home, Philip
noted in one of his many pocket books:

> I have directed Caesar to agree with the Labourers at Erthig within and
> without the Garden at the following rates being the same I give at Dyffryn,
> that is to say From the 1st of November to the 1st day of March ten pence p.r
> day, and throughout the rest of the year one Shilling p.r day, except four weeks
> in the year, by which is meant Harvest, when they are to stand at fourteen
> pence p.r day.

The wage of 10d. per day was what the labourers were being paid in January 1777,
when the head gardener, John Jones, was receiving 1s. 4d. a day (lower wages were
paid during the winter-months). Philip added a further note at the bottom of the page:
'N.B. This plan brings it to nine months at a shilling, and 3 months at tenpence. J. Jones
is allowed 4. men.'

    John Jones was not among those painted by John Walters, and it was not until
1830 that a gardener's portrait was hung in the Servants' Hall. Thomas Pritchard had
as a young man worked alongside the keeper Jack Henshaw, or 'Hencher'. His age is
given as 67 on the portrait:

95 Thomas Pritchard, 'old and run to seed' in 1830. He is sitting outside the Garden
House, home of several generations of Erddig gardeners

Our Gardener, old, and run to seed,
Was once a tall and slender reed,
Though in this Hall become a Bencher,
He often held the Pole for Hencher;
Of Cock and Partridge rung the knell,
And loudly call'd 'as dead as Hell.'

From Pond to Pool he was a Trotter,
And proved himself an arrant Otter,
When Fishing was the Squire's pleasure,
And Ale he drank above all measure.

We next record the Horticulture,
Wherein he seem'd a noble Vulture.

The Melons raised by Glass and Frame,
With Cucumbers of various Name,
The trees he pruned with stubby knife,
To bear their fruit for longer life.
He shone more bright in Marriage State,
And raised young plants from teaming Mate.

May he survive for many a year
And teach his Grandchildren to shear
Until old Time with scythe in Hand
Hath mowed his crop of Garden Land
For then the Best must leave them All
And sink to Earth at Nature's Call.

Pritchard is shown seated outside the Garden House, a charming building at one end of the kitchen garden at Erddig, conveniently near the greenhouses. The design of the windows and stone dressings suggest that it is by the same architect as the stables, either William Turner of Whitchurch or Joseph Turner of Hawarden, both of whom are mentioned in the Yorkes' accounts during the mid-1770s, when the Garden House was being built. With its Diocletian windows front and back, it is not without architectural pretensions, and the survival of fragments of a Chinese wallpaper in the main ground floor room suggests that it may have been used occasionally as a summer house by the Yorke family themselves. But the rooms at the back and upstairs were the home of several generations of Erddig gardeners.

Two of Thomas Pritchard's junior gardeners, William Price and James Phillips, spent most of their working life at Erddig and both are in the daguerreotype of the staff taken in 1852. They witnessed the return to fashion of formal gardening and the careful integration of a parterre and Irish yew walk into the early eighteenth century design. The fountains around which the parterre was designed were supplied by Blashfield's in 1861, and James Phillips must have supervised the cutting of the original 'L-shaped' borders surrounding them. That his conservatism pleased and amused the Yorkes was typical of Erddig:

Our Gardener here, James Phillips see,
A Bachelor of Husbandry,
Who did from garden-boy become
The finished grower of the Plum
Scarce ever absent from our ground
Then only some few miles around.
This Garden formed his chief delight,
And was as Eden in his sight.

96   James Phillips, who succeeded Pritchard as head gardener and who 'with foreign names, did not agree'

> Old-fashioned, in his notions, he
> With foreign names, did not agree
> 'Quatre-Saisons' 'Quarter-Sessions' meant,
> The 'Bijou' as the 'By Joe' went,
> 'Glory to die John' was the Rose,
> Which each as 'Gloire de Dijon' knows.
> No Green-house here 'twas his advice
> The Antique Frames would well suffice.

The verse that follows, written many years after Phillips's death by the second Philip Yorke, implies a comparison with the canal and pond in the Erddig garden:

> Invited by a friend was he
> To Leasowe Castle by the Sea
> And a day's holiday he took
> That he on that Estate might look.
> Little regard to it he paid,
> This one remark was all he made,
> That they, whose Gardens he was shown,
> Did 'a fine sheet of water' own.
>
> He in his boyhood once did try
> A verse of Psalm to glorify
> 'Blow up the trumpet in new moon'

'The time appointed for its tune'.
And thus to Marchwiel Church he brought
That instrument in Wrexham bought,
And on the solemn Feast-day played
To give effect to what was said.

For three and forty years his name
Was known to all who hither came:
Our gardens under his employ
Did great fertility enjoy:
And visitors did oft declare
They ne'er did taste so good a pear
As 'Winter-nellie', by him grown,
And at our local Contests shown.

This faithful steward, just and true
Died here, in eighteen eighty two,
At the full age of fifty eight,
Like 'shock of corn,' mayhap of wheat;
When 'as bare grain' his body sank
Were nigh four thousand pounds in Bank.
A search for next of kin was made,
And to a niece the same was paid.

When first appointed head gardener by Simon Yorke in February 1841, James Phillips was being paid £35 a year; but like his contemporary, the housekeeper Mrs Webster, employment at Erddig involved him in few personal expenses and he was able to put savings aside throughout a long working life. A letter to Simon from his brother General John Yorke shows that Phillips was remembered with affection by members of the family, long after they had moved away from Erddig:

89 St. George's Road,
January 19th 1882.

Dear Simon,
    We are truly grieved to hear of the sudden death of Poor Phillips so many years your trustworthy Gardener I thought him looking well when last I saw him, and indeed with the exception of slight lameness I perceived but little change in his appearance.

The roses with those troublesome foreign names were planted around an early eighteenth century sundial in the north-east corner of the garden. In this area there was originally a curious pattern of niched hedges, probably of yew, which are clearly shown in both Badeslade's engraving and in an early eighteenth century drawing of the garden. Their design was explained by the discovery of the timber footings of beehives

97   Some of the staff who worked under James Phillips during the second half of the nineteenth century

in the niches. Bees – so essential in a garden in which fruit trees were a principal feature – were as often as not tended by one of the gardeners; in the mid-nineteenth century by William Price, known as 'old deaf man':

> Oft as the bees inclined to swarm
> He would produce resistless charm
> By pots and pans together clap't
> And aught he would thereto adapt;
> The din thus made concerned him not
> So deaf he scarce could hear a shot
> And till their 'Queen' came out, the sound
> Proclaimed the fact for miles around.

John Davies, one of the next generation of under-gardeners, was also notoriously hard of hearing:

> John Davies now we well may deem
> A subject worthy of our theme
> Born, and brought up on this Estate
> No stranger he, within our gate
> Him, as our veteran we claim
> For since when first to work he came
> Full forty years of honest toil
> Have been expended on our soil.

98   John Davies, an under-gardener for over forty years

Though hard of hearing, and his sight
Is now no longer very bright
To our requests, on his reply
We may implicitly rely
Of those whom he had known before
And what was said and done of yore
While, grafted in his memory
Are plantings of each shrub and tree

Unsparingly he gives his aid
To each who needs it, man or maid
Though now and then inclined to ask
The 'whys and wherefores' of each task
Attentive to his Chiefs command
He does each job with willing hand
And, like a worthy honest man
Performs such duties as he can.

'Tis said that once in Marriage state
He took unto himself a Mate
Though when or where, or why or how
Concerneth no one now to know.
This did not last 'twould seem, for long
Whichever party in the wrong
But, when to amorous moods inclin'd
He seeks one, better to his mind.

He once, like hermit, sage and good
Found his vocation in the wood
To trim its walks, for such as pass
To burn the leaves, and mow the grass.
But there, 'twould seem, he felt afraid
Of Nymphs, which haunt the sylvan glade
And may be, shyness did express
For folks who wear such Classic dress.

Whene'er the solemn Church-bells call
'To worship O ye faithful, all'
His hearty song would praises win
From Cherubim and Seraphin
And through each week his days are spent
In godliness, and in content
Leading amidst this worldly strife
A righteous and sober life.

When Davies's work took him to the parterre in the main garden, the maids would tease him that, if only he cut the domes of box between the borders square, they would agree to marry him.

During the closing years of the nineteenth century, when Phillips's successor, Alexander Stirton, was head gardener, rhododendrons and many of the favourite Victorian flowering shrubs were introduced to Erddig. But the bones of Meller's formal design remained. By the time that George Roberts joined the staff in the 1890s, the gardens were at their most densely planted, most luxuriant.

The twenty years that Roberts worked at Erddig were, by the standards of other staff, a modest record. Those who as children knew him, remember a particularly warm-hearted man. Serving on the Parish Council and running the local Sunday School gave him, and many others in service, a greater sense of purpose and companionship than their everyday work could offer. He was photographed with his wife holding a portrait of her mother, Sarah Jones, who entered service at Erddig as a maid in 1860 and worked there for thirty-three years. It was not an autocratic and aloof squire who, in 1911, could write:

Our Children greet him as their friend
Pleased when to him their help they lend,
And honoured feel when asked to take
A turn at barrow, spade, or rake.
And, when at times we leave our home
Awhile in other parts to roam,
He tends each favourite plot of land
Filled by its Infant owner's hand.

A mutual intercourse attends
His greeting with our 'Feathered Friends'
As to the dovecot every morn
He brings the daily meal of corn,
Our snow-white Rabbits, known by name,
And pampered pets both bland and tame,
Await with eagerness his tread,
When bringing them their daily bread.

That sense of stability and contentment was about to be shattered.

Thomas Thomas was in his teens when he first worked as a garden boy at Erddig. On 23 December 1918 his parents wrote to Philip Yorke:

We are taking the pleasure of thanking you very much for your kind enquireing letter about our Son Thomas. We shall try and give as much details as we can remember of his history. We think that Thomas started to work at Erthig Gardens in January or February 1909 under Mr. Aitkin, Head Gardener, was promoted to the Glass Houses on Sept; 2nd 1912. He left Erthig about Sept; 30th 1912. He went to Tattenhall, Cheshire on Oct; 4th 1913 he left this place again towards Jan; 1914. Commenced work again at Frondeg Hall on Feb; 24th 1914 he left here and started at Hafod Colliery about July or 1st week in Aug. 1914. From Hafod he went to the Army Enlisted on Nov; 9th 1914 in the D. Company, 13th Battalion R.W.F. was in Training at Llandudno, and then Dec; 14th he was taken to Bangor Military Hospital and was operated on the same date of Appendicitus, was there for six weeks. About June 1915 he went to finish Training to Winchester, and here he joined the Machine Gun Section, on Dec; 1st 1915 he went out to France, soon after then they were in the Fighting line, in about Three Months he was promoted Lance Corporal and about Nine Months he was Full Corporal. After one Big Battle, I think it was on the Somme, he was Awarded the Military Medal, for Bravery on the Field. He had a slight Gun Shot wound in the Head. And was in General Hospital Dannes Carriers, France for about Six Days. I may say here Sir, that Thomas would not tell any of us what he had done for the Military Medal, and I am very sorry to Inform you that he never had the privilage of wearing the same, only the Ribbon. The Medal was sent to me on Aug; 9th

CORPORAL THOMAS THOMAS, M.M.,
(formerly employed in the Erthig garden)

As Garden-boy at Erthig,
between 1909 & 1913.

When first became a
'Tommy'. In 'Kitchener's
Army'.

The Military Medal,
awarded in 1917.

The Grave at Bouzincourt,
near Albert on the River
Somme.

When in 13th Batt., Royal
Welch Fusiliers.

99   Thomas Thomas, a garden boy killed during the First World War

1918 a little over Three Months after he was Killed in Action on the 22nd Day of April 1918, and is Buried in Bowzincourt Ridge British Cemetery North North West of Albert. We are sending the Photo for you, but we are very sorry that we have not been able to get the Photo taken with the Decoration. We shall be very pleased to accept a Copy of his history written in verse. My Daughter is Thanking you very much for inviting her down to Erthig. She will be able to visit Erthig next Friday the 27th Inst., between Two and Three O'clock in the afternoon if it will be convenient to you Sir. And anything that you would like to know further she will be able to tell you. I am afraid that this Brief history of our Dear Son Thomas has been badly put together. Please excuse me as I am not used to this sort of work. Please accept our Heartfelt Thanks for the kind interest that you are taking in our Dear Son.

    I Beg to Remain
        Yours Faithfully.
          Joseph Thomas

Philip Yorke Esq.   Jan 11th 1919.
Dear Sir,

    I received the Three Photos (enlarged) of our Son Tom, which you have been so kind in sending with Mr. Gittins. The Enlarged Photos are very good and very beautifully done. Of which we are all very pleased. Indeed we are sure they will look well when put together in the Frame and your Beautiful verses with them. Indeed Sir, I dont know how to Thank you for your trouble in doing such Honour to our Son and ourselves. I am rather at a loss in knowing what to do with these Photo's, whether I am to return them back to you, or, are intended for us. I should be very much pleased for a line to explain, as I leave every thing in your hands. I hope and trust that we shall have the Photo of the Grave very soon.

    I Beg to Remain Sir
        Yours Obediently
          Joseph Thomas.

Philip Yorke Esq.
Dear Sir.

    I received your kind letter yesterday Evening. I am very sorry that the Photo has not come yet, if I wont hear something in the course of the next few days I shall write again to the Director of Graves. And I shall send you the Reply as soon as I shall receive the same.

    I Thank you very much for your kind sympathy and kind word to us as a Family. The last letter we had from the Medical Superintendant at Denbigh was to the effect that My Dear Wife was fair in Health, but, no sign of improvement Mentally, most the Pity, but we believe that she will come all right again, and that very soon we hope. All of us at home are very fair in health except colds. There is a great deal of Sickness in the District and many Deaths. I may inform you that the Presentation of the Decorated Heroes in Rhos is to take place tomorrow night Friday 21st at the Pavilion. There are 11 Gold Watches and 3 Photos in Oils for those that has been Killed 14 Heroes in all including our Tom.

I hope Sir that you and the Family are enjoying the Best of Health and again I Thank you for the interest and sympathy shown to us.

I remain Sir. Yours Obediently

Joseph Thomas.

Philip Yorke Esq.

Dear Sir,

I received your kind letter safe on Friday afternoon which you sent me, with Mr. Gittins. We as a Family were so pleased to read of your offer to us, and to accept the Picture as a Present from you. My Two Daughters went down to Erthig yesterday Tuesday June 3rd and were Welcomed by all there. I had followed the Instructions given in your letter I sent to Mr. John Jones on Monday and everything was done according to your directions. So Mr. Jones drove them home with the great Treasure which you Sir have been so good to give us in Honour of our Dear Tom which we have missed so much. We all feel very proud of the Present which you Sir, have been so kind in giving us. For which we Thank you very much, And we feel that we owe you a Debt that we can never Repay. The Verses, Photo's & Frame is admirably done. So well planned by you Sir. And we know that the Picture is a Real Gift from you. Many of Toms Friends have been here to see it. They all say that they have never seen anything like it before. They all appreciate the Verses very much. One passing the remark that he was sure we were proud of the Picture and Tom's History in Poetry. And I tell them that I cant find words to express myself as I would like to. I am sure Mrs. Thomas would be very pleased to see the Picture and to join with our Heartfelt thanks to you. I am sorry to tell you, that she is no better Mentally. Hoping Sir, that you are having nice weather while you are on your Holiday.

I Remain yours

Obediently.

Joseph Thomas.

9
Liveried Staff

The Yorkes' disregard for the trappings of formality, the deplorable state of their stables and the studied inelegance of their own dress amused some friends and disturbed others. For Elizabeth Cust the attitude of her future husband Philip was at times endearing, at times infuriating. 'I have got a great deal of fine lace for you to see', she wrote in April 1770, 'I *will* have you extravagant upon yourself.' For their near neighbour, the sporting writer 'Nimrod', Philip on horseback was simply 'a figure of fun'.

Elizabeth did her best to make Erddig and her husband presentable. In May 1770 she wrote to Philip:

> I wou'd have you on the receipt of this, go to the Hosiers, pray chuse the Stockings *yourself*. I will have the white ones *very handsome* and the others very neat Remember to order the Postillion's Jacket Caps all the things must come tomorrow Evening The Stockings I beg you will send as soon as possible as I want them to be mark'd. . . . our coach was here this morning for me to see; it looks well.

But ultimately Elizabeth had to give up the unequal struggle. She had more than enough on her hands recruiting female staff, and, later, bearing her seven children. 'Coachmen distress me exceedingly I am determined you shall have the care and plague of all the men', she told her husband:

> The servant, Mr. Birch sent me very reasonably demand'd £24, he was quickly despatch'd & we return'd to the former with fresh conditions which are thought better, not by enhancing the Wages nor by adding to the number of Servants (which wou'd be worse, I will tell you the regulation when we meet he wou'd have accepted them but the Gentlemen he was driving had secur'd him. . . . I hope we shall succeed in geting one before you return & have all the Liveries bespoke.

Whenever Philip engaged a groom, he was more concerned about the man's reliability than his appearance. On 13 June 1777 he agreed with his agent John Caesar that Charles Ebbrell, son of the long-serving spider-brusher at Erddig, should be employed as postilion; but on strict conditions:

If Charles Ebbrell means to offer me his services in a serious determined Resolution of fulfilling his duty and of continuing in his place and of being *sober*, *honest*, *clean* and *diligent* therein, I shall then encourage him to come to me; but if it is only to exchange a hard and laborious living of very uncertain profit, for one of mere Plenty, and Less Fatigue & he is to follow the evil and idle Examples of his London Brethren of the Whip, I do then desire for his good, and my own, that I may not take him from a more innocent Situation. Tho I am not used to speak very often and on trifles, I shall not the less narrowly watch his Behaviour, and shall be soon able to Judge of his merit, or defects. For obvious Reasons I do not mean to give more wages than what he had under my Mother. I shall give a pair of Boots and a great Coat once in two years, a full Livery and a working Jacket every year with a pair of leathern breeches and if he follows me to London I shall give him perhaps additional Livery, as my Servants have lately had, but this altogether in my option –
        Ph: Yorke.

Philip was scrupulously precise when it came to noting in his pocket book exactly what the terms of service were to be for the various footmen, grooms and postilions he took on:

June 1, 1774 Thomas Newcome came to my service as Butler. I agreed to give him my clothes and 25£ per annum.

May 24 1776 Agreed with my coachman Ambrose Campion who came to my service this day as follows to give him 20£ a year wages a full suit of livery with plush breeches 1 pr Buckskin breeches Waiscoat and Frock Great coat and boots in every second year and to provide himself out of his said wages with a frock coat for common work allow him also a jacket when neat.

Septr 26th 1784. J. Hughes came this day to my service as Groom at the Rate of Eight Guineas a year, and I am to give him annually a plain Hat, a pair of Boots, a pair of leather Breeches, and a thickest Frock and a thickest waistcoat, and a stable waistcoat no other Breeches than Leathern. A great coat once in 2 years.

Octr. 13th 1784. Rich'd Roberts came into my service as postilion. He is to have fifty five shillings this year, and to be allowed five shillings for the Boots he brought with him. In other respects he is to find his own washing and shoes and shirts, and I am to give him a riding Jacket and Cap and leathern Breeches and Boots, & a thickest coat and waistcoat, and a stable waistcoat, and a common round hat.

NB. Bob the Postilion had two pr of boots in the year 1782. I shall allow them boots only once in two years unless they are absolutely worn out.

17 November 1785 Edward Allen came into my service as footman at the rate of 12 guineas a year.

The employment of liveried staff was part luxury, part necessity. Philip's parliamentary duties took him frequently to London and to his constituency in Grantham, and such journeys made it essential to him to have a trustworthy coachman and honest grooms, and to provide them with serviceable clothing. During the late eighteenth century keeping male staff purely for ornament became increasingly expensive. Lord North's tax of one guinea per head per year on male domestics had been introduced in 1777 and a duty on hair powder followed in 1786, making full livery more of an extravagance. That these taxes received parliamentary consent suggests a reaction among the squirearchy and lesser gentry against the more ostentatious trappings of the higher aristocracy. It may be no coincidence that the word 'flunkey' is of late eighteenth century origin and that this period saw a trend towards greater informality in social manners generally. Certainly Philip Yorke was not in the least concerned in later life to cut a dashing figure on horseback, if 'Nimrod's' description of him is at all accurate:

He was generally clad in cold weather in an immense blue military cloak, the remnant of his military exploits in the Denbighshire Militia some twenty years before; his favourite hackney was a cream-coloured mare, with black mane and tail, perfectly proof against the rowels—also military trophies—of a pair of silver chain-spurs, which were never away from her sides, her rider being thinking of anything but the animal that was carrying him, from a natural absence of mind. To make his figure complete, he often wore a cocked hat; and when riding hard on the trot on a windy day, with his cloak flying one way and the old mare's long black mane and tail another, the antipodes to a Meltonian foxhunter could not have been more completely illustrated than by a sketch of himself when, to use his own words, he was 'taking his constitutional ride'. But, jesting apart, he was the worst horseman I ever saw in a saddle – in England, at least. He was asked whether he ever had been a fox-hunting in his life. 'I have not,' said he; 'in fact, I never could reach the hare.'

One of the striking things about the portraits of staff in the Servants' Hall is that, with the single exception of John Meller's negro, they are all so very informal: woodmen, gardeners, carpenters and maids are depicted quietly going about their business, or casually sitting at home. There is no suggestion of their being paraded as a household. Clearly it was their individuality, their personal quirks which the Yorkes wanted to see recorded.

By the mid-nineteenth century, this carefully contrived informality had taken on more than a hint of inverted snobbery. At grander country houses the first requirement of a footman, groom or coachman was that they should have the physique to show their liveries off to advantage. They were expected to be at least six foot tall, and to have a well formed leg which could if necessary be shaped to perfection with the judicious use

101 Edward Humphreys, photographed in 1852

of pads beneath their stockings. The second Philip Yorke's description of Edward Humphreys, coachman in the daguerreotype of staff taken in 1852, is a far cry from such refinements:

> Clumsy alike in form and walk,
> A roofless mouth impaired his talk;
> No outward ornament was he
> To Equipage or Livery.
>
> No 'Jehu' as we did agree
> For he did not 'drive furiously',
> But lumb'ring o'er the weary space
> Our ponderous Coach kept sober pace.

The Humphreys family experienced a series of misfortunes. Edward himself was seriously injured when climbing on to a coach, and although he worked at Erddig for the remaining seven years of his life, the accident ruined his health and left him crippled. His eldest son, Nehemiah, went to work as a groom in Yorkshire, where he died young. The second son, another Ned, was gamekeeper to the Yorkes, but caught a chill while out beating on a grouse moor and died after a long illness. Henry Humphreys was at first the black sheep of the family, then a source of great pride and finally of great sadness. After failing dismally as an office clerk, he joined the army, where he rose rapidly from private to captain, serving with distinction in the campaign of 1884 in the Sudan. That same year he was fatally injured in a riding accident in Cairo. When his younger brother, Thomas Humphreys, heard of the accident, he immediately sent a telegram to Simon Yorke asking him to break the news to their mother. A letter followed:

> Sir,
> I feel I must apologise for causing you to trouble yourself on our behalf, as I fear I did by my telegram this morning, but my reason for presuming to communicate with you was that I feared someone, seeing the announcement of my poor brothers accident in the morning paper, should call at the Lodge, and without care or thought announce the sad news to her, the consequence of which in her present state might have been serious. I knew that Mrs. Yorke or yourself or whoever you elected to send, would be able so to tell her the news that the effect upon her would be in some measure lessened. I am sure you will pardon my thus asking you to add another to the very many great kindnesses shown by Mrs. Yorke and yourself at all times and to all members of our family, for which I, and I am sure those who are left, will never cease to be sincerely grateful. I see by the London papers that my Brother was alive last night, but that no hope was entertained of his recovery.
> Trusting you will kindly forgive the liberty I have taken.
>   I remain, Sir,
>   Yours most respectfully
>   Thos. Humphreys.

Thomas himself had been born with only one arm, but worked successfully as a clerk for a firm of solicitors. Richard, the fifth son, went into the grocery trade; while the youngest of the family, Benjamin, became a miner.

Also in the daguerreotype of 1852 is the butler, Thomas Murray, 'with bottle clasped within his hand', and the footman, William Stephenson,

> . . . among the last who wore
> The Livery of the days of yore.

Murray followed the practice common among butlers in the nineteenth century of leaving service to run a pub, The Horns, in Wrexham. With a tradition of teetotalism among the later Yorkes, their reaction was unsympathetic, and the episode seen to point a clear moral:

> But, though to make it pay he tried,
> He soon fell ill and shortly died.

When towards the end of the last century another butler, Frederick Otley, tried his luck at The Green Man, again in Wrexham, the consequences were no less dire:

> This movement, be it under-stood
> Proved other than for future good,
> His wife, who canter'd out the wine,
> Broke into galloping decline. . . .

With the Yorkes' comparative lack of interest both in their cellar and in the niceties of etiquette, their more successful butlers had to have qualities not normally associated with their position. A letter of 22 September 1884 to the butler George Dickinson from a former employee, suggests that he was liked and trusted by his junior staff:

You doubtless will be surprised to have a letter from me especially under the conditions in which I venture to write this. While working today, however I fell a dreaming and my thoughts carried me back to Wrexham – and somehow – to Erddig. It was a pleasant imagination and when I remembered yourself and the other kind friends I know, I thought I would write if only just to let them know where and how I was.

If you have not already heard you will be surprised to hear that I am a soldier! Army Hospital Corps it is called. I have only been in a few months and I have been Promoted to Lance Corporal.

You will believe me when I say that I find it deuced uncomfortable. Straw Beds and blankets, Huts and sanded floors T'would wring the hearts of your pleasant friends and ladies.

. . . my promotion keeps me out of all dirty and unpleasant work, although it occasionally brings me some inconvenience. As for instance one day I found my sword indellibly stained (by some spiteful scoundrel) with oxalid acid. And on another occasion when all the lights had been put out, about 20 fellows hurled pieces of coal, at my poor cot, while I was asleep. . . . Pleasant living this for a Christian age? I should be unspeakably pleased to hear from and to have news of Erddig and its occupants. Mrs. and Miss Rogers and all the rest.

I shall be coming home at Xmas and shall then see you all. Of course it depends upon whether I shall survive this delightful treatment until then.

The experiences of both Henry Humphreys and John Wilde were a reminder to the

102 The Family Museum

male staff who remained at Erddig that the alternatives to service there could be both harsher and more dangerous.

Dickinson was a great favourite with the Yorke children. He helped them catch, chloroform and then mount butterflies to exhibit in the Family Museum, the room off the north end of the basement passage where there accumulated over the years a miscellany of old coins, fragments of Chinese figures, a swordfish blade, the odd Indian bus ticket, a hornets' nest and a highly polished human skull, all piled in a display case probably made in the Erddig joiners' shop. In her notes on the house written half a century later, Mrs Yorke remarks that the butterflies 'were chloroformed and arranged by the Butler Dickinson (who himself died under chloroform during a slight operation at Erddig – a curious coincidence).' Simon Yorke had a hatchment painted to record his years at Erddig: 'IN Remembrance of the Faithful Services of Mr. GEORGE DICKINSON Butler to SIMON YORKE Esqre for 19 Years. He died at Erddig Decr 30th 1888.' Hanging on the opposite side of the range in the Servants' Hall is another hatchment, reading: 'In Remembrance of the Faithful Services of Mr John Davies Butler to Simon Yorke Esqre For Nearly 10 years whose death took place at Erddig Octr 23^d 1868.' Dickinson's cases are still in the Family Museum; but are bare except for small heaps of dust beneath the rows of empty pins.

103 George Dickinson's hatchment in the
Servants' Hall

A short passage leads from the Family Museum to the Butler's Pantry. As a door in
the corner opens on to steps down to the cellar, the position of the pantry has almost
certainly remained unchanged since the house was built. The inventory of 1726 lists
among its contents:

1 Little closet with Shelves and Double doors.
1 Dresser & 11 Shelves.
1 old Japan copper cistern.
4 Oyl bottles. 1 basket to carry up Knives & Salvers.
1 Wooden Tray to carry up the Glasses.
2 Knive baskets, 1 lined with baiz
12 new Ivory hafted knives & forkes. 1 knife lost by Mr. Jones.
6 old white knives and forks.
1 Box to hold nails. 1 hair broom.
1 Large 3 pointed borer. 1 Dark Lanthorn.
1 Little borer. 1 mallet. 1 Tin funnell.
1 Hard Brush. 1 rasp. 12 Rubbers.
6 China plates. 4 plates another sort 1 Joyned.
12 Invisible china plates.

The mysterious reference to 'invisible china plates' refers to Chinese porcelain with
decoration incised in the paste before the application of the glaze-mixture, and all but
invisible unless the finished article is held against a strong light. There is now a plain
oak table in the room and a lead lined sink with a draining board and racks above.
Among several discoloured prints is one of George V reaching out from his bed in a
hospital train near the Western Front, to pin the Victoria Cross on the tunic of one of
his troops, while a Yorke kinsman, Sir Charles Cust, assists 'the King's fine action'.
    However late the family's dinner might be, the silver had to be washed, polished
and put away in the strong room before the butler and footman could go to bed. On the

104   Nineteenth century liveries, usually hung in the Butler's Pantry

baize-lined shelves of the safe were arranged the Yorkes' superb late seventeenth century Monteith engraved with Chinese-style figures, the silver sauceboats of 1736 inherited from James Hutton, the tankard of twenty years later, also bearing the Hutton arms, and a score of lesser pieces. The footman then slept with his bed in front of the only door to the safe. In a nearby cupboard in which their liveries were hung, generations of footmen inscribed their names.

In the room next door there was, in the late eighteenth century, a billiard table. No doubt this end of the basement passage was usually a male preserve, with easy access to the cellar and to the lamp room, where there were racks for wine in current use. In the 1790s the first Philip Yorke had the billiard room decorated with the coats of arms illustrated in his book *The Royal Tribes of Wales*, and thereafter it was known as the Tribes' Room. The lamp room was, until well into the twentieth century, for the use of the male staff. But by the 1920s there were only maids to clean the forty-odd oil lamps needed when the Yorkes were entertaining and no footmen to resent this intrusion into their territory.

The social and political changes brought about by the First World War had more immediate effect on the male than on the female staff. Most of the men had anyway left to fight, and by the time they returned few owners of country houses could afford to pay their wages and had learnt to manage with a much reduced female staff. Some former footmen and butlers readily adapted to the changes of the post-war years. For others the revolution was too traumatic.

In the 1912 group photograph Frank Lovett was included in the front row, a salver in his hand:

Frank Lovett stands upon the left
Of crimson plush and drab bereft,
Which garb his predecessor wore
In scene of sixty years before.
A worthy butler he will make
When he that higher post shall take
And glad may be that lord or squire
Who does his valued help acquire.

Near Newport he first saw the light
(Though not that place in Isle of Wight
But in a latitude much higher
Where Salop touches Staffordshire).
Wherever be his future place
We trust it may not quite efface
The memories of this present year
And of a happy sojourn here.

A few months before the photograph was taken, Lovett had injured his hand in an accident. He must have valued the letter that he received from Philip Yorke, because he kept it and later passed it on to his son:

Erddig Park,
Wrexham,
Feb. 15. 1911

Mr. Frank Lovatt [sic],
We are all so very glad to hear the good news that all is going so satisfactorily & well with you & hope that before long your hand will have made a complete recovery of its former power of usefulness.

We are glad that you are having your well-earned holiday at your home & sincerely hope that all your Friends & Relatives there are well & prospering.

Do not trouble about returning until your Doctor is sure of your being strong enough for your duty but all here will be very glad to see you again, when you do return.

Between now & Easter, all will be very quiet, with only an occasional visitor or two.

All here send their best wishes for your speedy and thorough restoration to health, & with my thanks also for your kind letter,

I remain, very faithfully yours,
Ph. Yorke.

Lovett returned to service at Erddig and was promoted to butler. The entries in his account books are neat and repetitive:

1913 March	1st	Telegraph Boy	2*d*.
March	3rd	Telegraph Boy	2
March	5th	2 letters stamped	2
March	7th	Parcel	4
March	10th	Parcel	4
March	12th	Organ man	3
March	12th	2 Railway Guides	2
March	12th	Rouge for Silver	1.0
March	14th	Parcel	4
March	16th	2 letters	2
March	19th	Parcel to post	4
March	19th	Beer for Ladies Maid	1.6
March	19th	Beer for Mrs Gillam	2.0
March	25th	Stamped 2 letters	2
March	30th	Beer for Chauffeur	3
March	30th	Beer for Dining Room	2.6

In October 1913 Lovett was lured away by an advertisement for a post as chauffeur – not a position which Erddig was then likely to offer – and although Philip Yorke was disappointed at his leaving, he offered a good reference:

> I am sorry you have decided upon leaving my service where you have been only recently appointed Butler, but I wish you well, & hope you may like the new vocation which you are choosing.
>
> As to your character as Butler I may say that during the few months which I have known you in that capacity I have had every best reason to be very pleased & during the several years previous, in the capacity of Footman I have had all good opinion of you.
>
> I can therefore give you a very good character for the six years which you have spent with me altogether, but of course I know nothing as to how far fitted you may be for another capacity such as that of a Chauffeur.

Lovett's next surviving letter is undated:

> Sunday.
>
> Dear Sir,
>
> No doubt you will be very surprised to hear from me but being one of your old servants I thought I would let you know my whereabouts. As you will see I have donned khaki and doing my little bit for King & Country. I am pleased to say I am getting on well too as I have got 2 stripes and have been put in charge of the Divisional Headquarters officers mess. We belong to the 41st Division and expect to go out almost any day now whether to France or where we dont know. It is a very terrible war is it not but I shall go out with a light

heart trusting to God's providence for a safe return. I hope that you are enjoying good health sir and also that Mrs. Yorke & the 2 young squires are well.

> I am Sir
> > Yours obediently
> > (Corporal) Frank Lovett.

The opportunity to add a distinguished chapter to the record of service at Erddig was welcomed by Philip Yorke, and an exchange of several letters followed:

> Sir,
> I beg to thank you very much for your kind letter and for the wish to have a photograph of myself in khaki. I will gladly do so but at present I am fully occupied firing my course on the ranges. I hope to finish it next week and will sit for my photograph at once. The verses which you have composed about me are very good indeed & could not be improved by anyone. I quite approve of them and I thank you very much for your good opinion of me. I was born at Edgmond Nr. Newport, Salop on August 10. 1888. We are expecting to go out very shortly when I shall endeavour to do my best as I always have done again thanking you for your kind appreciation of my services I am sir your obedient servant.
> > Frank Lovett

On 3 May 1916, Philip replied:

> Corporal Lovett,
> Thank you very much for the Photos of yourself, both of which we all think are excellent, tho' the one which has been the most generally approved of by us & by all who knew you when here is the one in which you are wearing your cap, & we are therefore choosing that one for our Portrait Gallery, to which the verses are to be attached.
> We earnestly hope that you will keep your health & that when you get your first leave you will couple a visit here with a visit to your home at Newport, & I can promise you a very hearty welcome.
> I know Belgium & the north of France so well that it will add greatly to the interest of a letter from you if your locality may be told me, whether by name or at all events by description in any letters you may ever find time & opportunity to write to any of us here.
> I am now starting off to Wrexham to get your portrait enlarged, & for the present therefore will close, with our very best wishes for all prosperity, & the hope that we may before very long hear from you again.
> > Believe me to remain ever,
> > > very faithfully yours,
> > > > Ph. Yorke.

105   Frank Lovett, formerly a footman, shortly before he left for Italy, where he continued to correspond with Philip Yorke

Two years later Lovett renewed contact with Erddig, writing this time to Mrs Yorke, perhaps because he thought that Philip, then nearly 70, might not still be alive:

29.1.18.
Somewhere in Italy

Madam,

It is such a long time ago since you have heard from me that I feel rather ashamed at writing this letter but I am taking the liberty of presuming as one of your old servants that you will be pleased to hear of me again & to know how I am getting on. You will see by the address in this letter that I am a long way from old England now. I must say that so far the country does not appeal to me as it is so bitterly cold. We are right in the mountains so we get the brunt of it. However in the summer it must be beautiful out here. I am pleased to say that I have kept remarkably well & fit and although my duties do not necessitate my being in the trenches I am naturally continually in danger & have to endure a lot of hardships but we are all very bright & cheerful and all look forward to an early & victorious peace. I am sure too that all at home are enduring great trials and we all feel very grateful for all the noble work that the people at home have done especially the wonderful self sacrifice & devotion the ladies of England have shewn to all causes and appeals. I hope that you and Mr Yorke keep well also Master Simon and Master Philip. They must be quite big fellows and I am sure you feel very proud of them. Please remember me to Lucy and all the staff who I knew & who may still be with you. With my very best wishes, I am madam
    Yours obediently
    Frank Lovett

When he returned home, Lovett asked Philip Yorke for help in finding a job. This was willingly given:

7.5.21.

Mr. Lovett,

I need hardly tell you that it will give me the greatest possible pleaure to give you any help I can towards the object you now have in view & can safely assure you that I shall give you an excellent recommendation. You may refer anyone to me most certainly. I will enquire from amongst my neighbours who there may happen to be who require a Butler, & should I find any, I will at once let you know, & possibly you will yourself be hearing from that same person.

    I perfectly remember all your recent history & how that the last letter received from you was from Cologne.

    I am so pleased to hear that you are now married & with a little son, which both Mrs. Yorke & myself congratulate you very heartily upon.

    Thanks for your kind enquiries after all of us, & I am thankful to be able to reply that we are quite well.

We are very glad that you have happy memories of your sojourn here at Erthig & we wish for you & yours every prosperity wherever you may be going.

Believe me to remain ever very faithfully yours.

Ph. Yorke.

On 15 February 1923, a few months after her husband's death, Mrs Yorke gave Lovett a generous reference:

Frank Lovett was in our service as Head Footman for about five years and then became Butler for about a year. He was very capable honest and thoroughly satisfactory in every way. He only left to serve his country in the Great War where he distinguished himself and became a Sergeant. I shall be very glad to give anyone any further information they may require.

L. M. Yorke.

Although Mrs Yorke was in fact not strictly correct to say that war service had taken him away from Erddig – a slip which Philip would never have made – Lovett was successful in finding a post as butler at a house in Devon. But the war years left him disappointed and unsettled. He was drowned in 1934, leaving a widow and a young son, in circumstances which have led his family to believe that he took his own life.

Livery was last worn by a member of the Erddig staff in the winter of 1943, when a photographer from *Picture Post* came to the house. The only staff there then were John Jones, who had been coachman and had taught Simon and Philip to ride, and the housekeeper, Lucy Jones. Thirty years before Philip Yorke had written:

John Jones our Coachman, strong and stout,
Well known the neighbourhood about,
Here, on a pony at his side,
Teaches the Squire's son to ride. . . .

Our horses have his constant care,
Our dogs too his attentions share.
As driver none could him excel,
And all our Staff respect him well.
He keeps our trappings trim and neat –
Our equipages few could beat,
Although these have become, of late,
Not altogether 'up to date.'

When grave mis-hap, one luckless day,
Befell our Carriage on its way,
With calmness he was on the alert
A worse disaster to avert.

106 John Jones, coachman in 1911, with Simon Yorke

And once, when help at Fire we sought,
He 'mongst our band of helpers fought,
Who bravely quench'd the threat'ning Flame,
E'er summon'd help from Wrexham came.

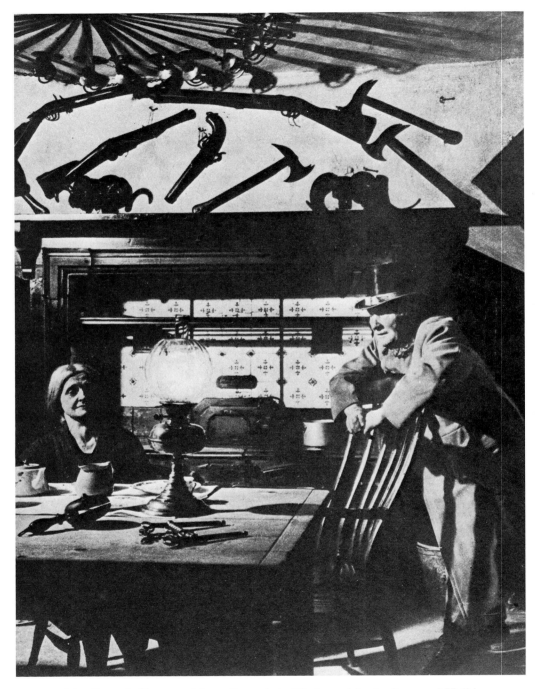

107   John Jones in livery and Lucy Jones (née Hitchman) in the Servants' Hall in 1943

From Pigeon-tower the dwellers all
Come fluttering round him at his call,
And cooing as he comes to deal
The corn which forms their daily meal.
At Garden-treats, to him we call
To start the scramble, send the ball –
And, at the Feast, his part to take
In helping Tea, and serving Cake.

His well earn'd leisure time is spent
On Fret-work, which is much his 'bent',
To which quite lately he aspired
Yet has therein great skill acquired.
While often when his work is done,
He seeks diversion with his Gun,
And sometimes will supply the Cook
With hare and rabbit, or a rook.

A dozen years have run their course
Since this, our Master of the Horse
Was here elected in the stead
Of one George Newns, now long since dead.
And may he long with us remain,
Nor yet the post of 'Chauffeur' gain,
Till carriages we cease to need,
And Horses yield to Motor-steed!

By 1943 John Jones had become the estate odd-job man and was ploughing up the Erddig garden to plant potatoes for the war effort. But, as the idea of a charade appealed to him and Lucy, he donned the livery and they posed for the *Picture Post* photographer in the Servants' Hall.

108   The Nursery corridor in 1973

10

Failures

Complaints about the idleness of servants, their unreliability, scarcity and sometimes criminal dishonesty are recurrent themes of much eighteenth and nineteenth century correspondence. To expect loyalty and trust, as the Yorkes did from their staff, would have been thought by many of their contemporaries an invitation to betrayal. Inevitably, there were times when the Yorkes were sadly disappointed by some of their servants, and the traditions of long and devoted service at Erddig made the experience all the more painful to them. Only occasionally does the verse they wrote about their staff hint at these failures. But bitter disillusionment did sometimes find expression in the family's letters and diaries. Even when they felt they had been betrayed, the Yorkes could rarely bring themselves to take down the portraits of offenders or revise their verse eulogies.

One of the Yorkes' saddest disappointments was young John Caesar. The lengthy correspondence during the 1770s between Philip Yorke and his steward, John Caesar, conveys a picture of a diligent and conscientious agent, given a great deal of responsibility by a squire who, because of his duties as Member of Parliament for a constituency in Lincolnshire, had to be away for months at a time. The elder John Caesar was similarly trusted by Simon Yorke and wrote regularly to keep him informed of progress in the garden. In a letter of 30 January 1750, Caesar had to report difficulties with junior staff:

> Honoured Sir,
> Since my last the weather continues Still the Same for the Snow is almost a foot Thick in many places about Erthig, and have not been able to do much business in the Garden; besides Nailing the Cherry trees, Plumbs Pears & planting Goosberries and Currant trees in the Nursery Yesterday and too day as it is a Frost, the Team is Carrying River Gravel to the new Garden Gate in order to lay on the Firr walk. Rob. Henshaw's Son did last Friday after I went to Llangollen Fair; in order to buy Heifers to eat Straw at Pentreemilin; took the Gun out of the House and shot Several of your pigeons; one of which he brought into the House; and call'd it an wood pigeon and said that one of the Dogs did kill it; and other two was found Dead in the Farm yard. This affair

was conceal'd from me till yesterday evening, at which time I examin'd him and found him guilty of the fact: which occasioned me to discharge him and told him not to come near the house any more. The Farmer and his Lad takes care with the Coach horses during your absence all things are well in and about Erthig and remain

     Your Dutiful Servt

      John Caesar.

Philip's mother Dorothy was a frequent visitor to the Caesar household and relied on Margaret, Mrs Caesar, to keep her up to date with affairs at Erddig. A letter of Dorothy Yorke's of May 1769 describes the elder Caesar's decline:

> I will tell you the state of his health without the least exaggeretetion, had from his wife; who is in the greatest trouble & affliction about him he keeps in his bed tell 4 in the Afternoon, for these last ten days has not taken an ounce of solid food, trembling & quite forgetful of any subject he hears an hour before; The tenents & other people are continually calling on him about business & he do's not know a word as soon as they turn their back what they have been saying to him. Margaret is as much present as she can, & they will let her, their boy surprizingly Careful about every thing relating to you. . . . the rest of yr servants are all very diligent & the place looks Charmingly pleasant.

Mention of Caesar's son is made in several other letters at this time: 'Jacky Caesar is a very Careful Lad and for one so very young transacts business very well', Dorothy wrote on 19 May 1769, continuing:

> your good nature and tenderness I much admire to his poor father but if you will take my advice I would by no means give this boy any Salary whilst he is his father's deputy you can at any time reward him as he deserves, your taken up with him in ye stead of Old C——r is certainly a favour & I know will be look'd on as such. & tho this is my advice yet I am as much in their interest as any friend they have. I have made Margt. a small present for the late trouble I have given her & I believe a better woman dos not live in her station than her self.

Dorothy Yorke was not deliberately mean. But her estimate of what was a fair wage changed little with the passing years, with consequent dissatisfaction amongst her staff. She also did her best to see that her son Philip was not over-generous, a fault which her husband had particularly warned against. There was never any doubt in her mind that the principal reason for not over-paying staff was that to do so was actually harmful to them, increasing neither their respect nor their usefulness. It was incidentally true that, at least until Philip's marriage, the family felt they needed the money themselves.

Fixing wages was complicated by the fact that different rates had usually to be paid when staff were working in the Yorkes' London house. Wages would also vary depending on whether the family was in residence. Inevitably Dorothy Yorke's view of what was fair was not always shared by her servants, and on more than one occasion their resentment was voiced. Writing to Philip on 30 November 1765, Dorothy had to report:

> Caesar was in a vast Bustle a few days before I came away proposed to ye Servants board wages half a crown weekly ye maids, & 3s. the men they did not relish this & y^r Father desire it might be Lay'd aside if disagreeable to them but they came with a request to me that they might have 4^s ye men & 3^s ye maids so I believe it is agreed tho Caesar has not answered my note to him they are to find nothing for themselves but ale Sugar and bread & they have some small stock to begin with. this will prevent Stangers soaking them whilst we are gone, as too many have got on that footing at Erthig. Caesar writes me word Liberality of Living causes Straitness of money He sends me Observations upon housekeeping when ye family was in London in ye year 1741: this foolish affair spoil'd my rest for a night or 2 but whilst I keep house I shall never pinch My Servants.

A few years later, in June 1769, Dorothy wrote in a similar vein to Philip, following a meeting with Mr Edwards, the agent of Chirk Castle:

> I ask'd his advice about yr workmens wages Henshaw & David Jones he assures me that if you part with them; you will have none under 12^d a day John Jones in a vast bustle least he should loose them out of the garden, especially Hen.w who takes Care of the Engine, & new ones he says must have a vast deal of direction from him, before they can be of any use in ye Garden.

At the root of the problem was the Yorkes' belief, shared by most other landed families, that working for them was a privilege to be more highly valued than mere financial reward. Their staff held rather different views.

Philip Yorke was courting trouble when he agreed with his mother to let young Jacky Caesar assume responsibility for all his father's work, but without payment. Dorothy reported in July 1769 that 'I have now all my discourses with the Lad who for his age & experiences is very Cleaver & diligent'. When the building of the foundations at King's Mill seemed to be unnecessarily delayed, she added, 'I do all I can to spirit Jacky Caesar up that there be no delay.' No doubt the Yorkes had every intention of rewarding young Caesar in time. But he was not prepared to wait. When he did officially succeed his father, he clearly felt that his wages were still inadequate. Before long the accounts were being adjusted so that Jacky Caesar received what he knew he deserved; at the same time the deficit left by his father of £185 was allowed to grow to over £600. The rift finally came on 5 January 1787:

John Caesar,
Your own mind and recollections, will suggest sufficient Reasons, wherefore, under the present circumstances, it was impossible for me to continue, you any further, in my service. I am very sorry to say I can see no marks of innocency, and mere mistakes of Figures, and omissions of charge in your accounts, tho Repetitions of this sort would disable you as a Steward; the Fluctuations of many of the year's totals could not be so continually varying by errors of that kind only, but must have had their source in traffick, very injurious to me and disgraceful to yourself; and I am very sorry to add that since you came to the management of this Estate near three years since, I have had reasons in my own mind, to dispute your integrity; You destroyed that letter (tho ordered to keep, and file all mine) which settled the Salary and altered it, when you brought it in charge to your own purposes and Emoluments. Perhaps on the whole your salary was not too much, but the manner of raising it, had a very bad aspect. I desire you will as soon as possible appoint Mr. Jones to meet you at Erthig and that you will deliver into his hands all my Keys and Papers, and inform him so far as possible in all unsettled business which comes to him to compleat.
  Ph. Y.

Philip Yorke's great-grandson was as proud, if not prouder, of his relationship with his staff; and he too was distressed when the relationship failed. He preserved an anonymous letter, dated 27 February 1894, which many in his position would have destroyed without a second thought:

Dear Sir, Pardon me for taking the liberty of addressing this note to you. Hearing of the alterations that is about to take place in connection with the workmen on your estate, I beg to give you due warning. Consider the course you are pursuing in sending a man off, a man that to my knowledge has been in the employ of your father for over 25 years. Kindly examine the character of his successor to see if it is up too the mark as it ought to be. I'm afraid if the examination was conducted out properly you would be astonished at the revealations. I am afraid there is some underhanded work going on, some false tale telling. If not then why should that poor man along with one or two poor honest men treated so and not the rest, some of which has not been in your employ twelve months. Ah dear sir beware of those two faced men, men that before your face are (yes Sir) and behind your back are thorough rouges. I hear sir that according to your present intentions you are about to throw honest trustworthy men out on the road and are going to keep some of the scum. I beg of you to pause before doing such a action and as I said before steer clear of those two faced men for they are nothing but wolves going about in the garb of lambs.
  One who has got his eyes open & knows
   them.

109   Mrs Penketh, cook at Erddig from 1903 to 1907

The letter was sent from Wrexham, addressed to 'Phillip Yorke Esq.'

If that incident was brushed aside, the Penketh affair certainly could not be. Mr and Mrs Yorke were humiliated publicly and in court. They had to read in the *Wrexham Advertiser* of 5 October 1907:

THE SERIOUS CHARGE AGAINST AN ERDDIG HOUSEKEEPER – EXTRAORDINARY PROCEEDINGS – Prosecutor Wishes to Withdraw – ACCUSED SENT TO THE ASSIZES.
At Wrexham County Police Court, on Thursday before F. Meredith Jones Esq., (presiding), H. Croom-Johnson Esq., and H. Rogers Esq. Mr. Yorke, J.P., of Erddig, charged on remand his housekeeper, a single woman named Ellen Penketh, with unlawfully converting to her own use various sums of money, amounting altogether to £201. 12s. 1d.

A photograph of Mrs Penketh found its way into one of the Yorke albums. She is prettily dressed, holding a posy of flowers, and distinctly young and attractive compared with the dour Mary Webster or the stern Harriet Rogers. But she lacked their sterling qualities. Like many other country house cooks, she made free with the whisky and cooking sherry. 'She's at it again', John Jones the footman was overheard to remark to Frank Lovett, as she approached unsteadily along the basement passage. Eventually, even the trusting Yorkes found out that their accounts with a Wrexham grocer, Messrs George Dutton and Company, were not in order. For a family that was almost entirely teetotal, the offence could not be lightly dismissed.

Excessive drinking was no new problem at Erddig. Writing to Philip in June 1768, Dorothy Yorke reported with undue optimism that 'Williams remains chief Butler, behaves with discretion in the place.' Almost exactly a year later she had to add: 'Poor William died the death of a Welch man immoderately he drank: buryd at Graesford.' They did their best to make discreet inquiries when taking on new members of staff. A postscript to a letter of the 1770s from Philip Yorke to his agent notes: 'Not a word of Deborah Lloyd's *sobriety* in Margery Taylor's Character; if you could have a confirmation of that, and in other things like her appearance & promises, I think you might take Her.' Other precautions are mentioned in Philip's letter to Caesar of 26 January 1775:

> I observe by the Returns, that Thomas Davies is perpetually Employed, to be sure you get something more out of him, than mere brewing; and this puts me in mind to recommend Aconomy in Small Beer; that you are careful it is not consumed by People out-of-doors, and who I know, will slip in, if the Cellar door be constantly left open.

When in 1897 the housekeeper, Miss Harrison, was dismissed for disposing of pheasants without the family's knowledge, a fellow servant told the Yorkes' agent that it was not unusual to find her in the kitchen, 'the worse for Beer'. The position of an employer wishing to take a strong line against drunkenness was considerably weakened if, as was the case throughout the nineteenth century at most country houses, staff were given a free quota of beer, in addition to their salaries. It was one of the triumphs of the Temperance Movement that an annual cash payment was eventually substituted. At Erddig beer money of £2 10s. was still being paid in 1912 to the junior maids.

The Penketh case could scarcely have gone worse for the Yorkes. Their intention was that Mrs Penketh should be charged with committing not a felony, but a misdemeanour, so that she did not have to appear at the Assizes. The prosecution's case was reported at length in the *Wrexham Advertiser*:

> Mr. Yorke was a merciful man, but felt that it was his duty at the time when the matter was discovered to take out a warrant against the accused. But he had received a very repentant letter from the prisoner, which he (Mr. Churton) did not intend to read. She had been in prison now for seven days, and having regard to all the circumstances, Mr. Yorke, believing that she had been led away by some person whom he need not mention, and who practically had been at the bottom of the whole mischief, had asked him to apply to their worships for their consent to withdraw the prosecution. There could be no question of compounding a felony because Mr. Yorke would have to make good all deficiency and did not expect the prisoner to do so.

This the court refused to accept. The Yorkes were not allowed to withdraw their charges, and the prosecution was ordered to give evidence.

The first witness was Mrs Yorke, who described numerous abuses of the household accounts which had cost the Yorkes over £200. Mrs Penketh's explanation was that £130 had dropped unnoticed out of her bag as she was emerging from a bank in Wrexham where she cashed the Yorkes' cheques; she had not been able to pluck up the courage to tell Mrs Yorke. After lengthy cross-examination by the defence, in which reference was made to Mrs Penketh's meagre salary of £45 a year, the magistrate decided that the case had to go before the County Court. Bail was offered on a surety of £10, which to applause Mr Yorke agreed to provide. This offer was subsequently rescinded when Mr Yorke got wind that Mrs Penketh intended to surrender her bail, and she was duly kept in custody.

The same painful evidence was repeated at the County Court. On this occasion the defence managed not only to win the sympathy of the jury, but to infuriate the Yorkes by referring to them as 'idlers on the pathway of life'. Although instructed by the judge to return a verdict of guilty, the jury sided with Mrs Penketh. It was not unusual in such cases for the employer, rather than his staff, to emerge discredited: although crime statistics of the period indicate a higher incidence of crime among domestic servants than in the population at large, they also show a high rate of acquittal of servants.

Philip Yorke could do no more than express his outrage in the verse he wrote to accompany the portrait of Mrs Penketh's successor, the worthy Miss Brown:

> Her coming we may here remark
> Brought to a close a period dark,
> For long on us did Fortune frown
> Until we welcomed good Miss Brown,
> One whom this latter did replace
> Did for five years our substance waste,
> As foul a thief as e'er we saw,
> Tho' white-washed by Un-Civil Law.

The years following Miss Brown's departure in 1914 saw the staff dwindle and the house decline, quietly at first and almost imperceptibly, then unmistakably and alarmingly, until by the 1950s it had reached a point of beleaguered hopelessness.

The fourth Simon went to Shrewsbury School and then to Corpus Christi, Cambridge, where he read for an Ordinary Degree. He tried desperately hard to succeed, particularly at rowing. His brother Philip followed him to the university, distinguished himself quickly and casually on the river – he rowed in the Frost Fairbairn Pairs at Henley – and then, perhaps so as not to compete with Simon, turned increasingly to acting.

Their father died in 1922, before Simon was 21. In 1924 Mrs Yorke organised a coming of age party for Simon at Erddig, when photographs were taken of their close relations and of all the staff present, grouped on the garden steps. The photograph of the maids is a misleading one: most of the servants had to be specially hired for the occasion.

William Gittins, son of the estate foreman, was too young to fight in the First

110 Simon Yorke's coming of age party in 1924. His brother Philip is looking away from the photographer because he had just been stung in the eye by a bee

111 Staff at Simon Yorke's coming of age party. Most of the maids had to be hired specially for the occasion

World War and was groomed to succeed his father. During his last illness, Philip Yorke summoned him and talked at length about the future of Erddig and how essential it was that the running of the estate should be in reliable hands. He hoped very much that Willy would in due course prove himself an estate foreman and agent as respected as his father, somebody whom the young and inexperienced squire could rely on for sound advice.

Willy Gittins had to choose between continuing his family's tradition of loyal service to the Yorkes, or seizing the opportunities open after the war to a young man of energy and initiative. Much of what he saw at Erddig worried him. Just how blind the Yorkes were to what was going on was shown by their attitude to their head gardener, Albert Gillam. When his photograph was added in 1914 to the gallery of servants' portraits, Philip Yorke's paean was generous even by Erddig standards:

Here Albert Gillam we describe
Who hails from out a five-fold Tribe
Of Husbandmen who made their mark
Whose Father was the Patriarch.
Ne'er did our Borders look more gay
Than they have done beneath his sway,
And highly we appreciate
The one to whom this doth relate.

While well contented to fore-go
All competitions at a Show,
He on our home expends his art
Holding our interests at heart;
And, (which we most of all admire),
Scorning not work-a-day attire,
Assistant with un-sparing hand
The staff of men at his command.

While praising here his useful life,
No less deserving is his Wife.
She is of healing-arts possest
For such as are by ills distrest.
At Orchard lodge these two reside
Close to the Garden's southern side:
Where time is profitably spent
On Poultry-rearing arts intent.

When those who view our Gardens ask
Who undertakes the arduous task
Of tending all the spacious ground
And that which is within it found,

112　Albert Gillam, the last head gardener employed by the Yorkes

> To such we joyfully confess
> In Gillam we a prize possess,
> And, tho' but recent on the scene,
> He a great power for good has been.

In Gillam's estimation Erddig was finished. There was no real prospect either for the
house and garden or for its underpaid staff. He tried to interest young Gittins in having
a share in a deal he was making with a local tradesman for all the wheels of the seldom
used family carriages. Gillam advised the Yorkes that certain vehicles were no longer
safe. These were then taken out of commission and the wheels removed and sold.
Willy Gittins wanted to have nothing to do with this. He gave in his notice, set up a small
firm of his own and in due course was managing one of the most successful building
companies in the Wrexham area.

A letter of Simon's written to his mother just before the May Races in 1925 already shows the petulance with which he was to deal with his financial affairs, with such relatives as Albinia Lucy Cust, the authoress of *Chronicles of Erthig on the Dyke*, and with his Trustees:

> I am so glad you have been able to kill the worm in the State bed. Don't you think that it would be as well to get an expert to repair the Buhl, because it is pretty valuable stuff –
>
> I hope something will be done about my cash at or before the Trustee Meeting. It is a perfect disgrace not having been able to get my £500 when it was due last November. I wonder how they think I am going to live here – I hear we were overdrawn £1000 before last Rent Day; a pretty good start!
>
> . . . Alba is not in Cambridge, which is in a way a blessing. I called on George but found him out (another blessing).

One of the first things Simon did on assuming responsibility for Erddig was to fall out with the agent dealing with most of the tenanted farms. After much bitterness Simon broke with the firm completely, at just the time that some continuity might have helped with the running of the estate. His mother shared her worries about the future of Erddig with Philip, writing to him in 1929: 'Simon, as you know, is a funny boy and never could make up his mind.'

Philip meanwhile was preoccupied with the theatre. In 1930 he joined the Northampton Repertory Company, acting first in Somerset Maugham's *The Letter* and later as the second Chinese servant in *The Chinese Bungalow*. This final flowering of the Yorkes' penchant for *Chinoiserie* also found expression in his occasional appearances at church fêtes, dressed as a Chinaman and playing an euphonium. Although not a particularly good actor – he would plaintively ask, 'Oh, do I have to express passion?' – he was popular with audiences, largely because of his friendliness and quirky sense of humour.

Clearly better suited to the role of theatre manager, Philip persuaded Gwen Nelson and other Northampton Repertory friends to join a company of his own, the Country Theatre Players. They successfully toured several south coast resorts, until their bus finally broke down in Bexhill-on-Sea, which suited them so well that they played there for five years. In 1934 Philip organised a theatrical expedition to Canada, where he was immediately interned for failing to have the necessary papers in order. He wrote to the *Bexhill-on-Sea Observer* of his ordeal:

> The 'Immigration Hotel' consists of a spacious appartment some 56 yards in length, with fourteen tiers of spring mattresses, containing twelve beds apiece, but as there are only nine unwilling guests of various nationalities these 168 beds seem somewhat superfluous. They give one, however, that feeling of sufficiency which Wordsworth felt so strongly in King's College Chapel.

When not engaged in theatricals, he gave much of his time to church missionary

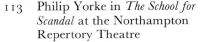

113   Philip Yorke in *The School for Scandal* at the Northampton Repertory Theatre

work, preaching sermons of unorthodox theology. He began to think seriously of taking Holy Orders and went so far as to enrol briefly at Ridley Hall, Cambridge. A favourite sermon, and one which he regarded as particularly important and original, concerned the life of St Mark. Other commentators had, he believed, failed to grasp the significance of the Gospel account of Mark losing his linen garment on the night of the Last Supper. It was surely more than probable, Philip suggested, that Mark's mother would have found another, ill-fitting pair of pyjamas for him, and that the figure later described as sitting by the deserted tomb in 'a long, white garment' was none other than the modest author of the Gospel. As far as Simon was concerned, Philip spent his time irresponsibly. They rarely met and Philip saw most of his mother when they went on holidays to Spain together.

The Second World War further weakened Erddig socially and physically. Simon had inherited none of the martial qualities that had won his great-uncle General John Yorke distinction in the Crimea, where he was wounded at Balaclava. One of Simon's first responsibilities as a soldier was for a large steam roller. Almost immediately and unaccountably it disappeared. Then Simon, always poorly sighted in one eye, lodged a splinter in the other while chopping wood. After a series of humiliations he was invalided out of the Army.

114　The final flowering of the
Yorkes' taste for *Chinoiserie*

Appearances now mattered still less than during the First War. An American camp occupied the park; birch and sycamore saplings grew in the rank grass of the formal garden. An old friend of Philip's Northampton Repertory days, Diana Carroll, visited Erddig on 20 February 1945 and wrote home with her impressions:

Great luck yesterday afternoon. Having failed to ring up Erthig as they're not on, being a lovely afternoon I thought I'd walk, & arrived before 3.30. Asked for Mr Yorke & was shown upstairs to Sitting-room on front (they enter by side door in basement) & there was Philip writing a letter, dressed as a sergeant. He sprang up saying what luck as he was going back to Northern Ireland that evening after leave, & almost any other day he hasn't been at home – but in London or elsewhere.

Mrs Yorke appeared soon, incredibly aged – I wouldn't have known her, not that I remember her well before. She is over 80 & very thin, & I think has had a stroke as the right side of her face looks stiff. But wonderfully on the spot, considering. . . . We had tea at 4, & then I walked to the station with Phil for the 5.8., he merely having a pack on his back. . . . He is in Army Education Corps & hasn't been abroad & I don't think will make any great efforts to take initiative about it. . . . Just like himself, with rather whimsical comments on things – says he thinks a little constructive work he can do is occasionally to put a non-left point of view over in talks & discussions. . . . Erthig is partly shut, under dust-sheets, but they've got two women I think, one an evacuee, & two men in the garden. What I saw of it looked rather overgrown, no wonder. . . .

Of all the changes brought to Erddig by the war, the most damaging proved to be the nationalisation of coal. At least as early as the eighteenth century, coal had been a valuable source of income for Erddig, with royalties from all minerals extracted from beneath the estate. A further benefit was in kind: most weeks a cart came from Bersham Colliery bringing coal for the house. In 1904, for instance, over 118 tons were consumed in the Hall itself, 29 tons in the sawmill, 10 tons in the stable yard, 18 tons in the laundry and over 4 tons in the blacksmith's shop. There was no question of the workings of the mine being taken underneath houses on the estate, and they were certainly never allowed to threaten Erddig itself. When in April 1914 the second Philip gave a speech at a supper for all his employees to celebrate twenty years of ownership of Erddig, the first person he singled out for praise was Mr Lloyd-Jones, mineral agent of the estate:

> All of you present know Erddig, as a beautiful spot on the Earth's Surface, but Mr. Lloyd-Jones can go a step further and tell us what it looks like beneath the surface. . . . For forty three years he has had to do with the mining interests of the Estate, for thirty eight of which he has been sole manager. He knows the underground workings, as it were, on a map, and except for his vigilance in taking care that the workings do not endanger the foundation of homesteads, it might be said that this house itself would fall as well as man.

In 1947 coal was nationalised. Officials of the Coal Board approached Simon to warn him that there was no exemption for buildings of historic interest, and of their intentions to take workings under Erddig itself. When Simon protested vehemently, he was told that there was absolutely nothing he could do. Thereafter he refused to have any dealings with the Coal Board. Their staff were not admitted either to assess damage, or to carry out running repairs. In the 1940s and 1950s faces were worked directly beneath the house itself; it fell 5 feet at one end and 3 feet 6 inches at the other. Its back was broken. The roof leads, instead of sloping to direct rain water away to the gutters and downpipes, now funnelled water towards the centre of the building, where it poured through into the state rooms. Dry rot would have spread more rapidly had it found sufficiently nourishing levels of humidity; but with virtually no heating at Erddig and with reasonable ventilation thanks to the broken windows, conditions were not ideal. Wet rot thrived, however.

Simon Yorke's solution to these problems was to give up any hope of saving the house and garden, and instead to buy outlying parcels of land whenever they came on the market. In this way he saw himself consolidating the estate, even if Erddig itself was doomed. There was no question of reroofing the sawmill building when it was burnt out by a disgruntled tenant. The other buildings around the outer stable yard were allowed to disintegrate gradually, until they were for the most part roofless shells enclosing chaotic piles of collapsed timbers, enveloped in ivy and brambles. Visitors were not allowed to see anything but the outward signs of decay. When the hunt met at Erddig, they were not admitted to the house and if lady members were bold enough to ask for a lavatory, they were brusquely directed to the bushes. The few neighbours who did penetrate were offered tea in the agent's office, off the basement passage.

115   The sawmill in
1973

There were long-standing rights of way in the park which enabled local people to enjoy walks to the Cup and Saucer and along the banks of the Clywedog. But wheeled vehicles of any sort, whether motor propelled or not, were strictly prohibited. Perambulators were no exception. If Simon Yorke met a car on one of the drives, it was ordered to leave without turning round, and had to back as far as the park gates, with the squire advancing as the vehicle retreated.

During the 1940s and 1950s Simon still kept one or two staff. His housekeeper, Miss Lloyd, 'lived in', usually with several dogs she had rescued from the local home for strays. One had cancerous sores which it rubbed on the walls of the back staircase; some were incontinent, and others, particularly Michael, bad-tempered and aggressive. When on one occasion the postman complained of being bitten, Simon found his manner offensive, and decided there and then that mail would never again be delivered by the Post Office, but would instead be left at one of the lodges.

Simon believed he had found a solution to servant problems when, after the war, he took on three German girls prepared to accept very low wages. For them, Erddig was a convenient means of setting up a boarding house in Llandudno. Shortly before they left, a procession of carpets and packing cases left the house through the outer stable yard. Subsequently the shelves for sheets and blankets in the housekeeper's room, neatly labelled in German, were found to be empty. The only carpets of quality left in the house were the vast and heavy Axminster in the Saloon, and the threadbare Feraghan in the Drawing Room.

Another solution to his staffing difficulties was to let houses on the estate on the understanding that part-time help would be given at Erddig. When the Hughes family moved into Bryn Goleu, earlier the home of Thomas and James Rogers, part of the

116   The haybarn in 1973

agreement was that Mr Hughes would run Scout camps in the park and Mrs Hughes would clean the house and prepare meals for Simon Yorke. His breakfast of bacon and eggs had to be ready on the Dining Room table promptly at 9 o'clock. It was normally eaten in solitude at about midday. Linda Hughes was allowed to pick fresh fruit in the garden, and in one year bottled twenty-eight pounds of blackberries, mostly gathered from what had been the parterre in front of the Saloon windows. The rest of the garden was scarcely penetrable.

Simon's isolation was further increased by his detestation of the telephone. Not only was an early telephone removed from Erddig, but Simon strongly discouraged any of his tenants from installing one, for fear that messages might be relayed to him.

117   The haybarn and outer stable yard in 1978

Similarly, tenants were expected to manage without cars, and in most cases without electricity. Isolation fed, and was fed by, Simon's sense of failure, his painful awareness of betraying his parents' longing for Erddig to be a family home for future generations of Yorkes.

Yet, paradoxically, Simon was to be vindicated. Somebody better able to cope with the problems facing him, a more energetic and optimistic owner, would have felt compelled to tackle Erddig's difficulties decisively and ruthlessly, selling off parts of the park, demolishing useless outbuildings and perhaps a wing or two of the main house, would have taken well-meaning advice to part with silver and furniture so that what was left could be properly looked after. Simon did the opposite. To the dismay of his friends he bought small parcels of outlying land to consolidate the estate; he refused to let the Coal Board carry out temporary repairs; he neither sold nor threw anything away. It was a policy which could only be justified on the grounds that if, by some miraculous turn of events, the house could be saved, nothing would have been lost irretrievably. However improbable, such a miracle was still a very remote possibility. As it happened, the inadequacies of the last Simon Yorke, like those of the first, served Erddig well.

On 6 May 1966 Simon set out to walk to Felin Puleston, taking a short cut across part of Manor Farm. He collapsed in the fields near Little Erddig. One of a party of girls riding their ponies down Hafod Road spotted his body lying face down in the grass.

He had never made a Will.

118 Philip Yorke

I I

Reconstruction

As soon as Philip heard the news of his brother's death he moved down from Pentre Clawdd and spent the night of 7 May sleeping on a chaise longue in the Drawing Room. Apart from Simon, Miss Lloyd had been the only other person living in the house, and she now locked herself into her bedroom at the far end of the south wing in the early evening. With no telephone or electricity, Erddig was appallingly vulnerable. But at least Philip had never been one for strict routines. Any attempt to plot his movements, to note when he might have his back turned, would certainly have ended in total frustration. The night of 8 May he spent in the Entrance Hall, the following night in the Saloon, the next in the Dining Room. An old camp bed from his Spanish touring days came into its own again. A .22 rifle and a box of ammunition were always to hand. Casual visitors to Erddig were reminded of these precautions by a scatter of ammunition across a writing desk in the Drawing Room, although closer examination would have revealed that the firing pin of the rifle was missing. In this nomadic way, and after a lapse of 200 years, the state apartments on the ground floor once again became a bedroom suite for the master of the house.

A table stacked with empty dog food tins was set up in the basement passage, with one end of a piece of string tied to the table leg and the other to a hook on the passage door. Any intruder who somehow managed to slip the bolts hastily put on all the basement doors would have been certain to topple the tins and set his dog Trixie barking furiously. Philip derived almost as much amusement from this contrivance as from his metal foil alarms, powered by torch batteries. These consisted of two pieces of metal foil placed on either side of a sheet of foam rubber with holes in it, concealed beneath a carpet. Any unwary footfall was enough to make the metal foil touch through the holes in the rubber, and a bell sounded shrilly. The device worked a treat, certainly as far as the detection of Philip's friends and official visitors was concerned. Finally a security firm was called in. The main doors were wired and the newly installed telephone linked directly to the local police station, where there were regular deliveries of crates of beer, by way of apology for the frequent false alarms. But the simple fact of being on the telephone must have made more difference to the safety of Erddig than all these precautions.

During the daytime, security was the special responsibility of Mr Boot, an octogenarian retired butcher from Wrexham. Mr Boot would usually arrive on a motorbicycle in the early afternoon. Although a small man, scarcely more than 5 foot 4 inches tall, his black leather suit, crash helmet and imposing white moustache lent something of the dignity of a First World War French general to his garden patrols. His other responsibility was the preparation of tea in the Servants' Hall, for which Mrs Boot baked special cakes. Instead of paying Mr Boot a regular wage, which would have meant forfeiting some of his pension, Philip bought Mrs Boot's cakes at what was by any normal standards a wildly inflated price. The arrangement worked to the satisfaction of both parties, even though a label from one of the cheaper Wrexham food stores was occasionally found on the underside of a cake wrapper. Mr Boot's duties at Erddig ended at about 6 o'clock. He would report all the shutters in the state rooms secure, would click his heels, salute and announce that he was leaving for home.

Unlike his brother, Philip was no recluse. The two visitors' books reappeared, one for guests staying overnight, the other for those who came only briefly. The pages began to fill. The only person to stay for any length of time was an old friend from Northampton Repertory days, Mr Bertram Heyhoe, or 'Hooha' as Philip called him. Still loyal to a theatrical way of life, though only an occasional radio or television part now came his way, Hooha was as lively in the small hours as he was dead to the world between about 3 a.m. and midday. When showing visitors round the house during the morning, Philip had to warn his guests before entering each bedroom that it might well be occupied. Hooha had at one time considered settling down in what had been the night nursery, which was painted lemon yellow throughout. But usually he preferred to sleep in each in turn of the several four-posters.

Miss Lloyd, the only member of the staff to 'live in' during Simon's last years, moved into a minute cottage at Plas Grono. Philip preferred to manage without resident staff and had help with cleaning from ladies living on the estate. Mrs Hughes, from Bryn Goleu, took it upon herself to rescue as much as possible from the ravages of furniture beetle. When she first came to the house in Simon's lifetime there was a layer of wood dust on the floor beneath many of the best pieces, almost all of which were of veneered or gilt softwood and therefore particularly vulnerable to beetle. Each spring, Mrs Hughes emptied can after can of Rentokil. Mrs Cheetham, whose husband Fred was working on the roofs, and Mrs Alman, who with Harry Alman had been on the staff forty years before, came in to help. The survival of much of Erddig's furniture is due to them.

Repairs to slates and leads, clearing drains or mending a fault in the ram (the water-powered pump which fed the tanks in the roof from the Black Brook) were Fred Cheetham's responsibility. After Fred and Philip had together cleared the central vista in the gardens, and ruthlessly cut back the Portugal laurels flanking the main walk, it was possible once again to see the canal from the house. For gardeners he brought in several sheep and a goat, each known by name, which would come running when summoned by Philip's bleat. The only snags were that they tended to bark the best trees, and, given half a chance, would graze the Saloon as well as the formal garden. A mirror in the Chinese Room was broken when on one occasion a sheep furiously butted its own reflection.

119   The garden and Mr Yorke's gardeners in 1973

Although Philip's emergency rescue operation had given the house a breathing space, its long term future was indeed gloomy. Everywhere there was disintegration and decay. A carefully phased restoration was bound to cost vastly more than could ever be found from the income of the estate, whatever the Coal Board might offer as compensation. There were no close relations to inherit. Trying to sort out the legal position was far from straightforward. Shortly after Simon's funeral, his agent, Mr Kitching, had asked the new squire about the terms of his father's Will, a document which Philip had no recollection of ever having seen. The omission had to be put right without delay. The two of them set off immediately for Marchwiel church, to check from his father's memorial when exactly he had died. Mr Kitching then wrote to Somerset House. The Will revealed that although Simon had been left the house and almost all the estate, Philip was to have inherited three-quarters of the contents. For forty-four years he had been unaware that he was the owner of one of the most valuable collections of furniture in the country.

In Mr Kitching Philip found an adviser whom he trusted and who was determined, although then in his 80s, to see Erddig rescued if at all possible. He would explain how the law stood on a certain question, often to Philip's intense annoyance. Their interviews would sometimes end with Philip leaving his office outraged at the

120   The Drawing Room in 1973, when Philip Yorke was using it as a bedroom. A rifle
and ammunition were to hand on the writing desk

injustice of some tax requirement and inclined to hold Mr Kitching personally
responsible. Then a few days later he would be back to apologise and seek his guidance.
A distant cousin, Ralph Edwards, was also able to advise Philip. Ralph Edwards had
known the house in the 1930s, when he was already working on his great *Dictionary of
English Furniture*, and he was in no doubt of the exceptional quality and importance of
the Erddig State Bed, the green lacquer chairs, and the girandoles in the Saloon. As
Keeper of the Department of Furniture at the Victoria and Albert Museum and
adviser on furniture to the Historic Buildings Council for Wales, he had close contacts
with the National Trust. On 7 June 1966 he wrote to the Trust's Representative:

> I have just had a letter from Philip Yorke about Erddig. . . . From P.Y's
> account it would seem to have degenerated greatly even from the deplorable
> state it was in when I stayed there between the wars. He had not decided what
> he wants to do about it – or indeed what can be done.

Encouraged by Ralph Edwards, in September 1966 Philip invited the Chairman
of the Trust's Committee for Wales, Colonel Wynne Finch, and two of the local staff to
visit the house to discuss its future. After picking their way as best they could round the

potholes in the entrance drive, the party arrived at the west front, to find the house apparently deserted. The doorbell could not be heard ringing (in fact it rang down in the Servants' Hall) and the surrounding dereliction did not encourage them to think it might be in working order. But they were eventually answered by the sound of hammering from the direction of the stables. Philip was repairing the roof with the help of Fred Cheetham and was busy nailing down slates and patching holes with pitch, which they were boiling up on a small portable gas ring. Philip introduced himself from the top of a ladder.

After a tour of the house, the party all had tea in the Dining Room. It was while the workings of the Trust were being explained to Philip that a rabbit, hotly pursued by a fox, bolted out of the dense mass of brambles and saplings that lay beyond the garden pavilions and rushed in and out of the overgrown bushes of box in what had once been the parterre.

The following month the possibility of the Trust's acquiring Erddig was reported to its Historic Buildings Committee. The minute of that meeting noted that:

> The Committee recommended acceptance and expressed the view that every effort should be made to save this remarkable house and its contents in spite of the severe financial problems which it is likely to pose.

Philip was advised to offer the house to the Treasury in payment of death duties on the understanding that it would be transferred to the National Trust, to have the contents valued so that the best pieces could be exempt from death duties, and give the Trust all the details of the workings of the estate so that a full financial report could be prepared. It all sounded so simple: far, far simpler than events were to prove.

Six and a half years were to go by before Erddig finally passed to the National Trust. That delay, which could so easily have proved disastrous, resulted first and foremost from the threat of renewed mining beneath the house. Philip had spoken more than once of oak panelling under stress groaning and even cracking at night, of the difficulty of opening doors which had swung freely the day before. More mining meant inevitably more damage from subsidence. It was scarcely encouraging when at a meeting in July 1969 the Coal Board told the Trust that there was a possibility of relieving some of the stress already in the building, by so planning the new areas of extraction that subsidence was concentrated at the northern end of the house, which had sunk a mere 3 feet, thereby bringing it down to the same level as the southern end, which had sunk 5 feet 6 inches. Whatever technical arguments the Coal Board put forward, their proposal sounded like bending a stick to weaken it, and then bending it back so that it finally snapped. The Trust had reluctantly to tell Philip that it would be unable to accept the property until mining beneath had finished. That, the Coal Board said, would not be until 1972.

Although it did not look as though the actual transfer could take place until 1972 at the very earliest, there were other aspects of the transaction to settle, once mining ceased, which might otherwise waste precious time. But one stumbling block after another was encountered. The initially cordial relations with Philip Yorke gradually soured, until eventually he referred among his friends to the 'National Distrust'. Part of the reason for this disenchantment was that the Trust had encouraged Philip to offer the house and the contents to the Treasury in payment of his brother's death duties. They would have then been transferred by the Treasury to the Trust. But the effect of this advice was to connect the Trust in Philip's mind with the Treasury and the government. With the Yorkes' intense distrust of officialdom, especially government officialdom, nothing could have been more calculated to tarnish the Trust's image. As it turned out the anguish was all unnecessary, because when the tax liability was eventually calculated, it was found that duty could be settled by offering no more than a few of the most valuable pieces of Erddig furniture.

The Trust was not alone in finding negotiations difficult. In 1968 Philip was almost persuaded by Ralph Edwards to get the furniture repaired. An application for a grant was actually made to the Historic Buildings Council which agreed to meet 80 per cent of the cost on the very reasonable condition that the furniture should be stored away from Erddig until the restoration of the building was complete. Realising how Philip might react to this stipulation – he was already desperately worried that the whole scheme was a ploy to whisk the most valuable things away from Erddig for the benefit of one of the national museums – Ralph Edwards frantically telephoned the Council's Chairman and persuaded him to drop the condition. Nevertheless, a year later Ralph Edwards had to write to a Trust colleague:

> I have done my level best (and so has the Chairman) to get him to consent to making a start on the furniture. . . . First he said he would, then he said he wouldn't; every letter he writes flatly contradicts the contents of the one before. . . . As he has now postponed the repair of the furniture indefinitely, I think that there is a strong chance that the HBC will not feel able to hold the offer of the grant open and that if the situation developed unexpectedly favourably he would have to apply again. The prospect of the Trust obtaining control of the house and its contents at present seems to me extremely remote.

Not the least of the Trust's frustrations was that it proved all but impossible to get hold of accurate figures for what the income and running costs of the estate might be. Part of the problem was that Philip continued to employ both his and his brother's agent, as well as both their respective solicitors, and none of them knew for certain what the others were advising. Philip wanted the actual transfer documents to be dealt with by his old friend Mr Templer, who had in the past handled all his theatrical business but had never been involved in Erddig affairs. Mr Templer heard of the offer of the house to the Treasury in payment of Simon's death duties two years after it had been made, and then only from the Trust. The firm of agents who had formerly looked after Philip's estate were retained, while Mr Kitching remained responsible for what had been Simon's. For months the Trust tried totally unsuccessfully to obtain a plan of a piece of land owned by Philip which he said he might or might not include in his offer. What finally arrived was a sketch by Philip a few inches square on the back of a scrap of paper.

Acting as emissary for the National Trust was sometimes far from easy. Before one meeting to try to agree exactly what parts of the estate should be offered to the Trust, Philip was found at the back door, wheeling out the body of one of his 'gardeners' in a barrow. A pack of stray dogs had found their way into the garden and had driven the dozen or so sheep into a walled corner. There they had been mauled and killed. Philip buried the sheep himself, staining his shirt with blood from their torn throats. It was not an afternoon for talking about the National Trust.

Most visits, however, were as amusing as they were unfruitful. There was always somewhere in the attics or outhouses to be explored with Philip for the first time, some new document or report in the press which gave a completely new complexion to the whole future of Erddig. The more one knew the place, the more mesmerising it became. Philip made the most of its theatrical qualities, delighting in the bizarre devices he rigged up. Gas lights rescued from a refuse tip on the estate and fed from a Calor gas cylinder were strung across the ceiling of the Servants' Hall. In the Drawing Room similar attachments were screwed to a plank laid along James Wyatt's chimney piece, with two of the finest Erddig silver salvers placed behind the filaments in imitation of eighteenth century girandoles, to reflect the light.

When visitors were shown the stable yard, Philip gave the impression of being scarcely aware of its dereliction. Wrexham youths had used the windows for target practice and had peppered their glass with air gun pellets. Undergrowth engulfed a Volkswagen, one of several abandoned around the stables. It was impossible to make out which was which of the carts and carriages jammed into the coach house. The 1907 Rover was coated with grime, its hood decayed to the skeleton of the framework, its upholstery rotten and splitting. 'We haven't quite got round to having this one put right yet', was Philip's comment on opening the garage door. When four years later he heard that the Trust was having it restored he was pleased: 'Yes, the second gear *was* giving a little trouble.'

In February 1970 the Trust produced a financial report on the cost of restoring Erddig and maintaining it in perpetuity. The figure of £800,000 finally proposed for an endowment had necessarily to be approximate (and in fact proved to be a serious underestimate). But understandably enough, Philip's reaction was at first incredulous, and then bitter. He commented in detail on the suggested expenditure, singling out for particularly strong criticism the proposition that two of the lodges should be restored and occupied by staff as some protection against the vandalism prevalent in the Wrexham area:

> My brother always liked the idea of a lodge-keeper smoothing out a clean apron whenever she heard the sound of horses' hoofs and dropping a curtsey as the carriage went by, but in these days a cattle grid is regarded as more practical.

The idea of putting Erddig on the mains appealed still less:

> I know little of main water excepting that it is not as cold as ours and the

121   Philip Yorke in the Drawing Room, a few months before he gave Erddig away,
reading by improvised gas lighting, reflected in eighteenth century silver salvers

farmers don't like it for cooling the milk. It often has a brown colour and is
largely made up of disinfectants.

The Trust was accused of 'carefree abandonment of reason and accuracy when dealing
with other people's money'. There was ominous talk of his giving everything to the
Welsh Nationalists, a threat which had to be taken seriously because Philip had already
left Erddig to them in his Will, should the National Trust not accept it. He even went so
far as to let the Trust see a copy of a letter he proposed sending to the *Wrexham Leader*,
warning that in view of the delays, the Trust would have to make up its mind whether
to accept the offer by June 1970 at the latest. Only after frantic appeals from his

122 The stable yard in 1973

123 The stable yard in 1978

solicitor was the letter finally withdrawn. At the root of Philip's fears was the thought that he might die before a decision could be reached: he had already had a stroke and had not expected to outlive his brother.

By 1970, the tide seemed to be turning at last. At a meeting with the Coal Board in November the Trust was told that the main shafts beneath Erddig had run into faulting. No further mining was contemplated. An independent firm of mining consultants was commissioned to report on the dangers of future subsidence and their report was reasonably reassuring. Enough time had elapsed since the last large scale extraction of coal from beneath the house for major settlement to have finished, although some further damage would take place while stresses already in the structure worked themselves out. But the report warned that a geological fault which had put a stop to mining might shift of its own accord and trigger off movement outside the normal pattern of subsidence. That was a chance which the Trust had to take, and still takes. The Coal Board agreed to the consultants' recommendation that the area below Erddig needed to support the house should be defined and that there should be no more mining within that pillar of support. There was little objection to the proposal at the time, as the faulting encountered made it seem unlikely that mining would ever be practicable in that area again. The implications for the colliery however were grave. The area suitable for mining from Bersham was so reduced that there was a danger that the pit might well be uneconomic in future, and if it closed, 600 men would lose their jobs. Only later did the Coal Board discover that the very rich coal deposits directly beneath Erddig could have been safely extracted by running their faces in from a different direction; but by then they were committed to not violating the pillar of support. Compensation was to be generous. Philip wrote on 23 February 1972:

> We had a big day yesterday with the Coal Board, ... They are prepared to give us £95,000 to repair the main part of the house with about £30,000 more for the roof.
>
> I said it was not enough as they have left out one or two parts of Coal Board damage and they will do the garden wall and water in addition. I feel rather inclined to accept the money and go for a holiday.

The finances of Erddig began to take on a new complexion at about the time that the problems over future mining were being resolved. It had always been understood that money would have to be raised by selling off an area of some sixty acres with outline building consent, on the Wrexham side of the estate. With the building boom of the early 1970s, the value of that land changed dramatically. What had been worth little more than £1,000 an acre in 1966, was by 1970 estimated to be worth between £3,000 and £4,000 an acre. While the succeeding months saw frustration and resentment over the numerous delays, they also saw the astonishing explosion in land prices that was to give Erddig a secure financial future. By October 1972 the land at Coed-y-Glyn and the Ithens could reasonably be expected to fetch £9,000 an acre. Philip was not slow to appreciate that the boom in land prices made a great deal of difference to the Trust's financial report, and he wrote accordingly on 8 March 1972:

124   The family Rover, a 1907
model bought from a
chimney sweep in the 1920s.
By 1973 Philip Yorke
acknowledged that 'the
second gear *was* giving a
little trouble'

It is now pretty well established that building land round about Wrexham has recently jumped to somewhere between £10,000 and £20,000 per acre according to its desirability. . . . Erddig has now become a centre for people coming to try and obtain sites to build bungalows, or to acquire houses. This is rather different from when I offered the Erddig estate to the Trust about six years ago; and at that time I thought that the value of the land was insufficient for you to pursue your demands, so I added my own personal estates to build up the resources.

I now intend to subtract Pentreclawdd from the Erddig offer, so that my future will not be entirely in your hands.

If the house at Pentreclawdd is still desirable to you to house Erddig furniture while Erddig is being restored, it will still be available.

The Trust's Historic Buildings Secretary replied that he found this 'perfectly understandable', but stressed that until exactly what was on offer was clearly shown on a map, it would not be possible to revise the financial report, and this in turn would mean yet more delay.

At the end of the summer of 1972 the point had at last been reached when it was realistic to draw up a Deed of Gift. Just as the Deed was being drafted, Mr Templer, Philip's solicitor, had to go into hospital for a major operation which would clearly leave him unfit for work for several months. Putting a signature to a Deed of Gift

125   The Rover in 1978

making over what had been his family home for 250 years was going to be difficult enough. Philip had to make that decision without having ever met the solicitor now advising him.

It came as no surprise when Philip refused to sign the Deed when first presented to him on 8 February 1973. Partly to be at hand to try to explain some of the points worrying Philip in the Deed, partly to work on the collection of documents with the Trust's Research Adviser, Gervase Jackson-Stops, I spent the best part of a fortnight in mid-February staying at Erddig. Perhaps those days of trying desperately to keep warm in the Dining Room, burrowing around in bundle after bundle of letters and bills, and transcribing the most important information into a card index, may have helped to convince Philip that the National Trust was not remote and impersonal, and that we cared deeply about Erddig's future. By working through all the documents, we hoped to gather together every scrap of evidence that might have a bearing on the restoration of the house and how it could be shown to the public. Philip was as excited by our discoveries as we were ourselves. He would creep into the Dining Room with a fresh supply of logs for the fire, or paraffin for the stoves, trying not to disturb us. Then in the early afternoon when it was no longer possible to work by daylight, he would go off to the scullery to start the generator, jumping up and down on the starting handle and pouring petrol over the ignition mechanism. The knowledge that he had been successful filtered through to the Dining Room when a brass standard lamp, its cracked plastic shade decorated with goldfish, flickered into life; and a moment or two later the sound of Philip's two television sets, tuned into different programmes, could be heard from the Drawing Room.

Sadly, the discovery which pleased Philip most turned out to be a disappointment. He had always believed the family tradition that Gainsborough had touched up the early eighteenth century portrait of John Meller while working at Erddig on the first Philip Yorke's portrait, and he was thrilled when we found conclusive proof of this in one of Philip's notebooks: 'Gainsbro': New dressing Mr. Meller's pict.^{re} and servant, £5. 10. 0.' The entry had us all leaping to the conclusion that Gainsborough had touched up not only the picture of Meller, but also one of the servants' portraits. Philip was sure that he detected some particularly fine painting in Jane Ebbrell's head-dress. Only later we found in a second notebook:

Last pay.^t of my own Picture   31.10.0
For new dressing Mr Meller's ditto   5.5.0.
Present to servt.   0.5.0.

We had also forgotten that Gainsborough came to Erddig in 1779, fourteen years before Jane Ebbrell's portrait was painted.

The memory of cold and of candlelight must have stayed with many winter visitors to Erddig. Candlelight animated the gilt furniture, particularly mirrors, to superb effect. One night, in the small hours, I wandered about the house with a candle, looking for a tap without the label 'Not Drinking Water', and trying desperately to spot which doors were wired and therefore on the alarm system. The expedition ended in failure and near disaster: at the bottom of the stairs, I found myself confronted by an extremely suspicious though mercifully silent Trixie. My flickering candle animated the exotic figures of the Soho tapestry and they danced as they never did in daylight.

The cold was also a revelation. Snow somehow managed to force its way round or under the sash windows, and in the morning lay unmelted by my bedside. Philip did much of the essential housemaids' work. Electric heaters, powered by the generator, were put in our sleeping bags in the early evening. At about 9 o'clock the next morning he brought hot water for shaving and let us know that the gas for the shower – one of his proudest devices – had been lit.

With the last Philip's shower, Erddig's bathing and plumbing reached the acme of discomfort. In the mid-eighteenth century there had been a bath house in the park, fed by the Black Brook. It was not so elegant as that at Wynnstay, which had a Tuscan portico flanked by niches with eared architraves, or so substantial as the Cold Bath at Chirk, which was a two storey building with a hipped roof, clearly labelled in Badeslade's engraving of 1738 of the castle. A letter of 1778 from the first Philip to his agent suggests that the Erddig bath was much in demand:

I would have a Vellum Inscription put to the Bath Key as follows – Every person who shall borrow this key, is desired to return it immediately to the House; and I desire that this key may hang upon one certain nail in your second Room, Old Stone Parlour: If there were two keys to the Bath, one might be subject to perpetual Interruption.

126 A nineteenth century
shower, with pipes
and a pump to
circulate the water

During the nineteenth century the bath house was abandoned and hip baths in front of bedroom fires became established ritual. There was also an ingenious portable shower, no less demanding of staff time, which released hot water from a cylindrical tank supported on pipes, painted to look like bamboo and designed to circulate water pumped up from a catchment tray. This was in turn superseded when the last squire found himself his own maid-of-all-work. The shower Philip rigged up in the late 1960s consisted of a tank full of water placed on a high table and heated from beneath by a portable gas ring. When the water was hot enough, a rubber hose was fitted to the tank and then allowed to hang over a length of string tied above the bath and draped with polythene sheeting. Water dribbled out just long enough for a hasty wash, while the polythene confined splashes to the area of the bath. Philip's attempts to keep mattresses in the house free from damp were not always so successful. Mrs Hughes once confided that the bed in which I had been sleeping stood beneath a leak in the roof and water had been dripping through the tester the week before. Perhaps another Philip Yorke, nearly two centuries earlier, had that very bed in mind when he urged John Caesar to take every precaution against giving his guests damp mattresses.

On 16 February a revised Deed of Gift was again put before Philip and again he

127 Philip Yorke's
shower. The tank
was heated by a
Calor gas ring and
the water then
allowed to trickle
down a rubber tube
threaded through the
loops on the washing
line

found he could not bring himself to sign it. Several points were still worrying him: in particular, that the Trust could not be relied on to keep the Erddig collections together in the house, or if it did, that furniture might be brought in from elsewhere; and that the tradition of allowing the Boy Scouts and the local hunt to use the park might not be continued. On that occasion the Trust's solicitor had to leave empty handed. Aware of the element of blackmail, Gervase and I explained that work on the historical documents would have to wait until the future of the house was finally resolved.

It was the middle of March before a new Memorandum of Wishes had been drawn up. Some of the clauses added to the original transfer documents, worked out with the help of Philip's advisers, raised legal eyebrows, but seemed to satisfy Philip. What we all hoped was to be our final meeting was fixed for 6.30 p.m. on 14 March. The evening before, Philip, Gervase and I went to the Wrexham cinema – once the theatre where Philip's repertory company had put on *Rebecca* – to see *Clockwork Orange*. Perhaps this brutal film weakened his resistance the next day.

On the evening of 14 March 1973 Philip signed the three principal legal documents giving Erddig to the National Trust the moment they were put in front of him. The event was recorded in the visitors' book used by Queen Mary when she came to Erddig. Then one of Philip's executors suggested that we should go off for a celebratory drink. This seemed rather an affront to Philip's teetotalism, so instead we paid a more than usually extravagant trip to a Chinese restaurant, ordering every vegetarian dish we could find on the menu: king prawns, tomatoes, bamboo shoots and mushrooms in every conceivable combination. In the general excitement of our return I strayed into the Dining Room and set the alarm bells pealing. We were joined with amazing promptness by three Panda cars full of police. In the glare of their searchlights we all gathered on the entrance steps to hear Philip explain that false alarms were no longer his responsibility. He had just given Erddig away.

Four months later, in June, the sixty acres on the Wrexham edge of the estate were auctioned. The Trust found itself with an endowment of over a million pounds. Within a year the property market had collapsed and Development Land Tax, which would have drastically reduced the National Trust's profits from the sale, was on the Statute Book.

The repair of Erddig was as much a matter of reviving a community of staff, as it was of physical reconstruction. Ted Jones, who had the small-holding at Little Erddig and whose cattle grazed the park, was persuaded to leave his job with the Council to become estate foreman. Thirty years before he had helped John Jones plough up the kitchen garden. Now he and his team of three others set about the task of clearing the formal garden and making a start on half a century's backlog of estate repairs. Although Harry Alman and Fred Cheetham had known Erddig for years and had worked for Philip, they needed a younger man. Barry Roberts was recruited from the local fire service and came to live at Bryn Goleu Lodge. While the others were working with chain saws and burning brash, the enormous Barry could pick up and stack whole lengths of tree trunk.

128   Barry Roberts clearing the garden in 1974

129   The Garden House in 1973

When Albert Gillam was photographed outside the Garden House in 1914, the building was a model of trimness. By the 1950s it was empty and decaying fast. Then in the 1960s it once again became the home of Erddig's gardeners, this time Philip's sheep and goats. Animals wandered in and out; a few traces of Chinese wallpaper hung in tatters from the wall, the roof was collapsing, the whole structure was dangerous. The greenhouses outside its front door were completely engulfed in overgrown yews, with sycamore saplings pushing their way up through the broken glass. An ancient vine struggled to hold its own in a jungle of brambles and nettles.

The arrival of Mike Snowden and his family brought back to Erddig a gardener who is as highly skilled and dedicated as any of his predecessors. They moved into the Garden House after it had been reroofed and rebuilt internally. Mike had been lured

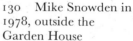

130   Mike Snowden in 1978, outside the Garden House

away from the National Trust's great garden at Bodnant, where he had been Head Plantsman. While Erddig's canal and pool were being dredged and reveted, he supervised the levelling and nourishing of the areas that had been cleared, at the same time bringing on in the nursery the trees, shrubs and plants that would eventually furnish the formal garden. A young fox, not very different in colour from Mike's Darwinian beard, trotted along beside him as he worked. His assistant gardener, Len Archer, re-established fantails in the restored dovecot, and like an earlier Erddig gardener, George Roberts, made himself responsible for controlling their numbers and feeding them. Before long Erddig was supplying other National Trust properties with fantails.

Philip's part-time house staff continued to clean, dust and polish, despite all the

131   The parterre in about 1900

132   The garden, 1974

133   The garden, 1978

chaos caused by repair work. Just as Erddig had been built by local men, so the firms responsible for its repair were local. The architect, Robert Heaton, had his office in Wrexham. Herbert Huxley lived nearby. As well as managing a highly skilled small building firm, he was his own head joiner. Other joinery work was carried out by Peter Smith. Both the blacksmith's shop and the joiners' shop were reroofed and brought back into commission. During the winter months estate timber was once again cut up in the sawmill building.

The craftsmen and women brought in to repair furniture, textiles and wallpapers set up their own workshops in the attics and in the north wing. Guidance was readily available from John Fowler, who had championed the rescue of Erddig after visiting it in 1971 and whose experience of a lifetime's work in country houses was to be invaluable. Graham Carr's skill in piecing together and repainting missing sections of the Chinese papers would have delighted Betty Ratcliffe. So too would Caroline Fellowes's painstaking cleaning of the suite of silvered chairs from the Saloon. Betty surely would have approved the laborious couching down of innumerable broken threads in the damask curtains by over 130 local volunteer needlewomen under the supervision of Sheila Stainton. The cleaning and cataloguing of the Library organised by Rosalind Powell-Jones would have satisfied even the meticulous John Meller.

134 Graham Carr remounting the eighteenth century Chinese painted panels in the Chinese Room, after dirt and stains had been removed

135 Jigsaw puzzles in the State Bedroom

136 The Library

137 The Dining Room

In 1974 the Victoria and Albert Museum mounted an exhibition called 'The Destruction of the Country House'. Two of the servants' portraits from Erddig and a mass of photographs were included, to illustrate how one house had been saved from the fate of the 170 demolished since the Second World War. All the staff at Erddig who wanted to see the exhibition came down by coach, some of them making their first visit to London. From the estate staff there were Barry Roberts and Ted Jones and his wife. Mike and June Snowden came and from among the house staff Mrs Hughes, Mrs Alman and Mrs Cheetham. After John Hardy of the Museum's Department of Furniture had spoken to them about the restoration of the State Bed, Philip took a party across the road to the Science Museum. Rather unsatisfactorily, they found that the front wheel of the penny-farthing there was a full half inch wider than any of those at Erddig.

Bibliography and Notes

GENERAL

Most of the documents quoted in this book are among the Erddig papers deposited at the Clwyd County Record Office at Hawarden. I have given their catalogue reference numbers at the beginning of the notes on each chapter. A few papers have been retained at Erddig for public exhibition. Some of the documents have already been published in Albinia Lucy Cust's *Chronicles of Erthig on the Dyke* (2 vols, London, John Lane, 1914). Wherever she altered the punctuation, spelling or whole words and sentences, I have reverted to what I believe to have been the original. The condition of a few documents has deteriorated in the last half century, and where these are no longer legible, her transcriptions remain indispensable.

The first Philip Yorke's poems about his staff I have quoted from his *Crude Ditties* (Wrexham, 1802), rather than the versions on the portraits, which were inaccurately touched up when the pictures were restored many years ago. I have not altered the spelling and punctuation of the second Philip Yorke's verse, except where his typewriter was obviously unco-operative.

For the later history of the house, I have relied to a large extent on the information given me by the late Philip Yorke. Where I have been able to cross-check his accounts, I have found that he was ready to improvise when it came to dates and chronologies, but that his memory for other details was usually reliable.

INTRODUCTION

Erddig MSS. 1126, 563.

Burnett, John, *Useful Toil*, London, Allen Lane, 1974.

Franklin, Jill, 'Troops of servants: labour and planning in the country house 1840–1914', in *Victorian Studies*, vol. XIX, no. 2, December 1975.

Girouard, Mark, *Life in the English Country House, A Social and Architectural History*, New Haven and London, Yale University Press, 1978. See also Lawrence Stone's review, 'On the grand scale', in *The Times Literary Supplement*, no. 3,997, 10 November 1978.

Howell, David, *Land and People in Nineteenth Century Wales*, London, Routledge & Kegan Paul, 1978.

McBride, Theresa M., *The Domestic Revolution*,

The Modernisation of Household Service in England and France 1820–1920, London, Croom Helm, 1976.

'Nimrod' (Charles Apperley), *My Life and Times*, ed. E. D. Cuming, London, William Blackwood, 1927, pp. 13–14.

1 SETTING UP

Erddig mss. 539, 1542/16, 1542/68, 549, 1431, 368, 547, 1542/79, 1542/106, 280, 1542/66, 869

Hardy, John, Lander, Sheila, and Wright, Charles D., *A State Bed from Erddig*, London, Victoria and Albert Museum, 1972.

Loveday, John, *Diary of a Tour in 1732*, Williamscote, 1890, pp. 79–81.

Waterson, Merlin, 'Elihu Yale', in *Smithsonian*, vol. 8, no. 7, October 1977.

2 ELIZABETH RATCLIFFE, LADY'S MAID

Erddig mss. 895, 888, 905, 889, 901, 385, 1542/238

Fowler, John and Cornforth, John, *English Decoration in the 18th Century*, London, Barrie & Jenkins, 1974, especially chapter 9, Ladies' Amusements.

Harris, John, *Gardens of Delight, the Art of Thomas Robins*, London, RIBA exhibition catalogue, 1975.

Waterson, Merlin, 'Elizabeth Ratcliffe: an artistic lady's maid' in *Apollo*, vol. CVIII, no. 197, July 1978.

Gervase Jackson-Stops drew my attention to the references to Elizabeth Ratcliffe in Lady Sykes's Journal, now at Sledmere.

3 CHIPS FROM THE BLOCK

Erddig mss. 1542/17, 1432, 394, 424, 563, 1542/215, 1092.

For information about the Rogers family and for permission to quote from their letters and papers I am indebted to Mrs Dennis Jones, the great-great-granddaughter of Thomas Rogers. Mr William Gittins has been similarly generous with information about his family, particularly his father.

Manuscript copies of the songs composed by Reginald Heber for the meetings of The Ancient Society of Royal British Bowmen were passed on to me by the Marquess of Anglesey and have now been deposited in the Clwyd County Record Office.

4 HOUSEKEEPERS, COOKS AND NANNIES

Erddig mss. 888, 280, 429, 284, 1069, 1022.

Philip Yorke retained his mother's diaries when the other Erddig papers were given to the National Trust, but he kindly made them available to me shortly before he died and they will, in due course, join the other papers at Hawarden. He also told me about Lucy Hitchman and took me to see her grave at Esclusham. Her letters to Simon and Philip are now at Hawarden, but have not yet been catalogued.

5 SPIDER-BRUSHERS TO THE MASTER

Erddig mss. 280, 563, 394, 293, 467.

The details of Bessie Gittins's and Edith Haycock's work at Erddig were tape-recorded in February 1977. Maggie Roberts kindly sent me her written accounts in 1975.

6 HARMONIOUS BLACK-SMITHS

Erddig mss. 539, 547, 278, 307.

Ifor Edwards, 'Robert Davies of Croes Foel, Bersham' in *Denbighshire Historical Society Transactions*, vol. 6, 1957.

Ifor Edwards, *Davies Brothers Gatesmiths*,

Eighteenth Century Wrought Ironwork in Wales, Cardiff, Welsh Arts Council exhibition catalogue, 1977.

7   WOODS AND WOODMEN

Erddig MSS. 563, 968, 283, 1542/219.

'Nimrod' (Charles Apperley), *My Life and Times*, ed. E. D. Cuming, London, William Blackwood, 1927, p. 58.
The Torrington Diaries, ed. C. Bryn Andrews, London, Eyre & Spottiswoode, 1934, pp. 174–5.

8   GARDENS AND GARDENERS RUN TO SEED

Erddig MSS. 539, 547, 277, 875, 556, 563, 1542/169, 1542/116, 984, 1134.

9   LIVERIED STAFF

Erddig MSS. 901, 563, 385, 280, 469.

F. L. Klingender, 'The portraits in the Servants' Hall', in *Picture Post*, 24 December 1943, pp. 22–4.
'Nimrod' (Charles Apperley), *My Life and Times*, ed. E. D. Cuming, London, William Blackwood, 1927, pp. 58–9.
I am grateful to Mrs Dennis Jones for the transcription of the letter from John Wilde, which was preserved amongst Harriet Rogers's papers.

The account of Dickinson's death is in Louisa Yorke's notes on the house, written into a volume of her husband's poems.
Frank Lovett's letters, kindly given to me by his son, Wing Commander F. W. Lovett, have now been deposited at Hawarden.

10   FAILURES

Erddig MSS. 556, 888, 563, 512, 1261.

Howard Knox-Mawer, 'Last days of Erthig', in *Anglo-Welsh Review*, Tenby, Five Arches Press, vol. 26, no. 57, Autumn 1976, pp. 70–176.
I am grateful to Philip Yorke and Bessie Gittins for their recollections of the Penketh case. For crimes committed by domestic servants see Theresa M. McBride, *The Domestic Revolution, The Modernisation of Household Service in England and France 1820–1920*, London, Croom Helm, 1976, pp. 106–7 and Pamela Horn, *The Rise and Fall of the Victorian Servant*, Dublin, Gill & Macmillan, 1975, pp. 133–48.
Miss Diana Carroll kindly wrote to me at length about the months Philip Yorke spent with the Northampton Repertory Theatre. For details of Simon Yorke's war experiences I am indebted to Lt-Col. H. M. C. Jones-Mortimer.

11   RECONSTRUCTION

Erddig MSS. 385, 563.

This chapter is largely based on National Trust files and my notebooks of 1971–8. Mr John Tetley and Mr H. V. Kitching kindly gave information about events at Erddig between 1966 and 1971.

Index

Accounts, *see* Estate accounts
Achievements (heraldic), *see*
   Hatchments
Acrefair, Clwyd, 95
Adam, Robert, 67
Agents: John Caesar the elder, 47,
   50, 51, 56, 101, 102, 135, 137,
   138, 139, 140, 152, 153, 154, 169,
   187, 188, 189, 192, 219; John
   Caesar the younger, 187, 188,
   189, 190; W. N. Capper, 129;
   Mr Hughes, 64, 90; Richard
   Jones, 26, 27, 76, 121, 150; John
   Williams, 22, 76
Agent's office, *see* Domestic offices
Aitkin, Mr, gardener, 162
Ale, 22, 105, 141, 155, 189, 192
Allen, Edward, 170
Alman, Harry, 207, 221
Alman, Mrs, wife of Harry, 207,
   228
Alport, Mr, 121
Alscot Park, Worcs., 44
Alsop, George, 58
Ancient Society of Royal British
   Bowmen, the, 68, 232
Anne, Queen, 52
Apperley, Charles ('Nimrod'), 14,
   58, 134, 168, 170
Apperley, Thomas, 14, 58
Archer, Len, 223
Archery, *see* Ancient Society of
   Royal British Bowmen
Army, life in during First World
   War, 162, 173, 178–9, 181
Attics, 13, 30, 56, 67, 98–9, 102,
   112, 116, Plates 57, 65; *cf.*
   Bedrooms

Badeslade, Thomas, 150, 218, Plate
   94; print of Erddig by 55, 121,
   134, 150, 158, Plates 70, 93
Bakehouse, *see* Domestic offices
Baker, Arthur, Plate 10

Balaclava, Crimea, 198
Baldry, G., Plate 5
Bangor, Gwynedd, 162
Banqueting houses, 55, 56
Baptism, of adults, 31
Barmouth, Gwynedd, 86
Barnes, Edward, 59, 76, 142–3, 145,
   Plate 86
Basement passage, *see* Domestic
   offices
Bath, Som., 38, 40, 47, 51, 52
Baths: bath house, 218–19; hip
   baths, 112, 219; showers, 218–19,
   Plates 126, 127
Bedrooms, 29, 98, 139; of staff, 13,
   30, 98–9, 102, 112, 116, Plate 57;
   State Bedroom, the, 14, 23, 29,
   44, 46, Plates 12, 13, 135
Beds and bedding, 27, 29–30, 56,
   98–9, 112, 139, Plate 57; State
   Bed, the, 27, 29, 197, 209, 228,
   Plate 13
Bee-keeping, 66, 158–9
Beeton, Isabella, 11, 85, 111
Belchier, John, 29
Belgium, 179
Belton, Lincs., 41, 136
Bersham, Clwyd, 121, 215; colliery,
   200
Bevan, Betty, 38, 101
Bexhill-on-Sea, Sussex, 197
Bicycles, 16, 88–9, 90, 228, Plates
   53, 118
Bicycling, 88–9, 90, 119
Billiard room, the, 13, 176
Billot, Lady, 26
Birch, Mr, coachman, 26, 52, 168
Birkenhead, 84
Black Brook, Clwyd, 95, 207, 218;
   diversion of, 135; waterfalls in
   valley of, 138
Blacksmiths, 121–31; Alan Knight,
   130; John Williams, 56; William
   Williams, 122–4, Plates 71, 72;
   Joseph Wright, 121, 124–6,

129–30, Plates 69, 73, 74
Blacksmith's shop, 69, 124, 130,
   200, 225, Plate 79
Blashfield's, fountain suppliers, 156
Blinds, *see* Furnishings
Boathouse, *see* Garden, features of
Bodnant, Gwynedd, 223
Book of Household Management, The,
   11, 111
Boot, Henry, 206, 207
Boot, Mrs, wife of Henry, 206, 207
Boulle (buhl), 29, 197
Boulter, Matilda, 112, Plate 10
Bow Meetings, *see* Ancient Society
   of Royal British Bowmen
Brew house, *see* Domestic offices
Bricklayers, 27; Jonathan Davis,
   Plate 10; Walter Davis, Plate 10
Bristol, Avon, 41
Brown, Miss, 90, 91, 92, 113–14,
   118, 193, Plate 54
Brown, Lancelot ('Capability'), 153
Brownlow, Frances, Lady, 58
Bryden, Dr, 112
Bryn Goleu, Wrexham, Clwyd, 64,
   201; lodge at, 221
Building industry: booms and
   recessions in, 10, 69, 215–16
Butler, Lady, 112
Butlers, 13, 173; duties of, 175–6;
   John Davies, 174; George
   Dickinson, 13, 173, 174, Plates
   64, 103; John Jones, 26, 76;
   Frank Lovett, 176, 177–82, 191,
   233, Plate 105; Thomas Murray,
   172–3; Thomas Newcome,
   169; Frederick Otley, 173;
   Williams, 192; Mr Wooton, 11,
   Plate 10
Butler's pantry, *see* Domestic offices

Cabinet makers, 24, 27, 43, 67;
   John Belchier, 29; Thomas
   Fentham, 44, 46, Plates 31, 35;
   John Linnell, 44

Caesar, John the elder, 47, 50, 51, 56, 101, 102, 135, 137, 138, 139, 140, 152, 153, 154, 169, 187, 188, 189, 192, 219
Caesar, John the younger, 187, 188, 189, 190
Caesar, Margaret, 188
Caesar, Nelly, 51
Caffoy, *see* Textiles
Cairo, Egypt, 172
Calcutta, India, 68
Calico, *see* Textiles
Cambridge, 197; Corpus Christi College, 193; King's College Chapel, 197; Ridley Hall, 198
Campbell family, 87, 88
Campion, Ambrose, 169
Canada, 105, 118, 197
Canal, the, *see* Garden, features of
Capper, Mr W. N., 129
Carmody, Mr, 138
Carpenters, 27, 55–75, 170; William Davies, 56; William Gittins, 64, 68, 69–72, 73, 113, 115, 129, 130, 146, 164, 165, Plates 45, 46; Willy Gittins, 69, 73, 193, 195, 196; Richard Hughes, 56; John Jones (1779), 56; John Jones (1911), 64–7, 69, 95, 165, Plates 36, 43, repairs done by, 67, 68, Plate 44; Robert Jones, 56; Charles Prince, 56; Edward Prince, 56–7, 59, *Frontispiece*; John Prince, 55, 56; James Rogers, 60, 63, 64, 201, Plate 42; Philip Rogers, 55, 56; Thomas Rogers, 12, 56, 59–60, 63, 82, 201, Plates 37, 38, 39; tools used by, Plates 38, 39; William Rogers, 56; Peter Smith, 225, Plate 41; . . . Williams, Plate 10
Carpentry tools, 60, 69, Plate 38
Carpets, *see* Furnishings
Carr, Graham, 225, Plate 134
Carroll, Diana, 199
Cars, *see* Motor Cars
Carving, 44
Cathedral Aisle, the, *see* Woods, features of
Cefn, Clwyd, quarries, 10
Cellar, *see* Domestic offices
Chairs, 24, 29, 30, 43, 44, 49, 77, 98, 99, 209, 225, Plate 21
Challinder, Mr, 77
Chambers, William, 38
Chancery: Court of, 22; records of, 22: Masters in, 23, 24
Chapel, the, 29, 88, 113, Plate 23
Chatsworth, Derb., 10
Cheese room, *see* Domestic offices
Cheetham, Fred, 207, 210, 221
Cheetham, Mrs, wife of Fred, 207, 228

Cheshire, Betty, 26
Chester, Ches., 35, 38, 42, 89
Chilton Foliat, Wilts., 88
Chimney-pieces, 55, 212
Chimney-sweeping, 77
China, *see* Porcelain
Chinese lacquer screen, *see* Furniture
Chinese pagoda, *see* Models
Chinese room, the, 44, 113, 207, Plate 134
Chinoiserie, 38, 44, 46, 197, Plate 114
Chirk Castle, Clwyd, 10, 58, 121, 122, 150; accounts, 121; agent at, 189; bath at, 218; gates, 121, 122, 130
Chronicles of Erthig on the Dyke, 7, 197, 231
Clocks, 35, 98
Clothing, 78, 116, 168, 170
Clywedog, river, Clwyd, 22, 201; diversion of, 135
Coaches and carriages, 51, 63, 119, 168, 171, 182, 185, 196, 212, Plate 51
Coachmen, 25, 30, 168, 170; Mr Birch, 26, 52, 163; Ambrose Campion, 169; Edward Humphreys, 171–2, Plate 101; John Jones, 95, 182–3, 185, 221, Plates 68, 106, 107; Mr Meacock, Plate 64; negro coachboy, 2, 30, 31, 33, 170, Plate 24
Coade stone, 135
Coal: amounts consumed at Erddig, 200; nationalisation of, 200
Coalbrookdale, Salop, 130
Coal-mining: at Erddig, 26, 147, 200, 210, 215; at Stansty, 127; subsidence caused by, 14, 127, 130, 200, 210, 215
Cobb, John, 49
Coed y Glyn, Wrexham, Clwyd, 111, 130, 215
Coleshill House, Berks., 98
Conway Castle, Gwynedd, 46, Plate 33
Cooks, 26, 52, 78, 85; Ruth Davies, 117; Mary Rice, 51, 58, 59, 101, 137
Copestake, Lizzie, Plate 10
Coracles, 71
Corbett, Mrs, 52
Cotes, Francis, 49, Plate 30
Country houses: organisation and stability of households of, 9–10; study and preservation of, 9
Crimean War, the, 198
Croes Foel, Bersham, Clwyd, 28, 121
Croom-Johnson, H., 191

Crude Ditties, 24, 78, 231; quoted 24–5, 58–9, 78, 122–4, 142
Cunliffe, Emma, 68
Cunliffe, Sir Foster, 68
Cup and Saucer, the, 138, 201, Plates 83, 84
Curtains, *see* Furnishings
Cust, Albinia Lucy, 7, 197
Cust, Brownlow, 41, 135
Cust, Sir Charles, 175
Cust, Elizabeth (later Yorke), 41, 168
Cust, Sir John, 41, Plate 30
Cycling, *see* Bicycling

Dairy, the, *see* Outbuildings
Dairy maids, 110
Damask, *see* Textiles
Davies, Ann, 101
Davies, John, butler, 174
Davies, John, gardener, 159, 161, Plate 98
Davies, John, innkeeper, of Ruabon, 105
Davies, John, smith, 121
Davies, Robert, smith, 28, 121, 122, 124, 127, 130, Plate 70
Davies, Ruth, 117
Davies, Sarah ('Lalla'), 104–5, 107–8, Plate 62
Davies, Thomas, 192
Davies, Thomas, smith, 121
Davies, William, 56
Davis, John, Plate 10
Davis, Jonathan, Plate 10
Davis, Samuel, 26
Davis, Walter, Plate 10
Death duties, 210, 211
Denbigh, Clwyd, 24, 164
Denbighshire Militia, 142, 170
Denmark, 89
Dickinson, George, 13, 173, 174, Plates 64, 103
Dogs, 2, 89, 92, 154, 182, 187, 201, 206
Dictionary of English Furniture, The, 209
Digby, Sir Kenelm, 36, Plate 27
Dining room, the, 79, 102, 202, 206, 210, 217, Plate 137
Domestic offices, 29–30, 78, 79–80, 102; agent's office, 78–9, 200, Plate 82; bakehouse, 29, 103, Plate 59; basement passage, 9, 112, Plate 9; brew house, 29; butler's pantry, 13, 29, 175–6, Plate 100; cellar, 29, 175, 176; cheese room, 29; housekeeper's rooms, 13, 29, 78–9, 89, 92, Plate 48; lamp room, 176; laundry, *q.v.*; meat pantry, 103; New Kitchen, *q.v.*; powder room, 29;

scullery, 29, 103, 217, Plate 56;
Servants' Hall, q.v.; servery,
78–9; still room, 79
Domestic service: attitudes to, 2–3,
9–10, 13–14, 85, 187; conditions
of, 82, 85, 110–11; literacy of
those in, 3; regional traditions of,
10; cf. Staff
Dovecote, see Outbuildings
Drelincourt, Mrs, 33
Drouais, François-Hubert, Plate 26
Druid, the, see Woods, features of
Drunkenness, 191–2
Dudmaston, Salop, 10, 58, 137
Duttons, Messrs. George & Co.,
grocers, 191
Dyffryn Aled, Llansannan, Clwyd,
78, 142, 154

East India Company, 22
Eaton Hall, Ches., gates, 130
Ebbrell, Charles, 168–9
Ebbrell, Jane, 2, 24–5, 26, 99, 104,
218, Plate 20
Edisbury family, 24
Edisbury, Francis, 55
Edisbury, Dr John, 23, 24
Edisbury, Joshua, 22, 23, 24, 26, 35,
55, 56, 67, 76, 121, 150, Plate 18
Edisbury, J. F., 88
Edward VII, King, 175
Edwards, Mr, agent at Chirk
Castle, 189
Edwards, J., 41
Edwards, Ralph, 209, 211
Egerton, Sir Robert, 111
Egypt, 89
Eisteddfodau, 69
Elections, 78
Electricity, 116, 203
Embroideries, 44; frames made for,
46
Emes, William, 122, 135, 137, 138,
139, 153, Plate 83
Emigration, 105, 118
Entrance Hall, the, 29, 67, 88, 206
Erddig, estate: continuity of
ownership of, 3
Erddig, house and outbuildings,
Plate 17; additions and
alterations to, 24, 26, 28–9, 42–3,
44, 46–7, 49, 55, 67, 78, 79–80,
102, 122; architecture of, 2;
Badeslade print of, 55, 121, 134,
150, 158, Plates 70, 93; building
of, 22, 55–6; condition of before
restoration, 2, 14, 200, 207–8,
209–10, 212, Plates 1, 9, 12, 14,
22, 40, 77, 108, 115, 116, 119,
120, 121, 122, 124, 129, 132; cost
of, 56; decline and deterioration
of, 193, 196, 198–9, 200, 209,

222; description of, 55–6;
opening to public of, 14, 16;
planning and layout of,
xxii–xxiii, 13, 78–80, 98;
restoration of, 221–5, Plates 134,
135; site of, 22, 107; visitors to,
26, 134, 200–1, 207. For
individual rooms e.g. Attics,
Bedrooms, Chapel, etc., see those
headings. For Outbuildings q.v.
Erddig MSS, the, 3, 7, 217, 220,
231–3
Erddig, parish: Parish Council,
161; parish meetings, 10
Esclusham, Clwyd, 95
Estate accounts, 56, 79, 124
Estate labourers, 113, 137–8, 154;
John Davis, Plate 10; Edward
Jones, Plate 10
Eustace, James, 26
Evans, Elizabeth, 110
Evans, John, 26
Evans, Sarah, 64
Eyton, Clwyd, 55
Eyton, Mr, of Leeswood, 26

Failures' Gallery, the, 112
Fairman, Jinnie, Plate 10
Fairs, 187
Family Museum, the, 174, 175,
Plate 102
Felin Puleston, Wrexham, Clwyd,
203
Fellowes, Caroline, 225
Fentham, Thomas, 44, 46, Plates
31, 35
Fire, 67, 183; danger of, 13
Fleet Prison, the, 22
Floods, 137
Flower room, the, 125
Flowers, see Garden, plants in
Foodstuffs, see Provisions
Footmen, 13, 176; duties of, 175–6;
Edward Allen, 170; Arthur
Baker, Plate 10; John Jones, 191,
Plate 67; Frank Lovett, 176,
177–82, 191, 233, Plate 105;
William Stephenson, 172
Fort St George, India, 22
Fountains, see Garden, features of
Fowler, John, 225
Fowlkes, Humphrey, 31
France, 162, 179
Franks, Mr, architect, 46
French, Lady: trustees of, 127
Frogmore, Berks., 90
Fron-deg, Esclusham, Clwyd, 105,
162
Fruit trees, see Garden, plants in
Funerals: of Harriet Rogers, 86; of
Thomas Rogers, 63; of Elizabeth
Yorke, 50–1

Furnishings, 24, 29, 55, 225;
accounts for, 24; blinds, 77;
carpets, 92, 112, 201; curtains,
225; see also Beds and bedding,
Tapestries, Textiles, Wallpapers
Furniture, 23, 27, 29, 43, 49, 52, 67,
71, 77, 98, 102, 103, 112, 206,
207, 211, 225; accounts for, 24;
Chinese lacquer screen, 23; of
domestic offices, 30; protection
of, 77, 207; of staff bedrooms, 30,
112; see also Beds, Chairs, Clocks,
Girandoles, Mirrors, Pier glasses,
Tables

Gainsborough, Thomas, 49, 90,
218, Plates 3, 19
Gallery, the, 28, 36, 38, 51, 52, 112,
Plate 22
Gamekeepers: Jack Henshaw, 56,
140–2, 154, 155, 189, Plate 85;
Ned Humphreys, 172
Games and amusements, 29, 68, 71,
88, 89, 113–14, 116, 152
Garden, 13, 24, 29, 55, 56, 69, 112,
126, 130, 134, 150–65, 185, 187,
198–9, 202, 207, 210, 221, 222,
Plates 74, 93, 94, 119, 131, 132,
133; features of: boathouse, 69, 71,
canal, the, 69, 71, 88, 130, 150,
153, 157, 207, 223, flower pots,
26, 152, fountains, 125, 156,
Plate 74, parterre, 13, 69, 156,
161, 202; plants in: flowers, 150,
154, 156–7, 158, 161, fruits, 42,
59, 134, 150–2, 153, 156, 158,
187, 202, shrubs, 13, 135, 150,
156, 158, 161, 207, 210,
vegetables, 150, 152, 156; cf.
Orchards
Gardeners, 30, 56, 58, 59, 76, 134,
147, 150–65, 170, 189, 207, 212,
Plate 119; Len Archer, 223; John
Davies, 159–61, Plate 98; Albert
Gillam, 195–6, 222, Plate 112;
John Jones, 51, 58, 59, 153, 154,
189; James Phillips, 12, 156–8,
161, Plates 96, 97; William Price,
156, 159; Thomas Pritchard, 2,
59, 154–6, Plates 95, 96; George
Roberts, 10–11, 161–2, 223, Plate
11; Mike Snowden, 222–3, 228,
Plates 92, 130; Alexander Stirton
110, 161, Plate 64; Thomas
Thomas, 162–5, Plate 99
Garden House, the, 156, 222, Plates
95, 129, 130
Gardens and Buildings at Kew, 38
Garrets, see Attics
Garrick, David, 58
Gates, 14, 121–2, 126, 127–30,
Plates 75–8

George III, King, 134
Gesso, 29
Gilding, 26, 29, 35
Gillam, Albert, 195–6, 222, Plate 112
Gillam, Mrs, wife of Albert, 178
Giller, Ed[war]d, 153
Gillows of Lancaster, 99
Girandoles (sconces), 29, 209
Girouard, Mark, 9
Gittins, Bessie, 18, 19, 110–12, 114, 115, 116, Plates 67, 68
Gittins, M. Louisa, 72, 73
Gittins, William, 64, 68, 69–72, 73, 113, 115, 129–30, 146, 164, 165, Plates 45, 46
Gittins, Willy, son of William, 69, 73, 193, 195, 196, 232
Glan-y-Wern, Llandyrnog, Clwyd, 87
Glassware, 53
Grantham, Lincs., 170
Greenaway, Kate, 92
Gresford, Clwyd, 110, 192
Griffiths, Ed[war]d, 153
Grooms, 168–9, 170; J. Hughes, 169; Ernest Jones, 93, 94–5, Plate 55

Hafod colliery, Ruabon, Clwyd, 162
Hardy, John, 228
Harrison, Miss, 192
Hatchments, 51, 174, Plate 103
Hawarden, Clwyd, 156; Castle, 10
Haybarn, see Outbuildings
Haycock, Edith, 18, 110, 111–12, 114, 115, 116, Plates 10, 67, 68
Hay harvesting, 26
Heaton, Robert, 225
Heber, Reginald, 67, 68, 232
Hedging, 153
Henley-on-Thames, Oxon., 193
Henshaw, John (Jack, 'Hencher'), 56, 140, 142, 154, 155, 189, Plate 85
Henshaw, Robert, 153, 189
Heyhoe, Bertram ('Hooha'), 207
Historic Buildings Council for Wales, 209, 211
Hitchman, Lucy (later Jones), 92–5, 181, 182, 185, 232, Plates 55, 107
Hogarth, William, 89
Holland, Mr, 26
Hopper, Thomas, 102
Horses, 2, 90, 93, 138, 154, 170, 182, 188
Housekeepers, 12, 13, 26, 76–95, 112; accounts of quoted, 77; duties and responsibilities of, 76, 77–8, 92; Miss Brown, 90–2, 113, 118, 193, Plate 54; Miss

Harrison, 192; Lucy Jones, (formerly Hitchman), 182; Sarah Lloyd, 77; Miss Lloyd, 201, 206, 207; Ellen Penketh, 90, 191, 192–3, Plate 109; Harriet Rogers, 60, 64, 82, 84–6, 90, 91, 110, 191, Plates 50, 51, 64, personal belongings of, 85, Plate 52; Mary Salusbury, 77, 78, 101; Mary Webster, 12, 80, 82, 85, 90, 158, 191, Plate 49
Housekeeper's rooms, see Domestic offices
Housemaids, 11–12, 13, 27, 51, 76, 77, 90, 92, 98–119, 170; leisure pursuits of, 113–14, 116; routine and duties of, 110–13, 115–16; Betty Bevan, 38, 101; Matilda Boulter, 112, Plate 10; Betty Cheshire, 26; Ann Davies, 101; Sarah Davies ('Lalla'), 104–5, 107–8, Plate 62; Jane Ebbrell, 2, 24–5, 26, 99, 104, 218, Plate 20; Jinnie Fairman, Plate 10; Bessie Gittins, 18, 19, 110–12, 114–15, 116, Plates 67, 68; Edith Haycock, 18, 110, 111–12, 114, 115, 116, Plates 10, 67, 68; Betty Jones, 51, 58, 59, 101, 102, 139; Ruth Jones, 108, 110, Plate 63; Sarah Jones, 161; Emily Pugh, 116, 118: Ann Roberts, 110; Maggie Roberts, 18; Eliza Sumpter, 110, Plate 64; Anne Williams, 26
House stewards, 76
Hughes, Mr, Agent, 64, 90
Hughes, Mrs, charwoman, Plate 10
Hughes, J., groom, 169
Hughes, John, gardener, 150
Hughes, Linda, 202, 207, 219, 228
Hughes, Richard, 56
Hughes, William, 145, 146, Plate 90
Hughes family of Bryn Goleu, 201–2
Humberstone family, 87
Humphreys, Benjamin, 172
Humphreys, Edward, 171–2, Plate 101
Humphreys, Henry, 172–3
Humphreys, Ned, 172
Humphreys, Nehemiah, 172
Humphreys, Richard, 172
Humphreys, Thomas, 172
Hurt, Mr, upholsterer, 27, 29
Hutton family, 52; arms of, 176, Plate 34
Hutton, James, 36, 40, 41, 42, 154, 176
Huxley, Herbert, 225

Illness and diseases, 38, 41, 72, 92,

164–5, 188; gout, 52; scarlet fever, 110; tuberculosis, 110; cf. Medical treatment
India, 23, 29, 112
Illegitimacy, 12, 41
Inventories, 13, 28, 29–30, 76–7, 98–9, 102, 103, 175
Ironwork, 14, 28, 46, 121–2, 124, 126, 127–30, Plates 70, 72, 75–8
Italy, 181, Plate 105

Jackson-Stops, Gervase, 217, 220, 232
Jacobitism, 26
Japanning, 35, 98
Jenkins, Richard, 26
Joiners' shop, the, 60, 69, 145, 225, Plates 40, 41, 43, 87
Jonathan, Mrs, 90
Jones, Alice, 112, 115, Plate 10
Jones, Betty, 51, 58, 59, 101, 102, 139
Jones, David, 189
Jones, Mrs Dennis, 232, 233
Jones, Edward, Plate 10
Jones, Ernest, 93, 94–5, Plate 55
Jones, F. Meredith, 191
Jones, John the younger (1779), 101
Jones, John (1725), butler, 26, 76
Jones, John (1911), carpenter, 64, 65, 67, 68, 69, 95, 165, Plates 36, 43, 44, 67
Jones, John (1911), coachman, 95, 182, 183, 185, 221, Plates 68, 106, 107
Jones, John (1912), footman, 191, Plates 67, 68
Jones, John, (1779) gardener, 51, 58, 59, 153, 154, 189
Jones, John (1779), joiner, 56
Jones, John (1779), plumber, 50
Jones, Lizzie, 102, 116, 118
Jones, Lucy, see Hitchman, Lucy
Jones, Mary, 77
Jones, Percy, Plate 10
Jones, Richard, 26, 27, 76, 121, 150
Jones, Robert, 56
Jones, Ruth, 108, 110, Plate 63
Jones, Samuel, 137
Jones, Sarah, 161
Jones, Ted, 221, 228
Jones, Thomas, 78, Plate 47

King's Mill, see Mills
Kip, John, 150
Kitchen, see New Kitchen
Kitchen maids, 51, 90, 92, 102, 110; Lizzie Copestake, Plate 10
Kitchen porters: Jack Nicholas, 99, 101, Plate 58
Kitchenware, 102–3
Kitching, H. V., 208, 209, 211

Knight, Alan, 130
Knockin, Salop, 82
Knole, Kent, 58
Knyff, Leonard, 150
Koeks, Adriansz, 52

Labourers, *see* Estate labourers
Lady's maids: Elizabeth Evans,
    110; Betty Ratcliffe, 12–13,
    35–53, 225; Ellena Rogers, 110;
    Harriet Rogers, 82; Mrs Wynne,
    26
Lamp room, *see* Domestic offices
Lamps, *see* Lighting
Landscaping, 134–5, 138–9, 153
Land values, 136, 215–16
Laundry, the, 29, 103–4, 200, Plates
    60, 61
Laundry maids, 26, 51, 77, 90, 92,
    102; Alice Jones, 112, 115, Plate
    10; Lizzie Jones, 102, 116, 118
Laundry yard, the, 13
Lawry, Simon, 154
Lead mining, 22
Leasowe Castle, Ches., 63, 157
Leeswood Hall, Clwyd: gates, 130
Legh family of Lyme Park, 58, 67
Library, the, 24, 225, Plate 136
Life in the English Country House, 9
Lighting, 88, 112, 176, 212, 218,
    Plate 121
Linen, 53, 76–7, 98–9, 201
Linnell, John, 44
Little Erddig, Wrexham, Clwyd,
    203, 220
Liveried staff, 168–85; attitudes to,
    170; requirements of, 170–1, 173;
    terms of employment of, 169–70;
    see also Butlers, Coachmen,
    Footmen, Grooms, Postilions
Liverpool, 53, 60, 82
Livery, 30–1, 168–9, 176, 182, 185,
    Plates 104, 107
Llandudno, Gwynedd, 162, 201
Llangollen, Clwyd, 86, 187
Lloyd, Miss, housekeeper, 201, 206,
    207
Lloyd, Deborah, 192
Lloyd, Sarah, 77
Lloyd, Thomas, 51
Lloyd-Jones, Mr, mineral agent,
    200
Lodges, 14, 130, 212, Plate 77;
    Bryn Goleu, 221; Forest Lodge,
    129, 130, Plate 77
London, 9, 26, 27, 52, 58, 78, 88,
    90, 121, 134, 150, 153, 169, 170,
    189, 199; despatch of goods from,
    52–3; house of John Meller in
    Bloomsbury Square, 24, 26; St
    James's Park, 138; street
    directories of, 44; Yorkes' house

in Park Lane, 41, 52, 53, 189
Long Mountain, Ruabon, Clwyd,
    46
Longueville, Miss, 36, Plate 27
Loveday, John, 26, 28, 29, 98, Plate
    22
Lovett, Frank, 176, 177–9, 181–2,
    191, 233, Plate 105
Ludlow, Salop, 115, 118
Lydney, Glos., 117
Lyme Park, Ches., 10, 58, 67

Mackreth, Miss, 90
Maddocks, J. C., 85
Magic lantern slides, 89
Maids, *see* Dairy maids,
    Housemaids, Kitchen maids,
    Lady's maids, Laundry maids,
    Nursery maids, Scullery maids
Manor Farm, Esclusham, Clwyd,
    203
Manual of Domestic Economy, A, 11
Marble, 29, 55, 125
Marchwiel, Clwyd, 31, 65, 85;
    church, 35, 158, 208
Mary, Queen, 220
Meacock, Mr, coachman, Plate 64
Meals, 2, 76, 102, 202, 207
Meat pantry, *see* Domestic offices
Medical treatment, 38, 40, 41, 92,
    110–11, 174; *cf.* Illness and
    diseases
Meller, John, 3, 10, 13, 24, 26, 27,
    28, 29, 30, 31, 33, 35, 42, 49, 52,
    56, 76, 77, 98, 102, 121, 130, 150,
    152, 161, 170, 218, 225, Plate 19
Meyrick, Diana (later Yorke), 78
Middlewich, Ches., 22, 55
Militia, Denbighshire, 101, 142, 170
Mills, 135, 137, 187; French mill,
    136; King's Mill, 135, 136, 189
Mineral agents, 200
Mirrors, 98, 99, 207, 218; *see also*
    Pier glasses
Mitton, Mr, of Hailstons, 26
Models: of Chinese pagoda, 38, 44,
    53, Plate 28; of Ruins of
    Palmyra, 38, 44, 53, Plates 31,
    32; stands for, 44, 46, 53, Plate
    31
Mohair, *see* Textiles
Mortar mill, *see* Outbuildings
Motor cars, 119, 201, 203, 212,
    Plates 124, 125
Motte in Erddig woods, *see* Woods,
    features of
Mourning, 50–1
Murray, Thomas, 172–3
Museum of the Year Award, 18
Musical instruments, 77, 112, 113,
    197, Plate 114
Myddelton family of Chirk Castle,
    137

My Life and Times, 134, 170

National Coal Board, 147, 200, 203,
    208, 210, 215, Plate 14;
    compensation paid by, 215
National Trust, the, 2, 14, 16, 130,
    209, 210, 211, 212, 213, 215, 216,
    220, 221; approach of to
    restoration of Erddig, 16, 18,
    217; negotiations with Philip
    Yorke, 210–21
Negroes, 2, 30–1, 33, 170, Plate 24
Nelson, Gwen, 197
Neo-classical style, 44, 46, 67
Newcome, Thomas, 169
New Kitchen, the, 13, 29, 78, 79,
    102, Plates 14, 15
Newnham, Herts., 36, 41, 52, Plate
    25
Newns, George, 185
Newns, John, 51
Newport, Salop, 177, 179
Nicholas, Jack, 99, 101, Plate 58
Nightingale, Florence, 110
'Nimrod', *see* Apperley, Charles
Northampton Repertory Theatre,
    197, 207; production of, Plate
    113
Northern Ireland, 199
Norway, 89
Nursery, the, 67, 92, 139, 207,
    Plates 37, 108
Nursery maids, 13, 51, 111; Sarah
    Davies ('Lalla'), 104–5, 107–8,
    Plate 62; Lucy Hitchman, 92–5,
    181, 182, 185, Plates 55, 107;
    Harriet Rogers, 60, 82

Ombre, 29
Orchards, 150
Ornamental water, *see* Canal, Cup
    and Saucer, Fountains
Osmond, Mrs, 90
Otley, Frederick, 173
Outbuildings: bath house, *see*
    Baths; blacksmith's shop, *q.v.*;
    dairy, 29, 134; dovecote, 162,
    185, 223; Garden House, *q.v.*;
    haybarn, Plates 116, 117; joiners'
    shop, *q.v.*; mortar mill, 69, 146;
    plan of, xx–xxi; sawmill, *q.v.*;
    stables, *q.v.*; timber yard, 60, 145

Palmyra, Syria, model of ruins of,
    see Models
Park, the, 14, 130, 134, 199, 201,
    202, 220; improvements in,
    134–9; opening to public of,
    139–40
Parry, Annie, Plate 10
Peacocks, 112

Penketh, Ellen, 90, 191, 192–3,
  Plate 109
Pennant, Thomas, 36, 49, Plate 26
Pensions and annuities, 12–13, 63,
  72, 73
Pentre Clawdd, Ruabon, Clwyd,
  22, 206, 216
Penylan, Ruabon, Clwyd, 19
Phillips, James, 12, 156–8, 161,
  Plates 96, 97
Phillips, Thomas, 68
Photographs: of staff, 60, 63, 64, 80,
  86, 90, 93, 95, 104, 110, 114–15,
  124, 156, 161, 164, 179, 185, 191,
  193, Plates 10, 11, 36, 39, 42, 43,
  45, 49, 50, 54, 55, 62, 63, 64, 66,
  67, 68, 69, 73, 90, 91, 92, 96, 97,
  98, 101, 105, 106, 107, 109, 111,
  112; of Yorke family, Plates 6–8,
  53, 110, 113, 114, 118, 121
Picture Post, 182, 185
Pictures (other than portraits), 28,
  36, 46, 52, Plates 22, 26, 27, 33
Pier glasses, 24, 29, 44
Pigeons, 187, 223
Pipe Rolls, the, 22
Plants, *see* Garden
Plas Grono, Ruabon, Clwyd, 14,
  22, 23, 60, 207
Plasterwork, 67
Plate, 53, 89, 175–6, 212, Plate 121
Plays, 58, 197, Plate 113; *cf.*
  Theatricals
Pope, Mr, 89
Porcelain, 44, 52, 53, 76, 80, 175
Portraits, 2, 30, 31, 49, 52, 68, 218,
  Plates 18, 19: of Erddig staff, 2,
  24, 30–1, 56, 57, 58, 59, 78, 101,
  170, 228, *Frontispiece*, Plates 9, 11,
  20, 24, 37, 58, 71; of servants
  elsewhere, 10, 58; of Yorke
  family, 46, 49, 218, Plates 2–5,
  29, 30; *see also* Photographs
Postilions, 26, 76, 168; Charles
  Ebbrell, 168–9; Richard Roberts,
  169
Powder room, *see* Domestic offices
Powell-Jones, Rosalind, 225
Powis Castle, Powys, 134, 137
Pratt, Sir Roger, 30, 98
Press-gangs, 60
Price, William, 156, 159
Prince of Wales, the: (1822) 68;
  (1977) 16
Prince, Charles, 56
Prince, Edward, 56–7, 59,
  Frontispiece
Prince, Edward the younger, 56
Prince, John, 55, 56
Prints, 55, 89, 121, 134, 150, 158,
  175, Plates 70, 93
Pritchard, Thomas, 2, 59, 154–6,
  Plates 95, 96

Provisions, 52, 76, 77, 78, 103, 138,
  189
Pugh, Emily, 116, 118
Puleston, Annette Fountayne, 86,
  88

Ratcliffe, Elizabeth the elder, 35,
  52, 53
Ratcliffe, Elizabeth (Betty), 12, 13,
  35–53, 225; letters from quoted,
  40, 42, 51–2, 53; work of, Plates
  25–8, 31–5
Ratcliffe, John, 35, 50
Read, Katherine, 46, Plate 4
Remnants of an Army, The, 112
Rhosllanerchrugog, Clwyd, 69, 165
Rice, Mary, 51, 58, 59, 101, 137
Richardson, Mrs, 51
Roads, condition of, 28, 39
Roberts, Alfred, Plate 10
Roberts, Aliza, 31, 33
Roberts, Ann, 110
Roberts, Barry, 221, 228, Plate 128
Roberts, Major David, 31, 33
Roberts, George, 10–11, 161–2,
  223, Plate 11
Roberts, Maggie, 18
Roberts, Richard, 169
Roberts, Thomas, 146–7, Plate 91
Robins, Thomas, 38
Rogers, Eliza, 82
Rogers, Ellena, 110
Rogers, Mr H., 191
Rogers, Harriet, 60, 64, 82, 84–6,
  90, 91, 110, 191, 233, Plates 50,
  51, 52, 64
Rogers, James, 60, 63, 64, 201,
  Plate 42
Rogers, Maria, 82
Rogers, Philip, 55, 56
Rogers, Sarah (formerly Evans), 64
Rogers, Thomas, 12, 56, 59–60, 63,
  82, 201, Plates 37, 38, 39
Rogers, Thomas, son of James, 64
Rogers, William, 56
Rose, Joseph, 67
Rowlinson, Mr, 67
Royal Tribes of Wales, The, 13, 49,
  176
Ruabon, Clwyd, 105, 108
Ruins of Palmyra, The, 44
Ruins of Palmyra, *see* Models

Salisbury, Wilts., 90
Saloon, the, 29, 44, 77, 201, 206,
  209, 225
Salusbury, Mary (Molly), 77, 78,
  101
Sandpatch (Sandbach), Ches., 22
Satin, *see* Textiles
Sawmill, the, 69, 145, 146, 147,

200, 225, Plates 80, 115
Saw pit, the, 60, 69, 145, Plates 87,
  88
Sawyers: Alfred Roberts, Plate 10;
  Thomas Roberts, 146–7, Plate 91
Sconces, *see* Girandoles
Scott, Louisa (later Yorke), 88, 89
Scott, Rev. T. J., 88, 112
Screens, *see* Furniture
Scuffle ovens, 103
Scullery, *see* Domestic offices
Scullery maids: Annie Parry, Plate
  10
Servants, *see* Staff
Servants' Ball, 114
Servants' Hall, the, 2, 9, 13, 29, 30,
  56, 78, 95, 102, 104, 112, 142,
  154, 155, 170, 174, 185, 207, 210,
  212, Plates 1, 107
Servery, *see* Domestic offices
Sherborne, Dorset, 90
Showers, *see* Baths
Shrewsbury, 38; School, 193
Shugborough, Staffs., 135
Silk, *see* Textiles
Silver, *see* Plate
Silvering, 24, 29, 44, 225, Plate 21
Simms, William, 26
Sledmere, E. Riding, Yorks., 232
Smith, Peter, 225, Plate 41
Smith, Selina, 84
Smiths: Robert Davies of Croes
  Foel, 28, 121–2, 124, 127, 130,
  Plate 70; *see also* Blacksmiths
Snowden, June, 228
Snowden, Mike, 222–3, 228, Plates
  92, 130
Society of Antiquaries, the, 49
Society for the Propagation of the
  Gospel, the, 67
Sontley, Marchwiel, Clwyd, 127
Spain, 198
Spring cleaning, 71, 112, 116
Stables and stable yard, the, 28, 29,
  30, 46, 60, 69, 156, 168, 200, 210,
  212, Plates 117, 122, 123
Staff: annuities granted to, 12–13,
  52; difficulties with, 90, 92,
  187–8, 192–3; dissatisfaction
  among, 188, 189, 190, 196; letters
  written by staff or their relatives,
  3, 7, 22, 26–7, 72–3, 82, 84, 85–6,
  95, 112, 152–3, 162, 164–5, 172,
  173, 178–9, 181, 187–8;
  misdemeanours of, 90, 187–8,
  189–90, 191–2, 193, 196, 201,
  233; numbers of, 30, 90, 92, 193,
  199, 201; outside activities of,
  161, 185; pensions granted to,
  q.v.; promotion of, 13, 102,
  111–12, 177; recollections of, 18,
  116; savings by, 12, 82, 101, 110,
  158; verses about, *q.v.*; wages of,

q.v. For references to particular categories of staff, e.g. Agents, Butlers, Carpenters, etc. *see those headings*
Stainton, Sheila, 225
Stansty, Wrexham, Clwyd, 126–7, 129; gates from, 126–30, Plates 75, 76, 78
State Bed, the, *see* Beds
State Bedroom, the, *see* Bedrooms
Statuary, 135
Stephenson, William, 172
Stewards, *see* Agents
Still room, *see* Domestic offices
Stirton, Alexander, 110, 161, Plate 64
Stoke Poges, Bucks., 90
Subsidence, *see* Coal mining
Sudan, 172
Sumpter, Eliza, 110, Plate 64
Sunday Schools, 161
Sweden, 89
Sykes, Lady, 53, 232

Tables, 29, 30, 46, 53, 67, 77, 98, 99, 103, 112, 152, 175, 176, Plate 44
Tapestries, 27, 28, 29, 44, 218, Plate 21
Tapestry weavers, 27
Tattenhall, Ches., 162
Taxes, 170, 221; *see also* Death duties
Taylor, G., 153
Taylor, Margery, 192
Temperance Movement, the, 192
Templer, J., solicitor, 211, 216
Textiles: caffoy, 28, 29, 77; calico, 77, 98; damask, 28, 29, 225; mohair 28; satin, 98; silk, 29, 99, Plate 35; velvet, 24, 29; *see also* Furnishings, Tapestries
Theatre companies, 197, 220, Plate 113
Theatricals, 16, 41, 58–9; *cf.* Plays
Thomas, Betty, 51
Thomas, Joseph, 164, 165
Thomas, Thomas, 162, 164–5, Plate 99
Thompson, Mrs, 51
Timber waggon, 145, Plate 89
Timber yard, *see* Outbuildings
Torrington, Lord, 134
Tortoiseshell, 29, 35
Townsend, J., 68
Toys, 69, 71, 95, Plate 37
Travels in Wales (1810), 49
Traverse, William (Billy), 152
Treasury, the, 210, 211
Trelawnyd, Clwyd, 22
Trevor, Sir John, 22, 24
Tribes' room, the, 13, 176
Turner, Joseph, 156

Turner, William, 156

Upholsterers, 27, 29
Upholstery, 29, 77; *see also* Textiles

Vandalism, 212
Van Dyck, Sir Anthony, 36, Plate 27
Vegeterianism, 2
Vehicles, *see* Coaches and carriages, Motor Cars, Timber waggon
Velvet, *see* Textiles
Verse (about Erddig staff), 2, 3, 7, 9, 10–11, 24–5, 30–1, 56–7, 58–9, 60, 64–7, 69, 71–2, 76, 78, 80 82, 90–2, 94–5, 101, 105, 107–8, 110, 115–16, 117–18, 119, 122–4, 142–3, 145–7, 155–6, 157–8, 159–61, 162, 171, 172, 173, 177, 179, 182–5, 187, 193, 195–6, 231
Victoria, Queen, 86
Victoria and Albert Museum, 209, 228
Visitors' books, 207, 220
Vyne, The, Hants., 135

Wages, 11–12, 26, 38, 52, 56, 76, 77, 79, 101, 111–12, 137, 138, 154, 158, 169, 170, 188–9, 192, 193, 207
Wallpapers, 43, 44, 56, 92, 156, 222, 225, Plates 134, 135
Walsh, J. H., 11
Walters, John, 24, 56, 101, 122, 141, 154
Wanley, Mrs, 52
War: Crimean, 198; First World, 92, 95, 162, 175, 176, 178–9, 181; Second World, 92, 185, 198–9
Water supply, 116, 125, 207, 212–13; *see also* Baths
Wat's Dyke, Clwyd, 22
Watson, Joseph, 58
Weather, 26, 46, 152, 153, 154, 187
Webb, Thomas, 22, 29, 55
Webster, Mary, 12, 80, 82, 85, 90, 158, 191, Plate 49
Welsh Nationalists, 213
West Room, the, 98
Whitchurch, Salop, 156
White, Gilbert, 36
Wilde, John, 173, 233
Williams, third carpenter, Plate 10
Williams, Anne, 26
Williams, John, 22, 76
Williams, John, blacksmith, 56
Williams, Maggie, 116
Williams, William, blacksmith, 122–4, Plates 71, 72
Williams Wynn family, 26

Williams Wynn, Sir Watkin, 4th Bart., 14
Williams Wynn, Sir Watkin, 5th Bart., 58
Willock, Mr, 52
Winchester, Hants, 162
Windows, 102, 156
Window shutters, 14, 26, 112
Windsor, Berks., 90
Withdrawing Room, the, 29, 44, 53, 77, 201, 206, 212, Plates 21, 120, 121
Wood, Robert, 44
Woodmen, 134–47, 170; Edward Barnes, 59, 76, 142–3, 145, Plate 86; William Hughes, 145, 146, Plate 90
Woods, 14, 46, 88, 89, 134–47, 152, 154, Plate 81; features of: Cathedral Aisle, the, 135, Plate 81, Druid, the, 135, Norman motte, 22, 134–5
Woolfe, Richard, 152
Wooton, Mr, butler, 11, Plate 10
Worcester, 94
Worrall, Mr, 138
Worthenbury, Clwyd, 113
Wrexham, Clwyd, 9, 14, 22, 64, 67, 85, 89, 101, 107, 110, 130, 134, 152, 158, 220, 225; building companies in, 196; church, 134; land values at, 215–16; Old Vicarage, 67; public houses in, 134, 172, 173; shops in, 207; station, 69
Wrexham Advertiser, 191–2
Wrexham Leader, 213
Wrexham, Mold and Connah's Quay Railway, 67
Wright, Joseph, 121, 124–6, 129, 130, Plates 69, 73, 74
Wristlesham, *see* Wrexham
Wyatt, James, 28, 46, 79, 80, 212
Wymondsold, Mrs, 41
Wynne, Mrs, lady's maid, 26
Wynne Finch, Col. J. C., 209
Wynnstay, Clwyd, 14, 58, 105, 218

Yale, Elihu, 22, 23, 29
Yale University, USA, 23
Yorke family, 2, 3, 7, 9, 12, 13, 16, 35, 36, 41, 44, 46, 64, 67, 68, 76, 77, 80, 82, 92, 102, 104, 107, 110, 112, 116, 125, 142, 156, 168, 170, 172, 173, 174, 175, 176, 187, 189, 192, 193, 195, 196, 211; arms of, Plate 34; attitude to and relationship with staff, 2–3, 7, 10, 12–13, 64, 110–11, 138, 168–70, 187, 188, 189, 190, 195; characteristics of, 2–3, 9, 16, 35, 67, 168, 170, 172–3, 191, 221;

line of succession of, 3, 6

Yorke, Anne, 152

Yorke, Anne Jemima, 36, 41, 43, 50, 51, 53, 154, Plate 29; letters from quoted, 36, 41, 153–4

Yorke, Brownlow, 58

Yorke, Diana, 52, 53

Yorke, Dorothy, 12, 35, 36, 38, 40, 41, 43, 44, 51, 52, 53, 76, 101, 188, 189, 192; letters from quoted, 36, 38–40, 41, 76, 101, 188, 189, 192

Yorke, Elizabeth, 42–3, 44, 46, 49, 50, 51, 56, 168, Plate 30; character of, 49–50; death and funeral of, 49–51; letters from quoted, 43–4, 47

Yorke, Etheldred, 46, Plate 4

Yorke, John (nephew of John Meller), 24

Yorke (General) John, 158, 198

Yorke, Lily, 87

Yorke, Louisa Matilda (formerly Scott), 7, 72, 90, 92–3, 95, 110, 111, 112, 113, 114, 174, 181, 182, 191, 192, 193, 199; diary of quoted, 88, 89–90, 92

Yorke, Philip I (1743–1804), 3, 10, 13, 14, 24, 29, 36, 38, 40, 41, 42, 43, 44, 46, 47, 49, 50, 51, 52, 53, 56, 58, 59, 76, 78, 79, 80, 88, 90, 99, 101, 102, 122, 134, 135, 137, 138, 139, 140, 141, 153, 154, 168, 169, 170, 176, 187, 188, 189, 190,

192, 218, 219, Plates 3, 31; antiquarian interests and historical sense of, 47, 49, 153; attitude to workmen, 138; character of, 35; description of, 170; letters from quoted, 47, 78, 102, 135–6, 137–8, 139, 140–1, 190, 192, 218; marriage of, 42; Parliamentary duties of, 170, 187; pocket book of quoted, 49, 154, 169–70, 218; verses by, 24–5, 58–9, 78, 122, 123, 142

Yorke, Philip II (1849–1922), 3, 7, 9, 10, 11, 63, 64, 67, 69, 72, 80, 85, 86, 88, 89, 90, 92, 93, 104, 108, 111, 112, 113, 114, 116, 124, 127, 128, 145, 146, 157, 162, 164, 165, 171, 177, 178, 179, 181, 182, 191, 192, 193, 195, 200, Plates 6, 53, 75, 105; charitable work of, 88; death of, 193; letters from quoted, 87–8, 127–8, 129–30, 177, 179, 181–2; marriages of, 86–8, 90; regard for staff, 88, 93; verses by, 10, 11, 64, 65–7, 69–72, 80, 82, 90–2, 94–5, 105–8, 110, 115–19, 124–6, 145, 146–7, 156–8, 162, 171, 182–3, 185, 193, 195–6; will of, 208

Yorke, Philip III (1905–78), 2, 3, 18, 19, 72, 92, 93, 94, 95, 114, 116, 130, 181, 182, 193, 197, 198, 199, 206, 207–13, 215–21, 228, 231, Plates 8, 55, 110, 113, 114,

118, 120, 121, 124, 127; attitude to Erddig, 18–19; death of, 19; education and c.v. of, 193, 197–8, 199; efforts to save Erddig, 206–30; letters from quoted, 18–19, 197, 212–13, 215–16; negotiations of with National Trust, 210–11, 212–13, 215–18, 219–21; religious views of, 198

Yorke, Simon I (1696–1767), 3, 24, 26, 27, 29, 33, 35, 152, 153, 187, Plate 2; epitaph to, 35; letters from, 27–8

Yorke, Simon II (1771–1834), 3, 10, 46, 52, 53, 59, 60, 102, 134, 139, 142, Plate 4; verses by, 59–60, 142–3

Yorke, Simon III (1811–94), 3, 60, 63, 82, 86, 158, 172, 174, Plate 5; letters from quoted, 63, 86; relationship with son, Philip, 86; verses by, 86

Yorke, Simon IV (1903–66), 3, 7, 9, 69, 72, 92, 93, 94, 95, 114, 130, 147, 181, 182, 193, 197, 198, 200, 201–3, 206–8, Plates 7, 46, 55, 106, 110; attitude to Erddig, 9, 200–3; character and habits of, 9, 197, 198, 201, 202, 203; coming of age of, 193, Plates 110, 111; death of, 203, 208; education and c.v. of, 193, 197, 198; letters from quoted, 197

Yorke, Victoria, 82, 85, 86, 172